The Human Tradition in America

CHARLES W. CALHOUN
Series Editor
Department of History, East Carolina University

The nineteenth-century English author Thomas Carlyle once remarked that "the history of the world is but the biography of great men." This approach to the study of the human past had existed for centuries before Carlyle wrote, and it continued to hold sway among many scholars well into the twentieth century. In more recent times, however, historians have recognized and examined the impact of large, seemingly impersonal forces in the evolution of human history—social and economic developments such as industrialization and urbanization as well as political movements such as nationalism, militarism, and socialism. Yet even as modern scholars seek to explain these wider currents, they have come more and more to realize that such phenomena represent the composite result of countless actions and decisions by untold numbers of individual actors. On another occasion, Carlyle said that "history is the essence of innumerable biographies." In this conception of the past, Carlyle came closer to modern notions that see the lives of all kinds of people, high and low, powerful and weak, known and unknown, as part of the mosaic of human history, each contributing in a large or small way to the unfolding of the human tradition.

This latter idea forms the foundation for this series of books on the human tradition in America. Each volume is devoted to a particular period or topic in American history and each consists of minibiographies of persons whose lives shed light on that period or topic. Well-known figures are not altogether absent, but more often the chapters explore a variety of individuals who may be less conspicuous but whose stories, nonetheless, offer us a window on some aspect of the nation's past.

By bringing the study of history down to the level of the individual, these sketches reveal not only the diversity of the American people and the complexity of their interaction but also some of the commonalities of sentiment and experience that Americans have shared in the evolution of their culture. Our hope is that these explorations of the lives of "real people" will give readers a deeper understanding of the human tradition in America.

Volumes in the Human Tradition in America series:

Ian K. Steele and Nancy L. Rhoden, eds., *The Human Tradition in Colonial America* (1999). Cloth ISBN 0-8420-2697-5 Paper ISBN 0-8420-2700-9

Nancy L. Rhoden and Ian K. Steele, eds., *The Human Tradition in the American Revolution* (2000). Cloth ISBN 0-8420-2747-5 Paper ISBN 0-8420-2748-3

Ballard C. Campbell, ed., *The Human Tradition in the Gilded Age and Progressive Era* (2000). Cloth ISBN 0-8420-2734-3 Paper ISBN 0-8420-2735-1

Steven E. Woodworth, ed., *The Human Tradition in the Civil War and Reconstruction* (2000). Cloth ISBN 0-8420-2726-2 Paper ISBN 0-8420-2727-0

David L. Anderson, ed., *The Human Tradition in the Vietnam Era* (2000). Cloth ISBN 0-8420-2762-9 Paper ISBN 0-8420-2763-7

The Human Tradition in
THE GILDED AGE
AND
PROGRESSIVE ERA

THE HUMAN TRADITION IN
THE GILDED AGE
AND
PROGRESSIVE ERA

No. 3
The Human Tradition in America

Edited by
Ballard C. Campbell

A Scholarly Resources Inc. Imprint
Wilmington, Delaware

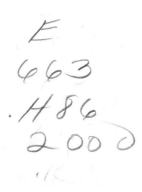

Scholarly Resources Inc.
104 Greenhill Avenue
Wilmington, DE 19805-1897
www.scholarly.com

Library of Congress Cataloging-in-Publication Data

The human tradition in the Gilded Age and Progressive Era / edited by Ballard C. Campbell
    p. cm — (Human tradition in America : no. 3)
   Includes bibliographical references (p.) and index.
   ISBN 0-8420-2734-3 (cloth : alk. paper), — ISBN 0-8420-2735-1 (pbk. : alk. paper)
   1. United States—History—1865–1921 Biography. I. Campbell. Ballard C., 1940– . II. Series.
E663.H86 1999
973'.09'9—dc21
                                    99-29786
                                         CIP

About the Editor

BALLARD CAMPBELL is professor of history at Northeastern University, where he has taught since receiving his Ph.D. from the University of Wisconsin in Madison. He specializes in the history of the Gilded Age and Progressive Era, as well as the political and economic history of the United States. His publications include *The Growth of American Government: Governance from the Cleveland Era to the Present* (1995) and *Representative Democracy: Public Policy and Midwestern Legislatures in the Late Nineteenth Century* (1980). Professor Campbell served as associate editor of the *American National Biography* (1999, 24 volumes), is coeditor of H-SHGAPE on the Internet, and is affiliated with the World History Center and the Ph.D. program in law, policy, and society at Northeastern University. He is finishing a book on American political development in the United States since the American Revolution.

I believe in aristocracy, though—if that is the right word, and if a democrat may use it. Not an aristocracy of power, based upon rank and influence, but an aristocracy of the sensitive, the considerate and the plucky. Its members are to be found in all nations and classes, and all through the ages, and there is a secret understanding between them when they meet. They represent the true human tradition, the one permanent victory of our queer race over cruelty and chaos. Thousands of them perish in obscurity, a few are great names. They are sensitive for others as well as for themselves, they are considerate without being fussy, their pluck is not swankiness but the power to endure, and they can take a joke.

—E. M. Forster, *Two Cheers for Democracy* (1951)

Contents

Introduction

Ballard C. Campbell

The Gilded Age and Progressive Era were marked by an array of changes matched by few other periods in American history. A frenetic release of energy ran through the United States between the end of the Civil War (1865) and World War I (1917). The economy underwent dramatic, accelerated growth as industrialization took off. The nature of work changed fundamentally, incomes rose, and modern retailing and consumption emerged. Millions of immigrants streamed to the United States, swelling the great metropoles and numerous smaller cities as well as filling in much of the nation's remaining open space. Electric lighting, telephones, typewriters, automobiles, aviation, X-ray photographs, filtered water, and taller and taller buildings were but a few of the technical marvels of these years. Education blossomed, especially at the high school and college levels, new understandings of the physical world and society challenged conventional beliefs, and printed materials and libraries proliferated. New forms of management refashioned the administration of business, finance, and civic affairs. Continuities with the past persisted, of course; yet it is hard to exaggerate the scale and scope of change that occurred in the Gilded Age and Progressive Era.

Citizens of the era regarded most of these developments as progress. Still, many people were not wholly pleased by what they saw. The rise of giant corporations, the power and wealth of the titans of industry, and the increased vulnerability of those dependent on wages troubled numerous observers. Some regarded the newcomers flooding to America as misfits in a culture dominated by white Protestants. The power of political bosses, who staffed governments with patronage appointments and raided public treasuries, disturbed many Americans. These and other criticisms raised during the Gilded Age and Progressive Era indicate that change could also be viewed as threatening and destructive. In fact, the period reverberated with debate over how society should cope with these trends. Americans were aware that their society was in transition, and they endlessly discussed the implications of this realization.

Change eventually forces individuals to confront a variety of new circumstances. How people reacted to these personal challenges constitutes one of the fascinating questions examined by historians. By recreating the settings in which individuals interacted with their environment, biography offers a window on human responses to change. The men and women featured in this volume faced numerous challenges. They were not the most famous of their time but neither were they ordinary. Each made a distinct contribution to history and is remembered in some way. These individuals are also representative of other citizens of the Gilded Age and Progressive Era. The biographies that follow touch on experiences that were common to African Americans, women, farmers, workers, business-people, union organizers, educators, athletes, Easterners, Westerners, politicians and governmental officials, immigrants, those whose family pedigree traced to colonial times, writers, military officers, people from humble backgrounds, and people born into comfort. The authors have made a special effort to assess the interplay between the unique personality of their subjects and the historical context in which they lived.

The stories begin in the 1870s, when national leaders attempted to repair the political wounds of the Civil War. These were also years when the nation embarked on a half-century of extraordinary economic expansion. Migrants were lured west by the dream of starting over and maybe even striking it rich. They were encouraged by the Homestead Act, which offered settlers who qualified a 160-acre parcel of land. Although most pioneers did not lay claim to these homesteads, millions carved out farmsteads in the western portions of the country during the last decades of the nineteenth century. Other migrants found opportunities in the lumber industry, in mining, and on cattle ranches and in railroad yards scattered throughout the Great Plains and the West. California's rapid growth exemplified this rush to tap the nation's natural bounty. The Golden State offered a variety of agricultural, mining, and lumbering opportunities, and its harbors at San Francisco, Los Angeles, and San Diego afforded numerous commercial possibilities. As California's economy diversified, the state came to symbolize the possibilities for getting ahead in the West.

The railroads made their appearance in the 1830s and by the outbreak of the Civil War had connected the East with cities in the Midwest. Rail construction boomed during Reconstruction, fed in part by feverish efforts to link small communities to larger commercial centers and in part by the desire to link both coasts. The completion of the first transcontinental route in 1869 was a monument to the triumph of technology over distance, and some migrants reached the West by riding the rails. As the nation's first big industrial business, railroads had an enormous impact on American life. Steam-powered transportation moved people and goods farther in less time than other modes and lowered the cost of shipping agricultural commodities and manufactured products. As costs fell, so did the prices that consumers paid.

The rails linked the expanded middle and western regions of the country to the rising factories of the East. The industrialization of the nation had a pronounced effect on the ways that Americans earned their living. As the nineteenth century wore on, a declining proportion of Americans devoted their lives to farming, and a growing share found jobs in manufacturing, transportation, and retail. Whatever their line of work, individuals faced stubborn obstacles in their quest to earn a living in the decades around 1900. Farmers were susceptible to the unpredictability of the weather and of the prices their products—increasingly sold abroad—fetched at market. Although there was a huge demand for labor in the United States, finding and keeping an industrial job depended on numerous factors, including the temperament of supervisors and the ability of managers to keep their firms afloat.

In the long run, Americans were marvelously successful in meeting most of these challenges; the economy became more productive, workers' wages rose, and the standard of living improved. In the short run, however, industrial employment meant meager wages, dangerous working conditions, and frequent economic depressions that forced periods of idleness. The overbuilding of railroads during Reconstruction triggered a financial panic in 1873 that spiraled into a prolonged industrial depression. During the hard times of the 1870s many men and some women turned to "tramping" from town to town in search of work and a meal. Neither Congress nor state governments offered help for these victims of the economic slump. The recurrence of depressions in the 1890s and early twentieth century convinced some people that the well-being of workers and business owners had become hostage to unpredictable swings between prosperity and stagnation in the new industrial economy.

Factory employment had an early start in Massachusetts, a fact that helps to explain why the Bay State was a leader in enacting laws that protected workers and children. Massachusetts established the Bureau of Labor Statistics in 1869, and four years later Carroll Wright became its commissioner. In his first major project, Wright investigated workers' standards of living; his study led to a series of reports that won him national attention. Wright's interest in the welfare of workers was mirrored by L'Abbé Jean-Baptiste Primeau, pastor to French Canadians in Worcester, Massachusetts. Primeau conducted his own survey among families in his parish, producing results that paralleled Wright's findings.

Despite similar findings, Primeau and Wright came to different conclusions about the implications of their research. Primeau worried that the lure of higher wages in America would erode the religious devotion of his French-Canadian parishioners. Wright doubted that French Canadians would climb the ladder of economic success unless they shed their immigrant ways. To Primeau, Wright's efforts to uplift French-Canadian workers smacked of Yankee prejudice. Both had a point, as John McClymer, a labor historian, explores in Chapter 1. Professor McClymer shows that earning a living and preserving religious identity posed a challenging dilemma. In Worcester, aspiring to an American standard of living unavoidably intruded on French-Canadian culture. In Massachusetts and elsewhere in America, economics and cultural values continually interacted.

An economy that grew steadily could ease tensions between ethnic identity and upward mobility. The key to this issue was how to expand the economy. A hotly debated question in the Gilded Age was what role government should have in this process. There were plenty of precedents for public promotion of economic development. The national government had granted land to railroads during the 1850s and 1860s to help finance their construction. Congress had enacted high tariff duties on imports, protecting manufacturers from the competition of cheaper foreign goods. Were these steps proper, or was economic development best left in private hands? Democrats in the Gilded Age customarily sided with the hands-off, or laissez-faire, position on this issue. They argued that government intervention bred centralized "paternalism," an enlarged bureaucracy, and unfair favoritism. Republicans tended to support a greater role for the national government. James G. Blaine, Speaker of the House of Representatives and the leading Republican in the generation after the Civil War, was an advocate of this position.

Charles Calhoun, a historian of Gilded Age politics, reviews in Chapter 2 the career of the Plumed Knight, as Blaine was affectionately known. Some Republicans supported Blaine's nomination for the presidency in 1876, but Rutherford B. Hayes went on to victory in one of the closest and most controversial elections in American history. Blaine moved on to the Senate and prepared to fight another day. His career belied the "spoilsmen" stereotype of politicians of his day, who were reputedly often corrupt and in league with business. Professor Calhoun argues that Blaine brought serious ideas to the practice of statecraft. His vision for engaging government in the development of the nation centered around protective tariffs, expansion of trade and diplomatic relations, and enforcement of civil rights for southern blacks. In 1884, Blaine managed to secure the Republican nomination but lost a close election to Grover Cleveland, the governor of New York. When Benjamin Harrison recaptured the White House for Republicans in 1888,

Blaine accepted an appointment as secretary of state, his second tour of duty in the office.

Congress followed much of Blaine's advice regarding tariffs and foreign trade, but it made no progress on the protection of blacks' rights. The Civil War had destroyed southern plantation culture, which had been built on slavery, and released four million African Americans from bondage. But the struggle also left a legacy of bitterness that lasted for generations in the North and the South. Federal troops were garrisoned in the South during Reconstruction (1866–1877) to protect the freed slaves, whose liberties and lives were threatened by resentful southerners. As white conservatives returned to power in the region, harassment of African Americans increased. Southern state governments enacted a battery of laws that restricted the rights of blacks. A few African Americans turned to the courts for relief. This step required extraordinary courage because filing a legal complaint constituted defiance of white rule.

Ida Wells, born a slave during the Civil War, exhibited such bravery when she sued a Tennessee railroad company that had evicted her from the whites-only passenger car in 1883. In Chapter 3, Christopher Waldrep, a legal historian, describes this incident and the trial in the Tennessee court where Wells sought justice. The verdict set Wells on a lifetime quest to protect blacks' rights. Her priority was the elimination of lynching, the mob-rule method for maintaining white supremacy in the region. Struggling to overcome the obstacles of her race and gender, Wells became an internationally known writer and crusader for racial equality at a time when most whites turned a deaf ear to racial injustice.

Inequalities among racial groups had parallels in the economic system. Disparities in income and influence were especially apparent in the great business firms that emerged during the Gilded Age and Progressive Era. The largest of these enterprises, usually organized as corporations, developed hierarchical networks that separated workers from managers. In their struggle for survival and profitability, many corporations expanded through mergers and acquisitions, sometimes in search of national markets for their products. Some businesses combined through a legal device known as a trust in order to evade laws that restricted corporate activity to a particular state. For Americans born into a world in which businesses were small and family owned, the appearance of corporate behemoths was a cultural shock. Many citizens recoiled in anger at the sharp practices of "robber barons." Responding to demands that government curtail unfair business practices, Congress enacted a modest antimonopoly measure in 1890.

The Populists joined the cry to tame the trusts. Populism was the nickname for the People's party, a group that challenged conventional politics in the 1890s. Populism's strength lay in the Great Plains, where agriculture predominated and farmers struggled to make ends meet. Prices for agricultural commodities had been declining for years, and they fell further during the depression of 1893–1897. Times were especially hard in plains states such as Kansas, where grain prices declined faster than the cost of transportation, supplies, and interest rates. This economic vise drove many plains residents and some southern farmers to the Farmers' Alliance, whose leaders lashed out at Wall Street financiers, railroads, and Congress. Politicians, they charged, served monopolists, not the people. One of the most articulate and electrifying Populist critics was Mary Lease, remembered for urging farmers to "raise less corn and more hell."

In Chapter 4, Rebecca Edwards, a historian of women and politics, removes the veil from the life of this remarkable woman. Mary Lease faced a bewildering array of hardships: the death of her father in a Confederate prison camp; poverty both as a child and as an adult; the death of her children as infants; the bankruptcy of her husband during the depression of the 1870s; and, in perhaps the cruelest cut of all, accusations of sexual impropriety during her campaign travels for Populists in the 1892 election. Mary Lease understood hardship, a perspective that she brought to a variety of reform and labor organizations that blossomed in the 1880s. Fighting to eliminate "oppression, injustice, and poverty," she found that the conservative views of men, including male Populists, constituted a formidable obstacle to the participation of women in public life. Despite this bias against women, Lease labored for Populist causes and campaigned for William Jennings Bryan, who ran as both the Democratic and Populist candidate for president in 1896. Populism crumbled after Bryan's defeat, prompting Lease to take up a new life in New York City, where she became active in the National Birth Control League. As Edwards demonstrates in her portrait of this spirited woman, Mary Lease epitomizes the tensions among gender, class, and protest politics in the Gilded Age.

The hard times of the 1890s put pressure on corporations as well as on farmers and workers. Railroads were particularly vulnerable to the economic slump. Rail lines required large amounts of capital for construction and maintenance, leaving them heavily leveraged with loans and stock issues. Revenue declined when business tapered off, hampering the ability of companies to meet their financial obligations. The depressions of the 1870s and the 1890s pushed numerous railroads into bankruptcy. Richard Olney, the subject of Ballard Campbell's Chapter 5, was a Boston attorney who specialized in providing financial and legal advice to railroads. Olney became the chief counsel and a director of several major railroads, including the Burlington lines, whose eastern terminus was Chicago. Olney's cautious, businesslike manner appealed to President Grover Cleveland, who appointed him attorney general in 1893.

Olney had barely settled into his Washington post when the panic of 1893 triggered an economic downturn and provoked managers to reduce workers' wages. The rail lines already faced a challenge from Eugene Debs, who initiated a campaign to unite all railroad employees into a single comprehensive union. When workers at the Pullman railway car factory south of Chicago walked off their jobs, Debs's new union pledged its support. This gesture of sympathy mushroomed into a massive work stoppage against railroads, which brought transportation in most of the country to a standstill in July 1894 and led to bloodshed in the streets. Incensed that a labor union blocked commerce, Olney used the resources of the national government to crush the strike and destroy the new union. Professor Campbell, a political and business historian, discusses the Pullman strike from the perspective of workers, railroad operators, and politicians. He argues that the conflict enhanced the power of the presidency and delayed the growth of unions as well as wounded the Democratic party.

Workers also clashed with owners in the mining industry. American business had an enormous appetite for resources, including industrial minerals. Mining operations ranged from coal fields in the Appalachian region of the Northeast to iron ore pits in the upper Midwest to copper and zinc fields throughout the Rocky Mountains and the West. Mining was arduous work that paid poorly and was extremely dangerous in an era before effective government safety regulations. At many locations owner-operators ruled the site with little outside interference. Fierce competition among small operators helped to keep wages down, setting the stage for strikes in the coal fields of the East and Midwest and the copper pits of the western mountains.

"Mother" Mary Harris Jones was on the scene at many of these clashes, offering her support for miners whom she urged to join the United Mine Workers Union and demand better conditions. Donna Gabaccia, a historian of immigrants and women, focuses in Chapter 6 on this unusual woman whose combative rhetoric and gritty determination made her the "most hated woman in America" to mine operators. But she was a darling to the men in the pits and the shafts. Uninterested in philosophy or mainstream politics, Mother Jones was a pragmatic activist. She joined picketing strikers around the country and thrived on taunting mine owners and capitalists despite several arrests and attempts on her life. Her mission was to "raise hell," which was her way of focusing attention on the gulf between the wealth of owners and the substandard wages of workers. Jones's style contrasted with the more genteel approach of the upper-class women of New York City who supported female garment workers striking in the early twentieth century. Defying conventions about age and gender, Mary Jones mounted a direct, no-holds-barred challenge to the economic power structure.

For those dissatisfied with work in the mines or on the production line, there was the prospect of striking out on one's own. The mountains of the West held precious metals, industrial minerals, and huge tracts of natural forests; the Great Plains contained vast expanses of grazing and farming land. Most of these natural assets could also be found along the Pacific coast, which boasted fine ports and commercial sites. The one resource that was in short supply was water. Ever since John Wesley Powell's geological survey of the Grand Canyon and the Colorado River, the idea of "reclaiming" land from its natural aridity by irrigation had gained adherents. One of the staunchest supporters of reclamation was Francis G. Newlands, the Nevada politician who is the subject of William Rowley's Chapter 7.

The ascension of Theodore Roosevelt to the presidency in 1901 boosted the cause of resource development. One manifestation of this thrust was enactment of the Newlands Reclamation Act of 1902, which provided federal assistance for transforming arid areas into productive farmland. Rowley, a historian of the West and land policy, traces the career of Francis Newlands, who amassed fame and fortune in frontier Nevada, was elected to the U.S. House, and capped his career by advancing to the Senate. An advocate of a national program for commercial development, Newlands was a progressive on some issues, such as federally sponsored reclamation, yet was extremely conservative on others, such as civil rights. These sorts of contradictions were not unusual in the Progressive Era, especially among Westerners. Professor Rowley discusses these crosscurrents during Newlands's years on the national political stage, the period when Roosevelt, William Howard Taft, and Woodrow Wilson occupied the White House.

The Progressive Era was a time of change in social relationships as well as in the conduct of politics. Clelia Duel Mosher, a physician, educator, and medical researcher at the turn of the century, discovered a significant shift in the attitudes of married women toward sexual relations. With information gathered from a series of unusual interviews that she conducted, Mosher combated Victorian rigidities concerning the role of women. She rejected the traditional wisdom that female behavior flowed spontaneously from inherent differences between the sexes.

In Chapter 8, Kathleen Parker, a social historian, reviews the life of this dedicated opponent of nineteenth-century views about female physiology. After receiving her medical degree from Johns Hopkins University, Mosher taught feminine hygiene at Stanford University in California. But she devoted most of her energy to disproving myths about the behavior of women. At a time before opinion surveys and the disclosure of intimate relations were common, Mosher's interviews provided rare insights into marital practices. Her data revealed the emergence of new attitudes among middle-class women about the purposes of sexual relations and the erosion of traditional conceptions about the obligations of wives. Parker's chapter also underscores the role that women played in challenging conventional thinking about feminine psychology and behavior.

If marital relations and suffrage ranked high on the list of women's concerns, surely baseball had a distinct appeal to men. Organized sports gained popularity in the early twentieth century, and baseball was easily the most popular. The emergence of the sport as a paid occupation and a business was connected to the growth of cities, the expansion of leisure, and the commercialization of entertainment. In Chapter 9, Steven Riess, a student of baseball and a sports historian, discusses these linkages in his profile of Christy Mathewson, one of the all-time great pitchers. "Matty," as he was generally known, embodied the qualities that Americans admired in their sports heroes: he was handsome, athletic, competitive, intelligent, gregarious, and religious (he did not play on Sundays). He was an ideal icon for a sport that was transformed from informal sandlot games into a profitable business with teams established in most of the nation's big cities. The World Series, the capstone of the baseball season, began early in the century and evolved into a national event on a level approaching the Fourth of July and Christmas. Mathewson led the New York Giants to several championships during his major-league pitching career (1901–1918), when his name probably was more widely recognized than those of most governors and senators. Riess's story is set in the first two decades of the twentieth century, when professional baseball acquired many of its modern characteristics.

Cities in the Progressive Era evolved into polyglot places with a mixture of nationalities and cultural groups. Native-born Yankees and migrants from England, Scotland, northern Ireland, Germany, the Scandinavian countries, and Canada (English and French) swelled urban populations in the nineteenth century. Large numbers of Irish had been arriving in America since the 1840s. They were joined by Italians, Greeks, Armenians, Poles, Russians, European Jews, and Mexicans after 1900. Asians and Hispanics had established a presence in the West after the Civil War. Maintaining public order and providing civic services in the cities became more complex by the end of the nineteenth century as immigration increased urban densities and ethnic heterogeneity. Paralleling this challenge was mounting criticism of political bosses and their machines, which thrived by providing favors and cultivating loyalties among the electorate. Reformers sought to remove partisanship from municipal government by hiring professionals to manage urban administration. Although the question of who should control urban government was a hotly contested issue, all sides agreed that cities should provide modern services and amenities such as clean running water, paved streets, good schools, and protection against crime and fire.

James Michael Curley entered Boston politics as these ideas were crystallizing. In Chapter 10, James Connolly, a political historian, evaluates this mercurial figure whose career illuminates social and political aspects of urban life at the turn of the century. Curley had an immense drive to succeed in politics, a goal that Connolly suggests was rooted in the historic conflict between the Yankees and the Irish. Yankees dominated the social order of nineteenth-century Massachusetts when the Irish first took their place as an urban proletariat. By 1900 the Irish had overcome many of their traditional liabilities, and they began to reach out for higher elective offices. The reorganization of Boston city government in 1909 offered Curley an opportunity to broaden his base among his Irish supporters. He combined an understanding of ethnic loyalties and working-class attitudes with skillful manipulation of the media to fuse a diverse electoral coalition in Boston. He was elected mayor on several occasions, partly on the strength of his talent for ridiculing upper-class Yankees, an act that he honed to a high rhetorical art. Professor Connolly argues that an irony of Boston's reform politics was its accentuation rather than diminution of ethnic identities.

Criticism of partisan politics and weak regulation of business were hallmarks of Progressive reform. Sentiments for political change peaked around 1910, when new political coalitions generated pressure for policy innovations in state after state. In California, reformers targeted the entrenched Republican leadership and the Southern Pacific Railroad as impediments to enlightened governance. Reformers rallied behind Hiram Johnson, a San Francisco attorney who had earned a reputation for prosecuting municipal graft. In Chapter 11, Philip VanderMeer, a political historian, examines the career of this complex individual whose attack on the Republican old guard meant confronting his father, a powerhouse in the party. The younger Johnson was a dynamic and tireless campaigner who toured the state by car in 1910 and rode a wave of voter enthusiasm for reform to the governorship. In 1911 the new chief executive presided over an outpouring of legislation that regulated railroads and public utilities; gave voters more say in politics through primaries, initiatives, and nonpartisan elections; and adopted reforms concerning conservation, education, and state finances. Professor VanderMeer's essay documents the importance of state government to the accomplishments of progressivism. In 1916, Johnson moved on to the U.S. Senate, where he supported the war against Germany but opposed the League of Nations and grew more conservative as the years passed. The shift in Johnson's views as he moved from the state to the federal level underscores the complexity of politics in the Progressive Era.

Shortly after Johnson went to Washington, Congress declared war on Germany. Woodrow Wilson called America's crusade against the Germans a war to "make the world safe for democracy." But the tradition of keeping the nation's professional military small rendered the United States ill prepared for a full-scale conflict. The war presented government with the mammoth job of building an army, navy, and logistical support system. For eighteen months during 1917 and 1918 military and civilian officials strained to recruit, train, transport, and deploy a U.S. fighting force. Eventually more than four million Americans served in uniform during the Great War. Two million doughboys were sent to France as part of the American Expeditionary Force.

The Allies' campaign depended on moving American troops and supplies across the Atlantic Ocean to Britain and France, missions menaced by German submarines. This threat was the primary concern of Admiral William S. Sims, chief of American naval operations in the Atlantic and a longtime critic of the navy's hidebound ways. In Chapter 12, Kenneth Hagan, a naval historian, explains Sims's dogged campaign to overcome American skepticism of the convoy system as a strategy to reduce shipping losses from German submarines. The success of convoying earned Admiral Sims the presidency of the Naval War College at Newport, Rhode Island. In addition to the expanded role of submarines, World War I debuted other military technologies, including airplanes, which were used for reconnaissance and bombing. This experiment captured the imagination of farsighted military planners such as Sims, who envisioned the day when planes would take off from and land on ships and be able to sink battleships.

World War I not only inflicted carnage on the battlefield but also disrupted life behind the lines. Paris was deluged with refugees who fled advancing German armies. The impoverishment of these uprooted civilians, plus Allied propaganda that depicted Germans as inhumane and brutish, tugged at the American conscience. Edith Wharton, an American novelist who was living in Paris when war erupted, wondered why the United States hesitated in joining the crusade against Germany, which she believed threatened refined civilization. Wharton was moved by the suffering of civilians in France and dedicated herself to helping the refugees who streamed into Paris. Alan Price, a Wharton biographer and professor of English, describes the turmoil in France in Chapter 13. Wharton's life opens a window on the upper class in America and literary circles in the early twentieth century. A friend of Teddy Roosevelt and major American writers, she was also an expatriate who relocated in Europe, in part to escape a disappointing marriage. Born to wealth, she devoted herself to helping the unfortunate at a moment of crisis in world history. The scale of her organizational activity, Professor Price conjectures, was tantamount to running a major corporation. The war was a major turning point in Wharton's life, as it was for so many individuals. Professor Price reflects on how the armistice in Europe marked the end of an era.

From Wharton and her dedication to assisting refugees in Paris to L'Abbé Primeau and his efforts in preserving the culture of French Canadians in Worcester, the individuals profiled in this book were affected by a matrix of changes that transformed the United States from comparatively simple, rural, and disconnected communities to a more complex, commercialized, and integrated society. They also weathered a series of unanticipated events in their personal lives. Ida Wells and Mary Lease lost parents as children. Mother Jones was widowed early in life. Divorce led Lease and Edith Wharton to relocate. Economic depressions affected the careers of James Blaine and Richard Olney. The upsurge of Progressive reform created political opportunities for Curley, Newlands, and Johnson. World War I left its mark on Mosher, Mathewson, Sims, and Wharton. Yet one should not overestimate the impact of unforeseen events or social changes on people's actions. Individuals' choices are also guided by their convictions. The men and women featured in this volume are living testimony to the capacity of human will and the tenacity of personal commitment.

1

Carroll D. Wright, L'Abbé Jean-Baptiste Primeau, and French-Canadian Families

John F. McClymer

What was a fair day's pay? Should it be enough to keep young children out of factory employment? Should employers be required to pay a minimum wage? These were some of the concerns that motivated Carroll Wright, commissioner of the Massachusetts Bureau of Statistics of Labor, to survey workers' pay and living conditions in 1875. L'Abbé Jean-Baptiste Primeau, a priest who ministered to French Canadians in Worcester, Massachusetts, was also interested in workers' standards of living.

Although Wright and Primeau asked similar questions and received parallel responses, the significance each man attached to individual economic success differed strikingly. To Primeau, the American standard of living threatened to entice immigrant families away from their French-Canadian roots. To Wright, upward mobility was an implicit goal in American life, but the rootlessness of some immigrants blocked their advancement. He believed that the transience of French Canadians marked them as "the Chinese of the Eastern States." Their pride offended by this ethnic slur, French-Canadian leaders offered a spirited defense of their communities.

John McClymer, an expert in labor history, traces this debate and what both sides learned from the experience. Although the cultural sniping between Wright and Primeau pitted Yankee against French Canadian, one could substitute other groups in this morality play without changing the plot. The larger story, Professor McClymer explains, was the tension that existed between achieving economic success in America and preserving traditional immigrant cultures. The challenge of accommodating both values posed a dilemma for many immigrants in their adaptation to life in the United States.

John F. McClymer is professor of history at Assumption College in Worcester, Massachusetts. He is general editor of Harcourt Brace's American Stories series of documentary narratives as well as author of the first volume in the series, *The Triangle Strike and Fire* (1998). He has written extensively on American social history.

1

The stranger in the stiff white collar immediately attracted notice. Visitors of any sort were rare in the South Works of the Washburn & Moen Wire Company in Worcester, Massachusetts. The company was Worcester's biggest industrial employer and the world's largest maker of barbed wire, telegraph wire, and innumerable other products. At 6:25 A.M., five minutes before work commenced, upward of a thousand men streamed through the gates, which were then locked. Anyone coming even a minute late lost that day's pay. A second offense cost him his job. There were no exceptions, no excuses. Visitors had to get a pass and even then were not free to wander about. An assistant superintendent or someone else in management always served as escort. But this visitor was by himself.

He carried a sheaf of papers and glanced about curiously before striding over to a small cluster of workers—die sinkers who made the devices through which the various sizes of wire were drawn. "Good day," he began. "I'm with the state Bureau of Statistics of Labor. We're conducting an inquiry into the wages and expenditures of workingmen and their families here in Massachusetts. I'm hoping one of you will be willing and able to assist."

"What kind of inquiry would that be, then?" one asked.

"And who are you to be askin'?" another put in.

"We're studying how families manage to make ends meet," the stranger said. "What can you earn, what kind of life can you provide for your families, that's what we want to find out. My instructions are to go to the biggest industrial centers in the state, Lowell, Worcester, Fall River, and seek out the biggest factories and shops. Then I'm to ask the first worker I see. The idea is to get information from enough families, maybe up to a thousand, so we can know pretty well what living conditions are like."[1]

"You still haven't said what you want to know, not so I can tell," the first worker interjected.

"We want to develop a budget for each family that'll itemize every penny that comes in and every penny that goes out."

"You mean you want to snoop into how much we put into the collection plate."

"Or whether a man spends two cents for a beer of a Saturday after getting paid."

The man from the bureau shifted his weight a bit uncomfortably. It was not easy persuading workingmen to trust him. Why should they? The bureau was only a few years old, and Colonel Wright had taken over as director only two years ago. "I know it might look like snooping," he began, "but my chief, Colonel Carroll D. Wright, has given orders not to pry into such things." He pulled out a document with the bureau's seal on the top. "'There is a sanctity to every household which even the state should not invade,'" he read. "The colonel's orders are that we are not to try to learn 'how much was thrown away from bad habits, or how much was squandered in extravagance.' We are only trying to determine if the workingmen of Massachusetts get a fair return on their day's labor."

"A fair return! That's a laugh. What's fair is what the foreman says is fair. 'If you don't like it,' he says to you, 'there's plenty that'll be happy to take your place.'"

"The bureau wants to know what's really fair," the agent began again. "I'll read you more of my instructions. Our 'particular work,' as Colonel Wright calls it, is to find out if the 'wage system' permits the laboring man 'with economy and prudence' to 'comfortably maintain himself and family.' That is, can he 'educate his children and also lay by enough for his decent support when his laboring powers have failed'? That's what the bureau means by fair. That's what I want you to help me find out."

"It sure isn't what Washburn & Moen means, I can tell you that right now," a worker murmured. "And what are you going to do once you've got all those facts? Stick them in some report that nobody will ever read?" he went on in a louder voice.

"Oh people will read it, you can count on that. Colonel Wright will make sure. So, will one of you help?"

The men exchanged glances. Should they trust the bureau? Who was this Colonel Wright? Could it really help their families if they agreed to cooperate? Could it hurt?

Enough said yes. The bureau's agents did not compile a thousand family budgets, but they did put together almost four hundred. Each budget detailed the family's size, the range in age of the children, the earnings of each working member plus all other sources of income. Each also itemized every expenditure, no matter how small. The agents did add in the nickel left in the collection plate on Sunday, the beer on Saturday, the penny candy for the kids. But they grouped them as "sundries." Only the sundry expenses commonly considered acceptable—the pennies for newspapers, the quarter for a union membership, or the church contribution—were identified as such. The money spent on tobacco or beer was not specified.

Agents visited each family twice. The first visit, during the day, allowed them to describe the family's housing and the condition of their neighborhood. Was there a garden? If so, were only vegetables planted or were there flowers too? How clean were the streets? Where were the outhouses? How clean were they? The second visit, in the evening when all family members were home, allowed agents to compile the budgets. How much did each working member earn? How much did the family pay in rent? What did family members spend on food? On clothes?

These second visits also provided an opportunity to describe how well the apartment or house was furnished and how well the family dressed. If there was a piano or a sewing machine or rugs on the floor, agents wrote that down. If the children were neatly dressed and clean, they noted that as well. Finally, agents put together detailed information about family members' diets. How often did they eat vegetables? What about meat and fish? Did they have pie with breakfast? That was the working family's big meal of the day. "You should breakfast like a king, dine like a prince, and sup like a peasant" ran an old saying. There were usually six hours of hard work between breakfast and dinner, another five or so before supper. A man needed his biggest meal in the morning. And he needed a substantial lunch. The rest of the family subordinated its needs to his, eating pork chops and steak for breakfast, not to mention pie or cake. At the noon meal the more prosperous families again ate meat, along with potatoes and perhaps more pie. For supper, some families had just beans and bread or potatoes left over from lunch. If a family was scrimping, agents learned, it might have only bread and tea. The worst-off families had this meager meal twice a day, always lunch and supper.

No. 92.   SHOEMAKER.   *French.*

EARNINGS of father, ... $396

CONDITION.—Family numbers 6, parents and 4 children from one to nine years of age; two go to school. Live in a crowded tenement of 3 rooms, situated in a very unhealthy locality, in the midst of filth and pollution. On outside of building is a sink-conductor, badly out of repair, and the sink-water, almost black, runs down the clapboards, causing an offensive stench which can be smelled at a great distance. The inside of house is on a par with the surroundings; it is poorly furnished, and seems the abode of poverty. Children pale-looking, sickly, and wretchedly kept. Father earns from $12 to $15 per week when he has work; but, on account of sickness and dullness of trade, finds it impossible to keep out of debt and live; sees no hope for betterment of condition until children are old enough to work. Family dresses miserably.

FOOD.—*Breakfast.* Bread, butter, sometimes salt fish or pork, coffee.
　　　Dinner. Bread, meat three days per week, salt fish or pork the remainder, potatoes; sometimes pie, water.
　　　Supper. Bread, sometimes brown bread or oatmeal bread, butter, tea, occasionally gingerbread. Cannot afford luxuries.

COST OF LIVING, ... $483 40

Rent,		$96 00	Fish,		$13 00	Sickness,		$19 00
Fuel,		30 50	Milk,		12 00	Sundries,		11 50
Groceries,		241 00	Clothing, shoes and					
Meat,		23 00	dry goods,		28 50			

Source: Sixth Annual Report of the Bureau of Statistics of Labor (Boston: N.p., 1875):251.

Carroll D. Wright, the architect of this investigation, was born in Dunbarton, New Hampshire, in 1840. He enlisted in the Civil War and rose through the ranks. After Appomattox, he studied law, passed the bar examination, and settled in Reading, Massachusetts. His new neighbors soon elected him to the state senate. It was not unusual for politically inexperienced Civil War veterans to be elected to office; in fact, these veterans dominated politics for two generations.

After serving a second senate term, Wright left the legislature to take over the fledgling Bureau of Statistics of Labor in 1873.[2] It was the first agency of its kind, and the thirty-three-year-old Wright was determined to demonstrate that the collection of reliable information was the crucial prerequisite to wise legislation. "All true and lasting progress," he maintained, "is founded upon knowledge." The budget study was his first major project. It proved, he confidently explained, that "the condition of the wage laborers of the Commonwealth" required "amelioration."[3] Massachusetts needed a minimum wage that all employers were required to pay, one high enough to allow hardworking and temperate laborers to support themselves and their families at a decent standard.

Such a law was only fair, Wright argued. If employers overextended themselves and could not meet their obligations, they could seek refuge in the bankruptcy courts. A minimum wage would give Massachusetts workers and their families a similar sort of protection. And the state's blue-collar families needed it. Most could not save money for hard times no matter how careful they were. Too many found themselves in debt even as they literally tightened their belts by cutting meat consumption to once a day or denying their children the milk they needed to grow properly. Few could do more than dream of owning their own home. As for being able to retire, virtually all male laborers worked for as long as they were physically able. Only a widower whose grown children were willing and able to take him in might retire. Otherwise a man worked until he dropped.

More than fairness was involved in Wright's campaign for a minimum wage. For him, as for many of his generation who served in the Civil War, the state was only as strong as its citizens. The industrial prosperity of Massachusetts rested on its workers, he insisted, just as the survival of the Union had rested on its soldiers. How long would prosperity last if the workers and their families did not share in it?

Wright's 1875 annual report really began the discussion in the United States of the notion of what came to be called a "living wage." It is a discussion still going on, and his definition of "fair and just" has proven as influential as his pioneering use of statistics:

> No one should receive such small compensation for his toil, that even when expended with economy and prudence, it fails to pay for his necessary cost of living; rendering him an involuntary debtor,

subjecting him continually to the demands of creditors who wish pay for the necessities of life he has consumed; obliging him to overwork his wife with home and outside duties; forcing him to deprive his children of education, that he may supply by their labor their cries for bread; finally, bringing him to the poor-house, to the state of a continual recipient of charity, or entailing him as a morally not-to-be-got-rid-of burden upon his children, relations or friends.[4]

This definition of a fair day's pay advanced a view of the government's responsibilities to its citizens that would in the twentieth century become normative, namely that the state has an obligation to protect those who cannot protect themselves. Protection might take the form of laws requiring school attendance, limiting the hours children can work, establishing a minimum age for child labor, stipulating fire-prevention and other safety measures, guaranteeing minimum wages, or providing workers' compensation in case of injury. Despite a hostile Supreme Court, which throughout the last third of the nineteenth century often ruled that state laws regulating these matters were unconstitutional infringements on the rights of corporations to "due process," this was an era of legislative activism. Massachusetts, thanks in part to Wright's efforts, frequently took the lead.

His 1875 annual report did not gather dust. Instead state after state across the North and West set up bureaus of labor statistics, undertook studies of living and working conditions modeled on his, and used the results very much in the way he envisioned, as proof that the state needed to protect workers and their families. By 1883 there were enough state bureaus for Wright to organize a convention of their chiefs.

Wright himself went on to become the first U.S. commissioner of labor in 1885. In 1893 he was named director of the census to speed up the processing of the census of 1890. In both positions he designed and supervised even more ambitious studies and, in the process, helped found the science of statistics. He also chaired the federal commission that investigated the Great Pullman Strike of 1894 and served on the commission of inquiry into the anthracite coal strike of 1902. Anthracite was then the main home heating fuel, and the strike threatened to leave millions of Americans in the cold.

Yet for all of Wright's credentials as a pioneer, some of the families who cooperated with his 1875 budget study had already had experience with systematic inquiries into their standard of living. At least this was true of French-Canadian immigrants living in Worcester, whose pastor, Rev. Jean-Baptiste Primeau, no sooner arrived in 1869 to found the first French-Canadian parish in the city than he undertook his own study of family living standards.[5]

Like Wright, he wanted to know how the families under his care were making ends meet. He too visited them in their homes, and he asked just as many questions. Who worked in the family? What did they earn? Did they take a newspaper? Who in the family could read? English or only French? Was the father planning on taking out citizenship papers? Was the family saving to purchase a home? He asked about what they ate, but—unlike the bureau's agents—he also swapped recipes for soup and stew. Most important, he talked with the families about a shared dream, a church of their own, perhaps someday soon with a school where children could learn French and Canadian history, where they would be exposed to the "right" sort of moral influence. Primeau did not discuss what each family might contribute. That would come later, he explained at the first meeting of the prospective congregation. His first duty was to be a shepherd, he told them. A shepherd must know his flock.

Primeau was scarcely the only pastor to undertake such a survey of the families in his parish. What is unusual is that the results of his visits were published, so we know specifically what he asked and how he interpreted the answers he received. We can compare his study and Wright's, a revealing exercise in several ways. First, although Wright and Primeau agreed on most facts with respect to wages, costs of various necessities, and related matters, they disagreed over what those facts meant. These conflicting views, one from inside the working world and one from outside, also can tell us a good deal about the perspectives of early investigators like Wright and of immigrant community leaders like Primeau. Finally, their disagreements and agreements illuminate the processes whereby immigrants found their way into the larger American society and native-born Yankees slowly learned to live with these newcomers.

In 1869–70 there were 1,743 "souls" in Primeau's flock, about three hundred fifty families. Most were headed by manual laborers. Shoemakers were the largest group, followed by day laborers and then by skilled artisans—blacksmiths, carpenters, and machinists. Only a handful had white-collar positions. There were a few grocers, a handful of clerks, a doctor, and a lawyer. There was one journalist, Ferdinand Gagnon, who was about to launch the most influential French-language newspaper in New England, *Le Travailleur* (The Worker). About one adult in six was an American citizen; about one in ten owned property, most often in Quebec. A majority could read neither French nor English. The families were almost all young; the average age of the fathers was thirty-eight, according to the 1880 census, and would have been even younger in 1869–70, when the curé made his initial visits. Almost all had children living at home, and although the great majority of these children were still very young, many were already working full-time. Most families could not manage on the father's wages. The two or three dollars earned by ten- and twelve-year-olds, supplemented occasionally by income from boarders and by what the mother could earn from taking in laundry or sewing, were needed to keep the wolf from the door. These were, in short, the same families Wright's survey showed to be living on the edge of subsistence. They ate meat or fish once a day; they frequently made do with a supper of bread and potatoes left over from lunch. Small wonder Primeau's recipes were for soup and stew.

Wright's agents described some of these families. Number 223 was headed by a laborer in a mill. Two sons, twelve and ten, also worked. "Family numbers 7, parents and 5 children from one to twelve years of age; one child goes to school. . . . Occupy a tenement of 4 rooms in a good locality, with neat surroundings. The house is moderately well furnished, but no carpets. Family dresses poorly, and looks pale and unhealthy, but neat. Tries to keep out of debt, but the father has to work all the time, as well as the children. Lost six days through sickness last year, and had to go without necessary clothing." Another family, number 224, also had a father who was a laborer in a mill. It also had two working sons, aged fourteen and twelve, but its overall condition seemed better to the agent. "Family numbers 6, parents and 4 children from three to fourteen years of age; one goes to school. Occupy a tenement of 5 rooms, in a good locality. House is moderately well furnished. Family dresses well and attends church."[6]

Some families were holding their own and some, teetering on the brink of financial collapse; others were indeed collapsing. Of one, headed by a day laborer with one working child, an agent wrote, "Family numbers 6, parents and 4 children from one to twelve years of age; one goes to school. Have a tenement of 3 rooms, in a poor locality. Sanitary arrangements are disgraceful; sink water running in the yard; privies over-running with filth. The house is poorly furnished and dirty; in fact, it is impossible to keep it clean. Family dresses moderately well."[7]

Primeau saw all of this poverty, but he did not see it in the same light that Wright did. Primeau's point of reference was village life in Quebec, not middle-class Massachusetts. As he told a visiting priest from Montreal, "The people of Notre Dame are neither rich nor poor. They enjoy a happy ease. There has so far [through 1872] been no lack of work in Worcester, and the price of labor is regular and high enough." Day laborers earned between $1.00 and $1.50 a day. Skilled shoemakers received between $2.00 and $2.50 a day; and the highly skilled, such as carpenters, could get up to $3.00. Servant girls made $3.00 to $4.00 a week in addition to their board. Living expenses, the curé continued, were moderate. Rents averaged

$12.00 a month. Heat cost another $4.00 to $5.00. "So in general, here in Worcester . . . people can under ordinary circumstances put more or less aside each month." On the whole, "we can say that materially speaking everyone lives well at *Notre Dame*, that a good majority can save up, that in fact a strong minority does save, and that very few accumulate wealth." Such was "the happy lot of the parishioners of *Notre Dame*."[8]

"Living well" meant quite different things for Wright and for Primeau. For Wright it meant that the father earned enough for his children to go to school, for his wife to stay home and not have to take in boarders or laundry, and for the family to set aside a little out of every pay envelope for the proverbial rainy day. A decent standard of living would allow the family to accumulate some of the nicer things in life such as a piano or a sewing machine. Such a family could afford to carpet the parlor.

Primeau also emphasized saving, but otherwise his view of the good life had little in common with Wright's. In March 1872 he offered up in his parishioners' name "this prayer of Solomon: 'Lord, give me neither poverty nor riches; give me what is necessary for life; for fear that if I have more, I might be tempted to renounce you . . . or that, if I am constrained by poverty, I might steal and might through perjury violate the name of my God.'" Riches, the priest continued, were especially dangerous in the United States. "Here, more than elsewhere, wealth . . . carries people closer to the Protestant or infidel class, which is dominant; it tends to make people enemies of their own faith; it pushes them toward contempt for their brothers." What was best, what the people of Notre Dame enjoyed, was a "happy mediocrity." Mediocrity, Primeau concluded, "accomplishes prodigies, . . . builds churches, and . . . maintains the sacred fire of the sanctuary." Primeau rejected, in short, precisely what Wright was calling for, an *American* standard of living. And he rejected it precisely because it was American, that is, Protestant. "We must," he urged his flock in 1872, "remain Canadian above all."[9]

Wright and Primeau would meet in 1881. The occasion was a hearing, called by Wright but organized by Primeau's parishioner Ferdinand Gagnon, into the living standards of the French-Canadian immigrants in Massachusetts. It was not a friendly encounter. In his *Twelfth Annual Report*, Wright had sought to make a case for a ten-hour day for factory workers.[10] One argument commonly put forward by opponents, especially employers, was that some workers, more often than not immigrants and frequently French Canadians, would put their additional free time to mischievous uses. The employers were correct, Wright conceded, but conditions should be "shaped for the better portion of the people" and not for the worst. "It is not too much to say," he continued, "that the sober, the industrious, and frugal operatives, and all who seek better things for them," including himself, "have to carry the loafers, the tipplers, and the saloonkeepers on their back." It was wrong, Wright maintained, to judge a law by how some might abuse it. "The well-behaved ought not to be punished by having conditions put upon them which hurt their welfare" in order to control the "ill-behaved."[11]

Had this been all he said, the debate over the ten-hour law would have remained within the usual bounds, but Wright directly took up the question of the French Canadians. They were, he wrote, "with some exceptions, the Chinese of the Eastern States." It was a hateful comment, one that reflected the racism of the day. Congress was about to pass the Chinese Exclusion Act. In California and other western states new laws prohibited Chinese from owning property, from attending the same schools as whites, and from holding a variety of jobs that required state licenses. And although Wright attempted to disclaim any racist intent by arguing in his next annual report that the "words 'Chinese of the East' are simply an expression used by economists to-day everywhere to denote the kind of labor that is migratory," the French Canadians of Massachusetts knew an ethnic slur when they heard one. Worcester's Charles Lalime claimed that the expression "hurt me somewhat" and led to his taking the lead in organizing a protest against the report. "We must meet Mr. Wright, and show him we are a white people," he proclaimed.[12]

Lalime's comment is revealing. Being "white" was not simply a matter of skin color in late-nineteenth-century America. Many immigrants, no matter how fairskinned, were viewed as nonwhite. University of Wisconsin sociologist E. A. Ross observed in 1912, for example, that doctors had concluded that "Slavs can stand dirt that would kill a white man." Further, everyone, including the most recent immigrants, understood that the United States was "a white man's country." Lowell's J. H. Guillet echoed Lalime. "Our French operative in the mills . . . have been opposed by the other help and abused on account of this name. For two or three weeks they were on fire for the people calling them 'Chinese' all the time. Some had to lose their places and go off; they could not stand it."[13]

What had Wright meant by the term "Chinese of the East"? The Canadian French "are a horde of industrial invaders," he wrote, who endeavored to crowd their children "into the mills at the earliest possible age" and who brazenly lied to truant officers to accomplish this purpose. When "at length they are cornered by the school officers, and there is no other escape, often they scrabble together what few things they have, and move away to some other place where they are unknown, and where they hope by a repetition of the same deceits to escape the schools entirely, and keep the children right on in the mills." If they finally did surrender their children to the schools, "then the stolid indifference of the children wears out the teacher with what seems to be an idle task."[14]

French Canadians did "have one good trait. They are indefatigable workers, and docile." They would take any job and work any number of hours. They lived, Wright went on, "in the most beggarly way" in order to "carry out of the country what they can thus save." Their only amusements, so far as the males were concerned, were "drinking, smoking and lounging." These descriptions reveal what Wright meant by "Chinese." He meant that the Canadian French were "so sordid and low a people" that Massachusetts should amend its laws so "that these people will either be coerced to conform to our established ways or else go where the already established ways of the country do please them." This solution was precisely the one supported by those calling for an end to Chinese immigration and the one about to be enacted on the federal level.[15]

For any public official to castigate French Canadians in such unbridled terms would have been bad enough. The fact that the official was Carroll D. Wright, one of the most respected men in the state, and that he presented this outpouring of insult and abuse as the result of his bureau's careful investigations made the situation even worse. And according to Worcester newspaper editor Ferdinand Gagnon, Americans in general shared Wright's low opinion of the French Canadians. Such people, Gagnon editorialized, based "their judgments on the exterior of life [and] do not find among the mass of our people that varnish of civilization which means more to them than the noblest of sentiments [found] under the humblest of circumstances." Yankees and other immigrants as well looked upon the French Canadians "with a begrudging eye" because "we are too numerous" and "are willing to work dirt cheap."[16]

H. A. Dubuque, a young attorney living in Fall River, added that Wright could insult the French Canadians with impunity because "we are weak today, without a voice in the English-language press to defend us and without influence in political circles."[17] So even though Gagnon and other French-Canadian spokespeople called upon their compatriots to protest against Wright's thirteenth annual report, they did not hold out much hope that anything would happen. But something did happen. Wright was nettled by the accusation that he had maligned the French Canadians without giving them a chance to defend themselves. As a gesture of "good faith," he offered them "a full and free opportunity to present such testimony as they might have showing their progress in the United States." His bureau would hold a public hearing on the question. As further proof of his good faith, Wright promised that the French Canadians could choose one of their own to chair the meeting—attorney H. A. Dubuque would be their selection—and that the chair could then determine which witnesses to call and what evidence to admit. Finally, Wright promised to print the entire transcript of the hearing in his next annual report.[18]

This extraordinary opportunity that Wright presented to the French Canadians was nothing less than a chance to prove they were "a white people." What did being "white" mean? The arguments they made and Wright's response provide as detailed a definition as Wright's diatribe had for what it meant to be called Chinese.

Ferdinand Gagnon took the lead in preparing for the hearing. His *Le Travailleur* was the oldest and most influential French-language paper in New England, and he sent questionnaires to pastors, journalists, and other leading French Canadians in over forty Massachusetts cities and towns asking for detailed information on how many of their fellow Canadiens owned real estate, were naturalized U.S. citizens, held public office, or owned their own businesses. How many of the children attended public schools? How many went to French-language parochial schools? There was a striking meeting of the minds here. Gagnon's plan was to confront Wright with exactly the sort of statistical evidence the bureau chief was famous for compiling himself. And he amassed exactly the sort of data that matched Wright's indictment. Had Wright said that the French Canadians cared nothing for American institutions? Gagnon would list every one of his compatriots who had become a citizen or run for public office. Had Wright charged that the French Canadians cared nothing for their children's education? He would count every child in public and parochial schools. And so with most of Wright's attacks upon the group. Proving oneself "white," in short, meant showing that one behaved like a Yankee.[19]

Gagnon was even prepared to acknowledge an element of truth in Wright's negative characterization of the group. In his first editorial on the subject, he had written "To be just . . . the conduct of large numbers of us lays us open to the criticism." Dubuque made a similar admission: "Colonel Wright reproaches us for certain failings which the French-Canadian press has already recognized."[20] Typical immigrants, Gagnon testified at the hearing, were poor and "burdened with a family." They had no real choice "but to go to the textile factories, and there accept what is offered to them." Often the wages were so low that they "are obliged to send children to the mills against the law of humanity, and, in Massachusetts, against State law." Children in the factories sometimes earned thirty cents a day for nine or ten hours of work. Gagnon insisted that the manufacturers were to blame. "Is it not the manufacturer [who complains] of the ignorance of the Canadian children [but still tries] to get them at their mills for a few cents a day?" Rather than blame the victims, he went on, the manufacturers should "cut the evil at its root, and refuse employment to these poor little ones, pay a little more to the adult members of these families, and give the children a chance to have an education." Whether Gagnon realized it or not, his testimony echoed Wright's own proposal for a minimum wage.[21]

He and his compatriots at the hearing also endorsed Wright's ten-hour measure for the same reason, that it was a more appropriate solution than blaming French Canadians for their own misfortunes. It was galling to Gagnon and the others that the same manufacturers who recruited cheap labor "at the bottom of our French Canadian country" should then "say that the French Canadians have been an obstacle to the system of ten hours of labor." The worst that could be said was that the "Canadians are peaceful, law-abiding citizens; and they accept the wages fixed by the liberality, or sometimes the cupidity and avarice, of the manufacturers." Were they "docile," as Wright had charged? "All they ask," he had written, "is to be set to work, and they care little who rules them or how they are ruled." H. A. Dubuque, who chaired the hearing, defended French Canadians based on their nonparticipation in strikes. The ten-hour movement had begun with a strike in Fall River in 1874. It had led to "intimidation, violation of law, rows, public demonstrations, which were converting the whole city into a state of rebellion." French Canadians, he went on, "wherever a strike has taken place," have "never taken part . . . and have staid [sic] at home like good law-abiding citizens." Their refusal to join their fellow workers "has created a prejudice against them, and made other nationalities believe they were opposed to the ten-hour law."

Docile or simply law-abiding, French Canadians still posed a danger to the ten-hour measure, Wright observed. It was not that they formally opposed it, he explained. Rather "manufacturers objected to taking up any reformatory movements for the elevation of a people that were not going to stay among them." The charge, as he had phrased it in his previous report, was that French Canadians were not "a stream of stable settlers" but a "horde of industrial invaders." Had it not "been the policy of . . . whom you might call the principal men [among the French Canadians] to advocate the doctrine of repatriation?" he asked Gagnon, referring to the efforts of the Province of Quebec to lure emigrants back with the promise of free land. "Yes, sir," Gagnon replied. "I have been an agent myself." But, Gagnon went on, "every thing is stopped" because so few families were interested in returning to Canada.

Repatriation, the Reverend J. B. V. Millette of Nashua, New Hampshire, interjected, "was a total failure." Wright asked about the policy of the Catholic Church on repatriation. "The Church in

Canada," Millette replied, "as represented by its bishops and priests, has done all in its power to stop immigration." Wright also wanted to know how the establishment of French Catholic churches in America affected the permanency of the French people in Worcester. "It brings on what in Canada was feared," Millette answered. This response led to a moment of epiphany for Wright, a moment when, as the philosopher William James would say, truth happened to an idea. Was he correct to think, Wright asked, that "during the last five years" the French Canadians in the United States had been passing through "a transitional state"? He did not mean simply that repatriation had failed, he explained. What he really wanted to know was if "the gradual establishment of churches here" was leading to "the permanency of the French population" in New England. The answer on all sides, including from Worcester's Father Primeau, was yes.

As the pastor of H. A. Dubuque's church in Fall River, the Reverend B. J. B. Bedard, phrased it, "It is quite natural for the clergy in Canada to desire the people living in Canada to stay there; but I do believe the American clergymen will be the first to raise their voice in favor of the permanent settlement of American citizens in the United States." Not only did the priests encourage naturalization, he went on, they urged their parishioners to "own property, real estate."

Wright somehow, despite his previous disdain for the French, grasped the full import of what Bedard and the others had told him. Indeed, he grasped it more fully than they did themselves, as their reaction to his next annual report would demonstrate. In his "Resumé," which he attached to the transcript of the hearing, he said, "When immigration began in earnest," the Canadians "came, as a rule, with not only the exhortation of the French Catholic priest of Canada to return when they had acquired some means, but with their own promises to the priest that they would return" still ringing in their ears. It did not take long, however, before "another influence began to be felt. The French Canadian loves his church, and is loyal to it." French-speaking parishes began to spring up, and the curé, "coming from Canada, it may be on missionary work, to take charge of the growing parish, soon found himself permanently established in New England, and his natural desire was to see his flock grow and prosper." With "strong French churches established," Wright observed, "repatriation is a failure."[22]

It was "very gratifying," Wright wrote, "to know that a wide and rapidly growing movement has arisen among the French Canadians within the past few years, towards becoming citizens, fully identified with us as a permanent and honorable part of our people." Indeed, he continued, their "complete assimilation with the

American people is but a question of time."[23] They were white because they were well launched down the road that would soon leave them indistinguishable from New England's Yankee residents.

What convinced Wright was not Gagnon's survey. It would have been easy, he commented in his "Resumé," to dispute the accuracy of the data. Instead he printed them as gathered, as a courtesy. Their accuracy was not important. What was important was that the French Canadians, at the urging of their priests, were becoming citizens, were becoming property owners, and were showing no interest in repatriation to Quebec. Even more important to Wright, and this is where his grasp of their situation went beyond that of the French Canadians themselves, was the fact that their efforts to remain Canadian were a stage in their assimilation. Their commitment to making their lives in New England, he wrote, is "strongly shown in the building of churches, the establishment of schools, societies, literary associations, etc." The growth of newspapers such as *Le Travailleur* with its masthead proclaiming devotion to "faith, language, and fatherland," also testified to the Canadians' ultimate assimilation. Ethnic institutions, Wright's interrogation of the clergy convinced him, promoted assimilation because they contributed to the permanency of the French-Canadian communities. The fact that the parishes were Catholic, that the schools, newspapers, and societies were Francophone, that all celebrated a French-Canadian identity, was incidental. Assimilation was "but a question of time."[24]

This was a hard truth, one the Canadians were not prepared to acknowledge. "The Colonel deceives himself," fumed *Le Messager* of Lewiston, Maine, in an editorial reprinted in *Le Travailleur*. "No one assimilates less than a Frenchman." Others before Wright "have offered them [Canadians] the kiss of peace in return for [them abandoning] their religious convictions or their fidelity to the traditions of their fathers," but history showed that the Canadian was "never a traitor to his country." Of course, Wright had not demanded, as *Le Messager* misleadingly claimed, that the French Canadians "abandon everything that is dear to them: their language, their religion, their customs." Nor had he insisted that "they forget Canada." He had done something far worse. He had written that they were in the process of doing these very things of their own volition, that assimilation was an inevitable consequence of their success in making a place for themselves in the United States. Far from assailing their religion, he had said that the French-Canadian parish was the key to the whole process.[25]

Wright's 1882 annual report gave even greater offense to French Canadians than his report of 1881—in which he had called them "Chinese"—because it directly challenged their own vision of themselves, the vision in Father Primeau's previous sermon. As *Le*

Messager phrased it, Canadians viewed themselves as "detached, regarded as strangers, not speaking the language of the country" while "framing, in the United States, a new fatherland whose point of reference is the memory of the dear and venerable fatherland." Canadians wanted to believe that they could be in, but not of, the United States. "Looked upon as strangers, they want to revive these memories and at the side of the Canadian church they will build the parochial school and the convent." Their task was to build a French-speaking, Catholic community in which they could perpetuate the customs of their parents. Their parishes, schools, convents, societies, newspapers, all were proof that they were succeeding. Wright's 1882 report so irritated them because he offered an alternative reading. They really had abandoned Quebec, just as those who stayed behind had accused them of doing. Their patriotism to the "old fatherland" was a matter of show, not substance. Their "Canadian" institutions were just so much evidence of the roots that they were so quickly sinking in New England's soil. What he did, in short, was voice their own misgivings and fears.

Unlike his surveys and other statistical investigations, Wright's analysis of the "Canadian French" and the process of assimilation won him no praise. The Canadians themselves denounced his report. And concerned native-born New Englanders simply failed to heed his assurances that the proliferation of ethnic institutions was in fact a sign of the eventual assimilation of the group in question. Instead, they flocked to organizations such as the Sons and Daughters of the American Revolution that catered to their view of themselves as the "real" Americans. Yet Wright had happened upon an important insight. The same visible signs of "foreignness"—the newspapers in a strange language, the shops featuring strange delicacies, the parades and fêtes in honor of Saint Jean-Baptiste or celebrating Mardi Gras, the churches with services in both Latin and French—that alarmed nativists that newcomers would refuse to become Americans and that reassured immigrants that they were true to the "old fatherland" were in fact signs of permanent attachment to the United States.

Father Primeau was one of those who unintentionally persuaded Wright of this assimilation. He had struggled for years with his flock to build up Notre-Dame-des-Canadiens. He had lived in the church basement in those early days, insisting that a convent and a school were more important than a rectory. He had taken only half his salary because he would ask no sacrifice of his parishioners he would not ask of himself. All of his self-imposed privations had been endured so that they could remain true to "faith, language, and fatherland." Yet at the very first meeting with Worcester's Canadians, Primeau had informed them that the new parish would be run on "American" principles. They were not in Canada, he had told them. In Canada there were parish councils, elected by the parishioners, that controlled the budget and held the deeds to church property. In America, the property belonged to the bishop, and he would control the budget. He would instruct the children in French and in Canadian history, he promised. And he was as good as his word. But he would also start a naturalization club. He would interpret the French-Canadian community to the Yankee community. He would defend its good name. His parishioners would also have to do their part. They would have to gain the respect of their Yankee neighbors by participating in the political process—by voting. They were Americans now.

Notes

1. I have invented this conversation but have taken all specific references to how the data were gathered and the goals the budget study was intended to serve from *Sixth Annual Report of the Bureau of Statistics of Labor* (Boston: N.p., 1875): 189–450.

2. James Leiby, *Carroll Wright and Labor Reform: The Origins of Labor Statistics* (Cambridge, MA: Harvard University Press, 1960). All biographical information comes from this source.

3. *Sixth Annual Report*, 194, 193.

4. Ibid., 194.

5. A Canadian missionary, L'Abbé T. A. Chandonnet, wrote a highly detailed history of the first years of Primeau's parish in *Notre-Dame-des-Canadiens et le Canadiens aux États-Unis* (Montreal, 1872), based on weeks of conversations with Father Primeau. Kenneth J. Moynihan of the Assumption College Community Studies Program translated it into English.

6. *Sixth Annual Report*, 295.

7. Ibid., 312.

8. Chandonnet, *Notre-Dame-des-Canadiens*, 100.

9. Ibid., 101, 29.

10. "Uniform Hours of Labor," in *Twelfth Annual Report of the Bureau of Statistics of Labor* (Boston, N.p., 1881).

11. *Twelfth Annual Report*, 470, 468.

12. *Twelfth Annual Report*, 150, 151; *The Canadian French in New England, Thirteenth Annual Report of the Massachusetts Bureau of Statistics of Labor* (Boston, N.p., 1881): 80.

13. *The Canadian French in New England*, 82.

14. *Twelfth Annual Report*, 150, 151.

15. Ibid.

16. "A Lesson," *Le Travailleur*, May 6, 1881. This and all subsequent quotations from the French-Canadian press are my translations.

17. "Colonel Wright's Report," *Le Travailleur*, May 17, 1881.

18. Carroll D. Wright, Introduction in *The Canadian French in New England*, 4–9.

19. "The Meeting in Boston," *Le Travailleur*, October 28, 1881, details the planning session French-Canadian participants in the hearing held to decide on a strategy. For the quotations from Wright, see note 12.

20. "A Lesson," *Le Travailleur*, May 6, 1881; "Colonel Wright's Report," *Le Travailleur*, May 17, 1881.

21. The full text of the hearing is in *The Canadian French in New England*, 15–87.

22. "Resume," *The Canadian French in New England*, 89–90.

23. *The Canadian French in New England*, 90.

24. Ibid., 90, 91.

25. "The Wright Questions," *Le Messager*, as reprinted in *Le Travailleur*, January 31, 1882.

Suggested Readings

Despite historians' reliance on Wright's reports and those of the researchers he inspired, they have largely overlooked his role in the debates over minimum wages, maximum hours, factory safety, immigration, and other social issues in the late nineteenth century. Paul Boyer, *Urban Masses and Moral Order in America, 1820–1920* (Cambridge, MA: Harvard University Press, 1978), mentions him only once. Michael B. Katz does not mention Wright at all in his *In the Shadow of the Poorhouse: A Social History of Welfare in America* (New York: Basic Books, 1986). Daniel Horowitz devotes a chapter to Wright and his 1875 report "How Workers Spent Their Money and Should Have Led Their Lives," in his *The Morality of Spending: Attitudes toward the Consumer Society in America, 1875–1940* (Baltimore: Johns Hopkins University Press, 1985). A critique of Horowitz is John F. McClymer, "How to Read Wright: The Equity of the Wage System and the Morality of Spending," *Hayes Historical Journal*, 8 (Winter 1989): 37–43. James Leiby, *Carroll Wright and Labor Reform: The Origins of Labor Statistics* (Cambridge, MA: Harvard University Press, 1960), remains the standard biography. Students of ethnic history have devoted little attention thus far to French Canadians. A good introduction is Charles W. Estus and Kenneth J. Moynihan, "Beyond Textiles: Industrial Diversity and the Franco-American Experience in Worcester, Massachusetts," in Claire Quintal, ed., *The Little Canadas of New England*, Third Annual Conference of the French Institute (Worcester, MA: French Institute, 1983), 104–119.

2

James G. Blaine
and the Republican Party Vision

Charles W. Calhoun

James G. Blaine was the leading Republican during the generation following the Civil War. Born to ordinary circumstances in Pennsylvania, Blaine started his career as a schoolteacher and a newspaper editor but later turned to politics, serving in the Maine state legislature, the U.S. House of Representatives, and the Senate. He rose to the speakership in the House and was the secretary of state under two presidents. He also sought the Republican party's presidential nomination on several occasions and gained it in 1884 only to lose the election to Grover Cleveland. Despite this disappointment, Blaine had a significant influence on the Republican party during his career.

Charles W. Calhoun, a historian of the Gilded Age, reviews the career of the controversial Plumed Knight. Professor Calhoun argues that Blaine's career contradicts the traditional wisdom about politics in the Gilded Age as issueless and insignificant. Blaine tackled economic issues, excelling in framing these subjects in terms that the general public could understand. By advocating protective tariffs, the development of trade ties with foreign markets, and subsidies to the states, Blaine demonstrated that Republicans of his era were not unequivocally wedded to laissez-faire approaches to government. Historians' fascination with corruption and cronyism during these years obscures this positive view of government.

Charles Calhoun received his Ph.D. in history from Columbia University. He is currently professor of history at East Carolina University and is a past president of the Society for Historians of the Gilded Age and Progressive Era. His publications include *Gilded Age Cato: The Life of Walter Q. Gresham* (1988) and *The Gilded Age: Essay on the Origins of Modern America* (1996).

In the intensely partisan struggles between Republicans and Democrats in the late nineteenth century, no one dominated American political life more than the Republican party leader, James G. Blaine. As a public man, Blaine possessed an extraordinary capacity to elicit the passions of both the masses and his fellow politicians. Tall and handsome with dark, piercing eyes, he had a personal charm and brilliance as a speaker that attracted a vast body of devoted followers, often called Blainiacs. As one contemporary observer noted, "Had he been a woman, people would have rushed off to send expensive flowers."[1] Yet although legions loved him, others hated him with equal intensity, especially those who believed allegations that he abused public office for personal financial gain. His personality was complex and multifaceted. To different segments of his generation, he was at once charismatic and repulsive— both the Plumed Knight of convention oratory and the Tattooed Man of damning political cartoons. But even though he was and remains a controversial figure, Blaine played a leading role in formulating his party's ideas. His principal goal was for the Republican party to embrace a nationalistic program of government action consistent with his vision of a progressive development of the nation. As much as any other individual, Blaine determined the political agenda of the late-nineteenth-century United States.

Blaine recognized implicitly what modern historians have stated explicitly, that the central fact of nineteenth-century American life was the transformation of the nation from a largely agricultural, rural, isolated, localized, and traditional society to one that was industrial, urban, integrated, national, and modern. In his time, this alteration was not yet complete, and he therefore advocated a powerful national government to foster the country's economic development. The lasting significance of his career lies in his effort to commit the Republican party to responsible, forward-looking national authority as against what he saw as the backward, parochial negativism of the Democrats.

James Gillespie Blaine was born January 31, 1830, at West Brownsville in western Pennsylvania. His family had once been fairly prosperous, but it faced more modest circumstances during his childhood. As a boy, James was a quick learner with an extraordinary memory, and he showed an early fascination with politics. According to one family friend, he was "a violent Whig partisan at the early age of seven."[2] When he was only thirteen he entered nearby Washington (later Washington and Jefferson) College. After graduation in 1847 he taught for a few years at the Western Military Institute in Kentucky. During his first term the young teacher attended a speech by his political idol, Henry Clay, at Lexington, where he wrote down every word that fell from the "majestic lips" of the "Whig oracle."[3] While he lived in Kentucky, Blaine saw the evils of slavery firsthand, confirming his hatred for the institution. On a happier note, he fell in love with Harriet Stanwood, also a transplanted teacher originally from Maine. The two married and eventually had seven children. Blaine taught at an institution for the blind in Philadelphia from 1852 to 1854. In the latter year he moved to Maine to enter the newspaper business with help from his wife's brothers. In Augusta he became editor of the influential Whig *Kennebec Journal*.

Like many men in his generation, Blaine used journalism to launch his political career. As the Whig party collapsed and gave way to the Republicans in the mid-1850s, Blaine championed the new organization. In 1856 he represented Maine at the party's first national convention, held in Philadelphia. Two years later he covered the Illinois debates between Abraham Lincoln and Stephen Douglas and formed an enduring veneration for Lincoln. The same year, Blaine won election to the Maine house of representatives, where he served from 1859 to 1862, the last two years as Speaker. Recognized as an adroit political organizer, Blaine in 1859 accepted the chairmanship of the Maine Republican state committee, a post he retained for twenty-two years.

In 1862, Blaine's constituents elected him to the national House of Representatives, where he served until 1876. In Washington he quickly attracted attention as an able debater, defending the Lincoln administration's conduct during the Civil War, including the enlistment of black soldiers in the Union effort. During Reconstruction he sided more often with moderate Republicans but did embrace the key element of the radical program, black suffrage. In the heated exchanges that characterized Congress in these years, Blaine did not hesitate to cross swords with established leaders such as Thaddeus Stevens or to match wits with other rising stars such as Roscoe Conkling. In one memorable exchange with Conkling, Blaine ridiculed the supercilious New Yorker for his "grandiloquent swell, his majestic, supereminent, overpowering, turkey-gobbler strut."[4] Conkling never forgot the derisive laughter that filled the House chamber, and for the rest of his life he did all he could to thwart Blaine's ambitions.

For the most part, however, the Maine representative won high marks, and at the beginning of his fourth term in 1869 his colleagues elected him Speaker. Thus, with remarkable speed he had become a force to be reckoned with in the national Republican party, having gained the speakership at a time when Congress stood at the center of the American political system. In the mid-1880s, Blaine recounted the major issues that confronted the nation in this era in his two-volume *Twenty Years of Congress*. He never wrote an extended work of political philosophy as such, but this book served as an implicit statement of his beliefs. Ostensibly a historical study, *Twenty Years* was an extended tribute to nationalism and government activism.

Much of what Blaine said in his book mirrored positions he took in congressional debates or in speeches on the political stump. At the end of the 1860s and nearly every year for the rest of his life,

Blaine made campaign speaking tours through several states on behalf of the Republican party and its candidates. In one typical fall campaign season he spoke thirty-nine times in eight weeks in Maine and then headed out to Pennsylvania, Ohio, and other western states. As probably the best-traveled politician of his time, he created a mass following for himself and the beliefs he articulated. With exquisite understanding of the American voter, he presented complex economic and social issues in comprehensible rhetoric that served the partisan purposes of the Republican party and also promoted his ideas. His willingness to undertake those grueling annual tours reflected his conviction that machine methods alone would not suffice to win elections, that his party must also appeal to the hearts and minds of what he called "the Sovereign People."[5]

As a partisan leader, Blaine naturally emphasized the issue differences between his own party and the opposition, but he went further and cast that conflict as the latest round in a century-old fight between two fundamentally different conceptions of the American Union and the role of government in society. In *Twenty Years* he pointed to an "enduring and persistent line of division between the two parties which in a generic sense have always existed in the United States:—the party of strict construction and the party of liberal construction, the party of State Rights and the party of National Supremacy, the party of stinted revenue and restricted expenditure, and the party of generous income with its wise application to public improvement."[6] The Democrats and Republicans of the Gilded Age, he maintained, simply carried forward these longstanding differences and offered voters the same fundamental choice between nationalism and localism, between government activism and government restraint. The Republican party should assume the mantle of the Federalists and the Whigs and offer the country a program to ensure a directed economic growth with efficiency and equity. Taking Henry Clay as his personal model, Blaine argued for a national currency and banking system, a well-crafted protective tariff, reciprocal trade agreements, and generous subsidies, all indispensable to move the country forward.

Blaine believed that the greatest impediment to the kind of program he envisioned was the prolonged controversy over sectionalism that had plagued the Union since its founding. Through several decades before the Civil War, Blaine wrote in his *Twenty Years*, the Democratic party, led by its southern wing, had dominated the federal government and, true to its strict construction-limited government doctrine, had thwarted the beneficent potential of national authority. Time and again the narrowness of Democratic party leaders had blocked Henry Clay's American System, which called for a protective tariff, internal improvements, and a national bank. When

Southerners carried their pernicious doctrine of states' rights to the point of rebellion, Blaine said, they launched "a challenge to civilization, and . . . a fight against the nineteenth century."[7] Thus, the Union victory in 1865 not only preserved the nation and freed the slaves; it also signaled the triumph of the activist theory of government as advocated by the Republican party. The great task of Reconstruction—securing this nationalistic outcome—met stout resistance from Andrew Johnson and the Democrats. But after three years of turmoil culminating in Republican victory in the 1868 election, Blaine believed that "the Government and the people of the Union were entitled to look forward . . . to the promotion of agriculture, manufactures, and commerce."[8]

But the fond hope of Blaine and other Republicans that the national government could now carry on the important task of fostering economic growth proved premature. Over the next eight years, conservative white Democrats employed a variety of means to regain control of state after state in the South. As a result, Republicans confronted a dilemma with serious implications for their ability to retain control of the national government: they could use force to prop up Reconstruction regimes and run the risk of alienating some Northerners growing disenchanted with "bayonet rule" in the South, they could concentrate on solidifying their northern support by waving the bloody shirt, or they could try to transcend sectionalism altogether by emphasizing economic issues important to both the North and the South. Republicans wrestled with these alternatives for decades. Blaine never fully resolved the problem for himself, but more and more the trend of his thinking was toward the last alternative—building a national constituency through appeals for a national economic program.

In the 1870s, however, he approached this delicate political problem with ambivalence. He showed little enthusiasm for further legislation on behalf of the Republican Reconstruction governments, but he also deplored the violence employed in the South to prevent blacks from voting. Stressing the protection of the rights of citizenship as a national obligation, he argued that "whenever and wherever the local authority fails, the strong arm of the Federal Government should be invoked and exercised."[9]

Yet during the course of the 1870s, Blaine balanced this sectionalist rhetoric with discussion of other matters, especially the money question. During the Civil War the national government had issued the so-called greenbacks, paper money unbacked by any promise to pay gold. After the war, inflationists argued for the continued or expanded use of these dollars; "sound money" advocates favored their measured withdrawal and a return to specie payments for those still in circulation. As a member of the latter group, Blaine sought to pin the inflationist heresy on the Democratic party while claiming financial soundness exclusively for the Republicans. Although he realized that debtors and other classes might suffer from the deflationary pressures of orthodox money policies, he took the political gamble that ultimately most voters would recognize the virtues of a "safe" currency of steady, reliable value. Neither laborers who earned a daily wage nor farmers who sold their crops wished to be paid in cheap money, he maintained.

Blaine predicted that the money question would be one of the leading issues in the campaign of 1876, the year he made his first bid for the Republican presidential nomination. In January he gave his candidacy a boost with a scathing speech in the House, attacking efforts to grant amnesty to Jefferson Davis. His campaign gained strength through the winter and early spring, but it suffered a serious setback when newspaper reports and a congressional investigation raised allegations that he had abused his position as Speaker in return for payments from railroads. In an audacious response, Blaine took the House floor a week before the Republican national convention and offered a dazzling defense that allayed the suspicions of many. He entered the convention with more than three-quarters of the delegates needed to win, and the capstone of his candidacy came in the nominating speech offered by Robert G. Ingersoll, who declared, "Like an armed warrior, like a plumed knight, James G. Blaine marched down the halls of the American Congress and threw his shining lance full and fair against the brazen forehead of every traitor to his country and every maligner of his fair reputation."[10] Nonetheless, in the end, Blaine could not overcome the doubts of reformers and the opposition of factional foes such as Roscoe Conkling, and he lost the nomination to Rutherford B. Hayes. In July, Blaine was appointed to fill a vacancy in the U.S. Senate, and he was elected to a full term early the next year.

By the time of the congressional election campaign of 1878, Blaine was telling audiences that "the currency question is the great question before the people" and that "the most fearful thing that could happen to this country would be the issuance of an unlimited amount of currency."[11] But in that year, for the first time since the Civil War, the Democrats won control of both houses of Congress with the bulk of their seats filled by Southerners. In response, Blaine again turned to the bloody shirt, but with a twist, for he now drew an explicit link between the festering problem of sectionalism and the economic issues he considered ultimately of much greater importance. In a Senate speech he pointed out that in the southern states thirty-five House seats and, hence, thirty-five electoral votes were based on the black population; by violence and intimidation, however, that population was denied the right to vote. Black suffrage had thus become "a hollow mockery," but disfranchisement raised an even broader question: "whether the white voter of the North shall be equal to the white voter of the South in shaping the policy and fixing the destiny of this country." As the result of "this ruthless seizure of unlawful power, . . . vast monetary and commercial interests, great questions of revenue, adjustments of tariff, investments in manufactures, in railways, and in mines, are under the control of a Democratic Congress whose majority was obtained by depriving the negro of his rights."[12]

As the prospects for racial justice in the South grew dimmer, Blaine gave increasing attention to economic questions. In 1880, once again a contender for the presidential nomination, he faced a formidable foe in former president Ulysses Grant, whose principal backers, the Stalwart wing of the Republican party, sought to keep the fading sectionalism issue alive. Blaine's Half-Breed faction fought to a deadlock with the Stalwarts in the national convention, and the party nominated a dark horse, U.S. Representative James A. Garfield, who agreed with Blaine on most economic questions. In September a Republican loss in the Maine state elections sent Blaine and other national party leaders in search of a new issue for the fall presidential campaign. The fact that Republicans had run well in Maine's manufacturing towns led Blaine and Garfield to focus on the protective tariff as the key to victory. Blaine was reported to have stormed into the party's campaign headquarters, shouting to workers, "Fold up the bloody shirt and lay it away. It's of no use to us. You want to shift the main issue to protection."[13] The story may be fictitious, but the shift was unmistakable. Within the Republican party the new strategy represented a triumph over the Stalwarts for Blaine's forward-looking Half-Breed faction. "From that time," Blaine later wrote, "the industrial question monopolized public attention."[14] Garfield won the November election, and the party's new ideological emphasis received the sanction of electoral success.

In recognition of Blaine's campaign services, Garfield invited him to head the State Department in the new administration. As secretary of state, Blaine charted an activist foreign policy especially devoted to cultivating closer commercial ties with Latin America. But Garfield's assassination and his replacement by Vice President Chester A. Arthur brought Blaine's cabinet service to a close before the end of 1881. Finding himself a private citizen for the first time in more than two decades, Blaine turned to writing and produced the first volume of his *Twenty Years of Congress*.

With his book and continued speaking on the political stump, Blaine sought to shape Republican doctrine to meet the needs of the industrializing nation in the 1880s. Even before the 1880 campaign he and other Republicans had advocated a protective tariff, but now Blaine moved to make protectionism the centerpiece of the party's program. In *Twenty Years* he devoted a whole chapter to the history of the tariff and its benefits to the nation. Describing the first tariff act passed by Congress in 1789 as "a second Declaration of Independence,"[15] he portrayed customs legislation as a signal example of national government activism in defense of American interests. He argued that during the nineteenth century when protective tariffs were on the books, the country enjoyed prosperity, but the lowering of tariffs always led to panics and depressions. Barely acknowledging other influences in the country's ups and downs, Blaine's portrayal of the American economy as virtually one-dimensional and delicately brittle was overdrawn. Modern-day scholars disagree about the impact the tariff has had on the nation's economic growth, but in his day, Blaine was convinced that protectionism made sense. "The record of tariff legislation, from the very origin of the government," he wrote, "is the record of enlightened selfishness; and enlightened selfishness is the basis of much that is wisest in legislation."[16]

Blaine's writing and speaking kept him in the public eye, and his popularity as a Republican spokesman continued to grow. In 1884 he at last won the party's nomination for the presidency, defeating President Arthur. The Democrats named Grover Cleveland, whose reform image had gained him a landslide victory in the New York gubernatorial race two years earlier. As governor of the nation's most populous state, which was pivotal in any presidential contest, Cleveland was a formidable opponent. Precedent dictated that presidential nominees should remain at home and leave overt campaigning to others, but Blaine broke with tradition and made an extended speaking tour. Again he celebrated the virtues of Republican economic policies, especially the tariff. With superb political instincts, he believed Americans would respond readily to arguments concerning their own material well-being.

Blaine contended that all Americans, regardless of station or occupation, prospered under protectionism, but he laid particular stress on its benefits to labor. He saw it as fitting that the Republican party, which had come into existence resisting slavery, should serve now as "the protector of free labor," using the tariff to rescue the laborer from "the servitude of poverty."[17] In launching his campaign he urged Republican newspapers to keep up "a steady flow in editorial columns on tariff, protection, [and] *wages*—especially *wages*."[18] On the stump he argued that since labor constituted upward of 90 percent of the costs of any manufactured article, to reduce the tariff and invite importation of cheap foreign goods would subject American workers to a ruinous competition with their low-paid counterparts abroad.

Of course, Blaine was no enemy to business. Indeed, it was the perception of the Republican party as the party of business and of himself as an apologist for capitalists that he hoped to counteract with his emphasis on the tariff's benefits to labor. He knew that among the voters, laborers far outnumbered employers. Hence, he stressed that "the man who is working for day wages will be found as keenly alive to the effect of a change in the protective duty as the stockholder whose dividends are to be affected."[19] He sought to portray Republican policies, especially protectionism, as the key to harmony between capital and labor and to domestic tranquility in the society at large. The abandonment of protectionism, he argued, "would produce a conflict between the poor and the rich, and in the sorrowful degradation of labor would plant seeds of public danger."[20]

Blaine denied the charge that a high tariff led inevitably to high prices and monopoly. Protectionism, he claimed, insulated Americans from foreign competition and thus stimulated the proliferation of producers at home, whose spirited domestic competition tended to keep prices low. He admitted some upward push on prices but justified it by the higher wages paid American workers. He also disputed the argument that a high tariff damaged the American export trade and particularly hurt farmers with products to sell abroad. He asserted that in the twenty-four years since the launching of the protective system in 1861, U.S. exports totaled 33 percent more than during all the country's previous history. Again, his history was somewhat one-dimensional, for he slighted other factors in the expansion of exports and ignored the question of how much trade might have grown without the inhibiting effect of a high tariff.

But the main point Blaine wished to make to farmers was that the home market, not the export trade, was the key to their prosperity. Noting that farmers sold vastly more at home than overseas, he stressed the harmony of agricultural and manufacturing interests in the industrializing nation. By encouraging the development of factories that used agricultural raw materials and paid the wages of laborers who demanded foodstuffs, the protective tariff helped generate a market that guaranteed farmers' ability to sell their commodities.

In answer to those who complained that excessive tariff revenues contributed to a surplus in the Treasury, he suggested applying the money to the national debt and also giving generous pensions to Union army veterans, improving the nation's defenses, and distributing excess revenues to the states. Finally, he denied the claim that protection led to overproduction and periodic gluts of manufactured products, which in turn led to financial depressions. Rather, he said, excessive production in manufacturing came from the increasing use of labor-saving machinery, which simply underscored the need to protect American manufacturing firms from the influx of cheaply produced foreign products that would come with a reduced tariff. Thus, Blaine played down the difficulties associated with the protective tariff and urged Americans to have an almost childlike faith in its powers to meet any problem. In sum, he asked, who could "measure the injury to our shops and our homes, to our farms and our commerce" if protectionism were abandoned?[21]

Undergirding all of Blaine's economic program was his deep belief in the responsibility of the national government to take positive action for the public good. By 1884 the bloody shirt had all but disappeared from his rhetoric, and during his campaign he tried to convince Southerners that they derived great material benefits from Republican policies. Noting the New South's quest for industrial development, he urged people in the region to embrace tariff protectionism and to put aside bitter memories of the war and Reconstruction. On a campaign swing through West Virginia he invited Southerners to "join in a union not merely in form, but a union in fact, and take your part in the solution of the industrial and financial problems of the time."[22]

The effort failed. The Republicans lost in the October state elections in West Virginia, and the prospect of a Democratic sweep in the Solid South prompted Blaine again to urge northern solidarity to turn back a states' rights triumph. He spoke out once more against the suppression of the black vote. He warned Northerners that they should "fully comprehend what it means to trust the National credit, the National finances, the National pensions, the protective system, and all the great interests which are under the control of the National Government, to the old South, with its bitterness, its unreconciled temper, its narrowness of vision, its hostility to all Northern interests, its constant longing to revive an impossible past, its absolute incapacity to measure the sweep and the magnitude of our great future."[23]

Despite the setback in the South, Blaine continued his midwestern tour, speaking to large enthusiastic crowds that seemed to warm to his nationalistic economic message. He traveled as far west as Wisconsin before turning back toward the East and a planned climax of parades and speeches in the Northeast. But climax turned into calamity in New York City. On the morning of October 29, Blaine met a group of ministers whose spokesman, Samuel D. Burchard, praised the Republican candidate and denounced the Democrats as the party of "Rum, Romanism, and Rebellion."[24] Blaine failed to catch this unfortunate insult against Roman Catholics, but Democratic reporters did and published it in newspapers throughout the country. Up to that point, Blaine had been courting the votes of Irish Americans (most of whom were Catholics) by accusing the Democrats of being pro-British, as shown by their low-tariff ideas. Now the Democrats charged the Republican nominee with condoning, if not sharing, a blatant prejudice against Catholics. Blaine later repudiated Burchard's slur, noting that his own mother had been a Catholic, but it was difficult to repair the damage with less than a week to go before the election.

To compound his problem, on the same day as the ministers' meeting, Blaine attended a dinner at a posh New York restaurant with Jay Gould, Andrew Carnegie, and scores of other wealthy businessmen. He addressed the assembled millionaires, reminding them that they owed much of their wealth to the policies of the Republican party, especially the protective tariff. The next morning Democratic newspapers sported front-page cartoons depicting a ragged poor family turned away from "The Royal Feast of Belshazzar Blaine and the Money Kings."[25] The Democrats played Blaine's misstep for all it was worth, hoping to undermine the appeal of his protectionist arguments with labor.

On top of these distressing incidents at the close of his campaign, Blaine's presidential bid suffered from defections by the so-called Mugwumps, self-styled reformers within the Republican party who professed to favor less partisanship and more "honest" government and who could not overcome their reservations concerning his alleged corrupt practices. Moreover, Roscoe Conkling's refusal to aid Blaine's campaign cost him the support of some of the old Stalwarts in New York and elsewhere. Still, despite all these handicaps, Blaine came within a hair's breadth of winning the presidency. Cleveland won his home state of New York by just 1,149 votes out of over 1 million cast, and the state's 36 electoral votes made the difference between victory and defeat. If 575 people had voted the other way in New York, Blaine would have become president.

The Republicans had begun 1884 with little hope of success in the presidential race, largely because a serious economic recession cost them support as the party in power. Yet Blaine's vigorous campaign, picturing the downturn as a momentary setback and touting Republican economic policies as the key to restored and permanent prosperity, reversed the gloomy outlook and brought the party close to success. Indeed, in losing, Blaine gained 400,000 more popular votes than Garfield had garnered in victory in 1880. Blaine lost the presidency in a virtual dead heat, but he had won the admiration and thanks of legions of party members high and low and had succeeded in placing his stamp on Republican party doctrine. Party officials urged him to publish an edition of his campaign speeches because, as one put it, "they will be read and preserved by admiring millions as an epitome of the whole Republican creed."[26]

After his defeat, Blaine continued to invoke the specter of the "old" South in his rhetoric, but once again he emphasized the sectionalism issue's economic dimension, especially its impact on labor.

In the South, he argued, the Democrats' racist policies locked blacks into a permanent underclass where they lived at only a subsistence level. Southern blacks received wages one-half to one-third those of northern whites, and the differential steadily drove whites' wages down. Thus, Blaine said, the Democratic party was doubly culpable. By threatening to expose the white American worker to the danger of European competition through a reduced tariff and "by unfairly making the colored laborer his fatal competitor in all the fields of toil," the Democrats stood "as the enemy of every interest of the American workman."[27]

In the strike-ridden mid-1880s, Blaine saw the political wisdom of giving even greater emphasis to the Republican party's free-labor ideology. He defended workers' right to unionize and "to exert strong power through combination,"[28] but he warned against "the error of treating the laborer & the capitalist as belonging to fixed & permanent classes. The laborer of today by industry and economy may become the capitalist of a few years hence."[29] He thus endorsed the Horatio Alger myth so useful to the capitalist class in defusing labor discontent, but he also called for further government action in the interest of working people. At the state level he favored legislation providing arbitration of labor disputes, limiting hours of work per day, and outlawing child labor. At the national level the principal influence on working conditions remained, of course, the tariff. He admonished organizations such as the Knights of Labor to consider how wages in the United States could be kept above the European level without protective duties.

Blaine welcomed President Cleveland's December 1887 annual message devoted solely to a call for reduced customs duties because it set the stage for the presidential campaign of 1888 to be waged squarely on the tariff issue. Blaine probably could have won a second nomination in 1888, but he withdrew early in the year. With the Maine statesman's blessing the party turned to Benjamin Harrison, whose campaign speeches echoed Blaine's economic emphasis. Blaine joined in the campaign, taking special care to deny Cleveland's charge that protectionism had led to the development of trusts, a matter of growing concern to Americans. He argued that free-trade England had many more trusts than the United States. Moreover, recognizing both the advantages and disadvantages of modern industrial organization, he refused to brand trusts as all bad or all good. In any case, he doubted that national policy had much impact on them. Because corporations received their charters from the states, he argued, state legislatures were the proper bodies to control them.

A much more dangerous threat, he maintained, grew out of the development of powerful and rapacious international trusts—

uncontrollable at any level of government—that would result from the adoption of free trade. Such combinations would enjoy free rein to raise prices and reduce wages at will. All the more reason, Blaine declared, to maintain the protection of the home market.

The Republicans won both houses of Congress as well as the presidency in 1888, and Blaine assured president-elect Harrison that he would have "the amplest power for a useful, strong and impressive Administration."[30] Harrison invited Blaine to join in the work as secretary of state. For the first time in more than a decade the Republicans possessed real authority to act at the national level. With the McKinley Tariff Act they raised customs duties to a record peacetime high, thereby ensuring protection to producers of a wide range of commodities. They also increased government expenditures for veterans' pensions, internal improvements, and the navy, with spending reaching an unprecedented billion dollars. Passing a host of laws that included the Sherman Antitrust Act, the Meat Inspection Act, the Forest Reserve Act, and many others, the Republicans posted a record for domestic legislation unequaled until Theodore Roosevelt's second term. "Progress," Blaine explained, "means additional national ability and additional national expenditure."[31]

As head of the State Department, Blaine devoted much of his time to the cause of increasing foreign trade, particularly with Latin America. To further this goal and other objectives, in late 1889 he convened the Pan-American Conference, a meeting of delegates from throughout the Western Hemisphere. Although the conference produced few concrete results, Blaine emerged as the foremost American champion of its chief recommendation: the expansion of trade through reciprocity.

During the recent presidential campaign he had still maintained that it was "vastly more important not to lose our own great market for our own people in the vain effort to reach the impossible."[32] Now, however, he pointed out that both agricultural and manufacturing production exceeded the domestic demand, and it was time to seek new outlets. In the past, he argued, Congress had shown carelessness in tariff legislation, for whenever it had reduced or removed duties on goods from foreign countries, it had not demanded reciprocal favors. In 1890, Blaine made a dramatic appeal to Republicans to rectify past mistakes by inserting a reciprocity provision in the pending McKinley Tariff Bill. "There is not a section or a line in the entire bill that will open a market for another bushel of wheat or another barrel of pork," he argued.[33] Farmers had always been skeptical about Republican tariff policy. With farmer protest on the rise in groups such as the National Alliance and the nascent Populist party, Blaine touted reciprocity as potentially opening the markets of the forty million people of

Latin America to farm products from the United States. He denied charges from Republican critics that he was abandoning protectionism and claimed instead that because reciprocity offered the one sure way to defeat free trade, it represented the best safeguard for protection. Congress accepted the argument and passed the McKinley Act with reciprocity. Blaine's estimate of the law's effect was overblown, but his influence on tariff policy remained clear in the succeeding generation of Republican tariff legislation.

The test of the Republicans' activist program came in the 1890 midterm congressional elections, and the voters rejected it, giving the Democrats more than 70 percent of the seats in the next House. Within the party many Republican leaders had grown disenchanted with Harrison, largely because of his cold personality and his inability to satisfy their patronage demands. Some Republicans harbored the wish that Blaine could replace Harrison on their ticket in 1892. On the eve of the national convention, Blaine dramatically broke with the administration and resigned from the State Department. His name did go before the convention, but Harrison easily surpassed Blaine on the first and only ballot, 535 delegates to 182.

In fact, Blaine's poor health was a key argument against his nomination in 1892. Illness had kept him away from the State Department, and even out of Washington, for long periods, and the consequent extra load of work for Harrison in foreign affairs contributed to their estrangement. The death in early 1890 of two of Blaine's children had had a devastating effect on his energy. The loss of another son a week after his defeat by Harrison at the 1892 convention sent his spirits as low as they could go. He took little part in the campaign that fall beyond writing a magazine article extolling the twin policies of protectionism and reciprocity. Harrison lost his bid for reelection to former President Grover Cleveland.

Blaine was back in his Washington home in the fall of 1892, and there his illness, diagnosed as Bright's disease, deepened. He died January 27, 1893, just four days short of his sixty-third birthday.

Blaine's ideas lived on, however. When Cleveland and the Democrats seemed unable to cope with the devastating depression of the 1890s, the nation turned again to the Republicans. In 1896, William McKinley waged a vigorous campaign for the presidency, drawing on the central elements of Blaine's program: a "sound" currency based on the gold standard, tariff protectionism, and reciprocity. He crushed Democrat William Jennings Bryan, and the Republicans emerged as the nation's majority party, a status they retained for more than a generation. McKinley frankly acknowledged that his activist policies owed much to Blaine's teachings. In his last speech before his assassination, the president paid tribute to the great party leader for his "broad American spirit."[34]

Blaine's chief accomplishment as a politician was in helping to educate the Republican party to a wider vision. Certainly he was partisan to the very center of his being, but at that center he believed that his party must represent more than mere party loyalty for its own sake. The American voter demanded more. Although highly intelligent, Blaine was neither a learned nor a sophisticated economic thinker; he proved less interested in theory than in pragmatic approaches to problems. He espoused what is now called trickle-down economics, but he honestly believed that the forward march of progress would mean prosperity for all and harmony for society. "The distinctive trait of modern times," he wrote near the end of his life, "is that the achievement of the highest is brought down to the service of the lowliest." "America justifies her birthright only as she—not relieves merely but—uplifts, enlarges, strengthens the individual man in the widest organized community."[35]

In many ways, Blaine's program was more talk than performance, and sometimes rather simplistic talk. But such simplification was natural for a politician whose chief aim was providing the average American voter with an understanding of government's potential. Blaine did as much as any other public figure of his time to win respectability for the notion that progress could best be achieved not through a laissez-faire approach but through the enlightened and benevolent operation of government. The nation's phenomenal progress, he concluded, "could not have been made except under wise laws, honestly and impartially administered. It could not have been made except under an industrial system which stimulated enterprise, quickened capital, assured to labor its just reward. It could not have been made under the narrowing policy which assumes the sovereignty of the *State*. It required the broad measures, the expanding functions, which belong to a free *Nation*."[36]

Notes

1. Julia B. Foraker, *I Would Live It Again: Memories of a Vivid Life* (New York: Harper and Brothers, 1932), 132.

2. Gail Hamilton, *Biography of James G. Blaine* (Norwich, CT: Henry Bill, 1895), 66.

3. Hamilton, *Blaine*, 85.

4. *Congressional Globe*, 39th Cong., 1st sess., 1866, 2299.

5. James G. Blaine, *Twenty Years of Congress: From Lincoln to Garfield. With a Review of the Events Which Led to the Political Revolution of 1860*, 2 vols. (Norwich, CT: Henry Bill, 1884, 1886), 1:551.

6. Ibid., 1:180.

7. Ibid., 1:177.

8. Ibid., 2:467.

9. *New York Times,* October 13, 1874.

10. *Official Proceedings of the National Republican Conventions of 1868, 1872, 1876, and 1880* (Minneapolis: Charles W. Johnson, 1903), 296.

11. *New York Times,* August 22, 1878.

12. James G. Blaine, *Political Discussions: Legislative, Diplomatic, and Popular, 1856–1886* (Norwich, CT: Henry Bill, 1887), 202–3, 206, 208.

13. H. Wayne Morgan, *From Hayes to McKinley: National Party Politics, 1877–1896* (Syracuse, NY: Syracuse University Press, 1969), 116.

14. Blaine, *Twenty Years,* 2:669.

15. Ibid., 1:185.

16. Ibid., 1:200.

17. T. B. Boyd, comp., *The Blaine and Logan Campaign of 1884* (Chicago: J. L. Reagan, 1884), 197.

18. James G. Blaine to Whitelaw Reid, July 27, 1884, Whitelaw Reid Papers, Library of Congress, Washington, DC.

19. Blaine, *Twenty Years,* 1:181.

20. Blaine, *Political Discussions,* 426–27.

21. Ibid., 427–28.

22. Boyd, *Blaine and Logan Campaign,* 104.

23. Ibid., 146.

24. Ibid., 191.

25. New York *World,* October 30, 1884.

26. William E. Chandler to James G. Blaine, November 6, 1884, James G. Blaine Papers, Library of Congress, Washington, DC.

27. Blaine, *Political Discussions,* 493.

28. Ibid., 490.

29. Blaine draft of a letter of acceptance for the Republican nominee for governor of Maine, 1886, James G. Blaine Papers, Library of Congress, Washington, DC.

30. James G. Blaine to Benjamin Harrison, November 9, 1888, in Albert T. Volwiler, ed., *The Correspondence between Benjamin Harrison and James G. Blaine, 1882–1893* (Philadelphia: American Philosophical Society, 1940), 41.

31. James G. Blaine, "The Presidential Election of 1892," *North American Review* 155 (November 1892): 519.

32. *New York Tribune,* December 8, 1887.

33. *New York Tribune,* July 15, 1890.

34. Alexander K. McClure and Charles Morris, *The Authentic Life of William McKinley* (N.p.: W. E. Scull, 1901), 310.

35. James G. Blaine, "Progress and Development of the Western World," in *Columbus and Columbia: A Pictorial History of the Man and the Nation* (Philadelphia: Historical Publishing, 1892), 36, 62.

36. Blaine, *Twenty Years,* 2:675.

Suggested Readings

The only full-length scholarly biography of Blaine is David Saville Muzzey, *James G. Blaine: A Political Idol of Other Days* (New York: Dodd, Mead, 1934). Edward P. Crapol offers the most extensive examination of his service in the State Department in *James G. Blaine: Architect of Empire* (Wilmington, DE: Scholarly Resources, 1999). Blaine clearly deserves a modern biography, and Professor R. Hal Williams is currently engaged in writing one. For politics generally in this period, one should consult H. Wayne Morgan, *From Hayes to McKinley: National Party Politics, 1877–1896* (Syracuse: Syracuse University Press, 1969); R. Hal Williams, *Years of Decision: American Politics in the 1890s* (New York: John Wiley, 1978); and Robert D. Marcus, *Grand Old Party: Political Structure in the Gilded Age, 1880–1896* (New York: Oxford University Press, 1971); and Robert W. Cherney, *American Politics in the Gilded Age* (Wheeling, IL: Harlan Davidson, 1997). Useful discussions of the tariff issue appear in Joanne Reitano, *The Tariff Question in the Gilded Age: The Great Debate of 1888* (University Park: Pennsylvania State University Press, 1994); and Alfred E. Eckes Jr., *Opening America's Market: U.S. Foreign Trade Policy since 1776* (Chapel Hill: University of North Carolina Press, 1995). For the presidential administrations in which Blaine served see Justus D. Doenecke, *The Presidencies of James A. Garfield and Chester A. Arthur* (Lawrence: University Press of Kansas, 1981); and Homer E. Socolofsky and Allan B. Spetter, *The Presidency of Benjamin Harrison* (Lawrence: University Press of Kansas, 1987).

3

Ida B. Wells, Higher Law, and Community Justice

Christopher Waldrep*

As an African American and a woman, Ida B. Wells had two formidable liabilities that prevented access to the domain of white males in the Gilded Age South. She further underscored her exclusion by directly challenging the southern legal establishment. Born a slave in 1862, Wells lost her parents to yellow fever when she was fourteen but managed to finish her education and become a schoolteacher in Tennessee. On a trip to Memphis in 1883 she was ejected from the "ladies'" passenger car, which the railroad company reserved for whites only. Wells sued and lost on appeal to the Tennessee supreme court, which was loaded with former Confederates.

Christopher Waldrep, a legal historian, focuses on this critical episode in Wells's life and discusses its impact on her career as a reformer. Embittered by her treatment in court, Wells inaugurated a campaign confronting the system that had denied her justice. Her greatest passion was the elimination of lynching, the most radical means of maintaining the South's caste system. Crusading to eradicate this evil, she challenged the mythology that black men frequently raped white women. In tracing Wells's devotion to the cause of racial equality before the law, Professor Waldrep examines the tension in American life between the promise of individual liberty for all and shortcomings of the nation's constitutional system.

Christopher Waldrep is associate professor of history at Eastern Illinois University. He received his Ph.D. from Ohio State University in 1990 and is the author of *Night Riders: Defending Community in the Black Patch, 1890–1915* (1993) and *Roots of Disorder: Race and Criminal Justice in the American South, 1817–1880* (1998).

When Gilded Age journalist Ida B. Wells launched her crusade against southern lynching, she took on a tradition hundreds of years old. Long before the beginnings of American history, rioters had used violence to defend community values. The most sophisticated articulation of this "doctrine of Vigilance" came in 1887 when historian Hubert Howe Bancroft defined law as the will of the

*Thanks to Lynne Curry for her comments on an earlier version of this essay.

community as a whole, the voice of the people. Bancroft did not define community, but he must have meant a neighborhood of shared values within a limited geographic space where residents had reached consensus on law and justice, right and wrong. According to Bancroft, a lynching really represented the ultimate provincial assertion that a small group of neighbors can best set the bounds of moral conduct without guidance from the broader polity or a higher authority. Many white people shared Bancroft's views.

Wells's campaign against lynching, then, amounted to an attack on ideas firmly entrenched in nineteenth-century white constitutionalism, an ethic of decentralized government. She began her career committed to the ideal of a higher law at a time when whites reiterated their dedication to local sovereignty. Wells's campaign against lynching coincided with her realization that she could not realistically expect whites to apply a color-blind law to race relations. Indeed, nearly a century of research into the workings of law shows that this expectation was hopelessly naive. A wide variety of social, economic, and political forces shape lawmaking and law enforcement. But the fictions societies choose to believe do influence governing. Mythology is the vehicle by which citizens learn the values and beliefs that inform the allocation of power and distribution of rights. Myths preserve and present the collective ideology in a narrative form. For a time, Wells favored a particular myth about law, one that she hoped would make a truly biracial society possible. Her insight that neutrally enforced law was an impossibility changed her life. She began to favor self-help for African Americans over preparation for life in an integrated society. But she never ceased to attack localism.

In 1862, when Wells was born a slave in Holly Springs, Mississippi, white southerners mythologized law as truly neutral. The common law, one judge insisted, "is not the result of the wisdom of any one man or society of men, in any one age, but of the wisdom and experience of many ages of wise and discreet men."[1] At the same time southern whites paid homage to higher law, they also believed that states and neighborhoods were best suited to interpreting and enforcing that law. Many also believed that throughout history republics thrived when they governed only a small territory such as a state or a county. Only in a limited space could neighbors build the consensus necessary to set boundaries between right and wrong. At its most extreme, this rhetoric of popular sovereignty could mutate into a justification for vigilantes and lynch mobs. When mobs formed they inevitably claimed to speak for the whole people. American revolutionaries took to the streets against British authority, insisting they represented the people against a government no longer legitimate.

In the 1850s, San Francisco lynchers claimed to act for the people in place of an impotent government. Their partisans insisted the people had the right and the duty to maintain a perpetual vigil over anything related to their own governance. When the servants of the people proved unfaithful, the people were obliged to "rise in their sovereign privilege" and overthrow their governors.[2] Since a vigilance committee acted for the people, it could not act unlawfully; to the contrary, it was acting in accordance with the "true" law.

Wells's challenge to this localism followed the Civil War, emancipation, and Reconstruction. Abraham Lincoln had found within the Constitution precepts that expanded national power. His party passed laws local-minded Democrats had thwarted for years, including laws providing for a national income tax, a central bank, federal support for a transcontinental railroad, and the abolition of slavery. The United States ended slavery with the 1865 Thirteenth Amendment and then enacted the Civil Rights Act of 1866. These measures challenged the states' powers. The 1866 law defined national citizenship for the first time and articulated the rights associated with that citizenship. Two years later the principles legislated in the 1866 Civil Rights Act became part of the Constitution as the Fourteenth Amendment. Republicans espoused a new nationalism, one that promised to define and defend the rights of American citizens.

Laws passed to protect the rights of black citizens reached even the little Mississippi village of Holly Springs, where Ida B. Wells began life. Holly Springs had a population of just three thousand, of which slaves had made up one-third. Wells's parents were artisans and had enjoyed that degree of independence common to slaves who had advanced skills. Wells's father, Jim, was a carpenter, the son of his master and a slave woman named Peggy. Jim's owner and father never put his son on the auction block; Wells wrote that her father did not know the worst horrors of slavery. Wells's mother, Elizabeth Warrenton, by contrast, had been sold and resold and had lost track of her original family. Like her husband, she had a skill prized by Holly Springs whites. Wells later described her mother as a famous cook.

The independence that Wells's parents enjoyed as slaves probably encouraged them to assert themselves after emancipation. But Reconstruction also encouraged Wells's father to claim political rights that he believed were guaranteed by the federal government; he refused to vote Democratic even when pressed to do so by his white employer. Jim Wells followed his political aspirations until he was cut down by a yellow fever epidemic. His wife died at the same time.

News of her parents' deaths reached Wells at Shaw University, now known as Rust College. She wanted to rush to the side of her six sisters and brothers, now orphans, but friends urged her not to set foot in disease-ridden Holly Springs. No passenger trains ran because no one wanted to go into a town ravaged by yellow fever. Wells, though, demonstrated the determination and stalwart courage for which she later became famous. Only fourteen years old, she took a freight train into Holly Springs and helped nurse her family. After the epidemic abated, Wells insisted on keeping her siblings together, finding work as a schoolteacher to support them.

Like most African Americans in the years after the Civil War, Wells embraced the notion of national citizenship rights. In this era, African Americans used whites' own universal-rights discourse to make demands. They deployed patriotic icons and quoted the Declaration of Independence. They wanted to participate in a society administered by laws enforced fairly. Wells condemned the racial segregation enforced by local authorities as a sin and aimed harsh criticism at those African Americans "tacitly conniving at it by assenting to their caste arrangements."[3] In an article published in 1886 she exhorted black schoolteachers to cultivate strong character in their students. With a noble character marked by "quiet deportment and manly independence," blacks could hope to "convince the world that worth and not color made the man."[4] In an article published a year later, Wells lashed out at African Americans willing to accept separate fraternal lodges and labor organizations. In these early writings, Wells envisioned a color-neutral, if not color-blind, society.

Wells understood that law had to be the backbone of such a society. In her diary, she recorded that she "firmly believed" that the law would protect her rights.[5] Whites had relied on race to allocate resources and maintain order; blacks such as Wells wanted to substitute law. In 1875, Congress enacted a new civil rights law requiring that "all persons within the jurisdiction of the United States shall be entitled to the full and equal enjoyment of the accommodations, advantages, facilities, and privileges of inns, public conveyances on land or water, theaters, and other places of public amusement."[6] The statute represented an attempt by Congress to throw out old informal neighborhood rules and patriarchies, creating a new society ruled by abstract, national standards.

Southern whites did what they could to thwart congressional efforts to end discrimination. In Tennessee, the legislature tried to forestall state suits inspired by the 1875 civil rights law by abolishing the common-law right of victims of discrimination to sue. The new statute gave proprietors of public facilities "perfect and complete" power to exclude persons from their establishments. After passage of this law, the railroads routinely charged blacks first-class fares but assigned them seats in shabby smoking cars. On some trains baggage cars doubled as "smoking" cars. In these cars, blacks and whites mingled, and conductors made no effort to control foul language and drinking.

In Tennessee, African-American voters put into office legislators they thought would support laws protecting their rights. The four African Americans serving in the Tennessee state legislature in 1881 vigorously fought against racial discrimination. Thomas A. Sykes urged repeal of the 1875 state statute. Newspapers praised Sykes as "a fluent speaker," and he adroitly steered his controversial bill into the legislature, where it lost only narrowly, 31–29.

Beaten on that front, Tennessee blacks tried another approach. State representative Isaac F. Norris proposed a ban on racial discrimination by railroads, but white lawmakers prevented his bill from coming to a vote. Instead, the legislature considered a compromise measure requiring separate but equal facilities for the races on railroad cars. Though a far cry from what blacks had proposed and though intended to guarantee segregation, the compromise bill was an effort to impose a statewide legal standard on local practices. Discrimination varied from railroad to railroad and proponents of the bill claimed it would "clarify a rather confused legal situation."[7] Black legislators cast the only votes against the bill, which was passed by an overwhelming majority. The law mattered little, though, because railroads ignored it.

Railroad companies sometimes called their first-class coaches "ladies' cars." Gentlemen rode with their ladies in these cars. Lower-class men and blacks of both genders rode the integrated cars. White Victorians regarded African-American females not as "ladies" but as "women" and, as such, easily shunted them into less-well-supervised second-class cars. Several courts had upheld this practice, ruling that railroad companies had considerable power to seat passengers where they wished.

In 1880 a black correspondent for the *New York Age* reported that trains serving Nashville segregated passengers by race. The next year blacks challenged segregation by purchasing first-class tickets and sitting in the first-class cars reserved for whites. The railroad companies feared the courts might rule against them and played a game of cat and mouse with protesters. On one train the railroad moved all the white passengers from the first-class car to another car and locked the doors. On another train the company steered whites onto a car normally reserved for blacks to avoid seating them with early-arriving black passengers. In none of these incidents did the company have the nerve to forcibly remove blacks from seats reserved for whites.

The railroads understood that the courts had given them considerable authority to police their own trains, but this authority had limits. State supreme courts agreed that the railroads had a duty to enforce order and maintain peace on their cars, and separating the races was a reasonable way to do so. The state courts could overrule unreasonable regulations or the caprice of railway employees, but the duty of maintaining order lay with the company. And maintaining order meant segregated facilities. The state supreme court in Pennsylvania showed itself almost obsessed with maintaining the boundary between black and white Americans. "From social amalgamation," the judges warned, "it is but a step to illicit intercourse, and but another to intermarriage."[8]

On September 15, 1883, Wells, now twenty-one years old, traveled by train from Memphis to Shelby County, Tennessee, where she had a teaching job. The train she rode had three cars: a baggage car behind the train engine and two first-class cars, one for black men and women and white male passengers and one for whites only. Since the train company switched the cars, using one car for blacks and whites on one trip and the same car for whites only the next, the two cars offered equal physical accommodations.

But a rougher class of people rode in the mixed car. As Wells boarded the train, she glimpsed a drunken man among the passengers on the integrated car and boarded the ladies' car, as she had done before without incident. When the conductor found Wells riding in the ladies' car, he told her she would have to ride in the mixed car. Wells refused, and the conductor tried to physically drag her from her seat. She still refused to go, biting the conductor on the hand, bracing her feet against the seat in front, and gripping the seat behind. It took three men to eject her from the car. Whites in the car stood on their seats to watch the show and applauded when the trainmen finally succeeded in removing her.

Wells hired a lawyer and sued the railroad. Under the Civil Rights Act of 1875 she could have gone to federal court and claimed the railroad had violated her Fourteenth Amendment rights. Starting in 1873, however, the Supreme Court had begun to restore the localism prevalent before the Civil War. The Court declared that the Civil War amendments had only a limited purpose, the "freedom of the slave race." The justices warned that shifting the power to protect citizens' rights from the states to the federal government threatened to bring "the entire domain of civil rights" into the federal courts.[9] This the Supreme Court refused to do. A decade later the Court remained steadfast in its determination to protect the powers of the states over their citizens. In the *Civil Rights Cases,* the Supreme Court declared portions of the 1875 equal rights law unconstitutional. There came a time, the Court declared in one callous passage, when former slaves had to join the ranks of mere citizens "and cease to be the special favorites of the law."[10]

Even with no federal help forthcoming, Tennessee state law looked promising. Wells's lawyer must have advised her that in 1881 the Tennessee legislature had charged that railroad companies habitually collected first-class fares from blacks and then relegated them to second-class smoking cars. The legislature required railroad companies to furnish truly first-class accommodations for African-American purchasers of first-class tickets. The next year the legislature amended the 1881 law, toughening its provisions. The new law declared that all purchasers of first-class railway tickets "shall be entitled to enter and occupy first-class passenger cars."[11]

Wells testified at the trial on her suit, describing her aborted attempt to ride ten miles from Memphis to Woodstock station. Her attorney called four black men as witnesses on her behalf. Three identified themselves as passengers in the integrated passenger car, and two reported they had themselves smoked in this car. G. H. Clowers and Silas Kerney both agreed that this car, where they had seen others also smoking and some people drunk, was not a "fit place for a Lady."[12]

The railroad also produced four witnesses. Conductor William Murry said the two cars offered truly equal accommodations. The railroad had made a rule, Murry explained to the court, that only "white Ladies and Gentlemen" could ride in the rear car on the train. This rule pleased most passengers, Murry claimed, and avoided "unpleasant associations and antagonism of race." Murry described Wells's resistance much as she did, admitting he "got the worst of it," bleeding freely where Wells had bitten him. Contrary to Wells's witnesses, Murry insisted that no one had smoked in the first, integrated passenger car. If anyone had done so, Murry claimed, he would have stopped it. Nor had he seen any rowdy or drunken behavior in that car. The only two drunken men on the train had been in the rear car. The other three witnesses uniformly agreed that Murry strictly enforced the rule against smoking in the integrated car. But these witnesses for the railroad supported Wells's claim in critical ways. Dr. J. E. Blades, a regular rider of the train to Memphis, agreed that Murry did not allow smoking in the forward car, but he conceded that smoking nonetheless occurred. Dick Moody, a porter on the train, further undermined the railroad's case by describing the forward coach as the "second class car" and not equal to the whites' "first class car." With its own witnesses conceding pivotal points to Wells, the railroad, not surprisingly, lost its case, and the judge awarded Wells $200.

When the railroad company appealed to the state supreme court, Wells's lawyer used soaring rhetoric to insist that law should be above racist appeals. Her chief attorney, a white Shelby County judge originally from Holly Springs, Mississippi, named James

Greer, insisted the railroad had failed to offer equal accommodations. Even the conductor's testimony indicated passengers in the forward car smoked, he reasoned, since the conductor said he repeatedly enforced the no-smoking rule. Greer reminded the justices that the railroad's own witnesses had described the forward passenger car as "second class." Greer described Wells as "decent, well educated" and called the act of throwing her off the train "monstrous." He denounced racial prejudice: "Waves of passion break against the doors of the temple of justice," he orated. He called race prejudice enforced by law "a startling proposition" and urged the court away from such a course.[13]

Wells and her attorneys faced a phalanx of former Confederates on the high court. Chief Justice Peter Turney had so enthusiastically supported secession that he raised the first Confederate regiment in Tennessee, acting even before his state had seceded. The rest of the judges had similar backgrounds. Horace Harmon Lurton served in Morgan's Cavalry, riding with the famed raider into Ohio. He was an uninspired thinker known chiefly for his hostility to foreign immigrants and any threat to states' rights. (Lurton nonetheless befriended William Howard Taft, and in 1909, Taft appointed Lurton to the U.S. Supreme Court.) William C. Folkes had been seriously wounded at the first battle at Manassas but had returned to the Confederate army anyway, losing a foot in a later battle. Even without his foot, Folkes continued his service in the army throughout the war. David Lafayette Snodgrass and Waller Cochran Caldwell had missed Confederate service only because they were children when the Civil War started.

The Tennessee supreme court found against Wells. Ignoring the conductor's testimony that his fight with Wells left him scratched, bitten, and bloody, Tennessee's highest court insisted Wells had been "politely assisted from the car by a colored porter." The court further ignored the rough behavior of passengers in the forward car, writing that the front car differed not at all from the rear car, as the railroad had furnished and equipped the cars identically. Ignoring the railroad's own witnesses, the court said Wells's testimony of having seen a person smoking in the front car had been contradicted by another witness. "We know of no rule," the justices concluded, "that requires railroad companies to yield to the disposition of passengers to arbitrarily determine as to the coach in which they take passage."

This defeat challenged Wells's hopes for a truly pluralistic society. Passion had overwhelmed the temples of justice. Wells wrote in her diary that she felt "sorely, bitterly disappointed." She had put her faith in the law, she wrote, and felt "utterly discouraged" and shorn of her confidence in justice through law. The words that follow are telling. Wells wrote that "if it were possible [I] would gather my race in my arms and fly far away with them."[14] Truly higher law independent of political manipulation promised a biracial society; law manipulated by former Confederates meant a racist society dominated by the color line. Wells's train trip to Memphis had turned into a journey that took her away from her faith that white lawyers could be bound by higher law. And Wells understood that without the myth of a higher law in place, a genuinely pluralistic society was not possible. The moment she lost confidence in truly neutral law marks the instant she hardened herself anew to life in a hopelessly segregated society.

Wells did not wait long to act on her new conviction. Seven days after learning of her defeat in court, Wells attended a meeting of the Negro Mutual Protective Association. The idea of a self-help organization came to Wells at a propitious time, just as she reeled from her loss of faith in the law. Organizers urged African Americans to find strength in their own people. Racial unity offered the only protection. The energy of the speakers impressed Wells and she came away from the meeting "very much enthused."

The Tennessee supreme court had thwarted Wells's effort to impose broader-than-local standards on Tennessee railroads, but the case ultimately allowed her to personally transcend locality in new ways. Wells's account of the lawsuit appeared in the religious weekly *Living Way,* and Wells soon purchased a third interest in the Memphis *Free Speech and Headlight.* The railroads gave free passes to journalists, and Wells traveled up and down the Mississippi valley, selling subscriptions. She was determined to make a living from her new occupation. Her travels paid off. Subscriptions to *Free Speech* increased all along the spur of the Illinois Central Railroad in the Mississippi River delta. For a woman to work as a correspondent and an editor was, Wells wrote later, a "novelty," but she had found her calling.

In the 1880s Wells became a writer. In 1892, Memphis whites directed the focus of her writing by lynching grocers Thomas Moss, Calvin McDowell, and Henry Stewart. Ultimately, the murders of Moss, McDowell, and Stewart changed Wells's identity from journalist to crusader against lynching. Before the lynching, Wells had accepted the idea that although lynching violated law and order, "unreasoning anger over the terrible crime of rape" prompted lynching violence.[15] She probably accepted Victorian stereotypes of gender in which male sexuality had a brutish side. Whereas women lacked passion, men struggled to keep their animal passions under control and did so only imperfectly. "Perhaps," Wells wrote of male lynching victims, "the brute deserved death anyhow and the mob was justified in taking his life."[16] But these three grocers had committed no crime against white women; rather they had been economically successful, Moss owning his own home. Their deaths challenged Victorian conventions. Rather than a response to male brutishness, their murders seemed a calculated conspiracy to eliminate economically successful African Americans. Race rather than gender had motivated the lynchers.

Black residents of Memphis responded as a cornered people. Many fled to Oklahoma. Wells herself advised black Memphis residents to leave Tennessee for the West, quoting Moss as urging his fellow blacks to move West just before lynchers murdered him. African Americans not leaving Memphis lashed out at whites with an unprecedented unity. They boycotted the streetcars. The superintendent and treasurer of the City Railway Company came to Wells's office in hopes she would call on blacks to patronize the streetcars once again. "The streetcar company had nothing to do with the lynching," one of the white men protested. Wells answered, "We have learned that every white man of any standing in town knew of the plan and consented to the lynching of our boys. . . . The colored people feel that every white man in Memphis who consented to his death is as guilty as those who fired the guns."[17]

Wells responded to the lynching of her friends the grocers by trying to prove black males no more capable of rape than whites. In May 1892, she wrote, "Nobody in this section believes the old thread-bare lie that Negro men assault white women."[18] Wells investigated a series of cases where whites alleged rape, finding every time that the supposed white female victim had willingly agreed to the liaison. Alice Walker, author of *The Color Purple*, brilliantly captured Wells's determination to circle the wagons of her race: Walker imagines Wells urging her to "Deny! Deny! Deny!" that black men ever raped white women. "It will be used against black men and therefore against us all."[19]

Wells's denials prompted such an angry white reaction that the antilynching crusader considered a move to Oklahoma herself. She clearly could not go back to Memphis; the Memphis *Commercial Appeal* reprinted her editorial and called for its author to be lynched. Her friend and fellow journalist T. Thomas Fortune offered a more appealing option, calling on Wells to move east instead, and she agreed to at least visit New York. A mob destroyed the Memphis offices of the *Free Speech* on May 27, 1892, while Wells was en route to New York. She took a position on the *New York Age*.

Wells's work for the *New York Age* taught her that merely putting her story in print could not sway the communities and neighborhoods where white lynch mobs found sustenance. Wells published a detailed analysis of lynching in the *New York Age*, documenting instances of white women fabricating rape charges that led to lynching. In some cases these women felt enough remorse to confess what they had done. Wells quoted one woman as admitting "a strange fascination" for her black lover. When neighbors saw him going to her house, "I hoped to save my reputation by telling . . . a deliberate lie."[20] Wells mounted an assault on the myth of white feminine purity, and her publisher was determined to put her words in the face of white America. The *New York Age* printed ten thousand copies of that issue to be distributed across the United States, one thousand copies on the streets of Memphis. The reaction of the northern press to her explosive revelations disappointed Wells. She had assumed it had remained silent only because it did not have the facts. But after a year of printing her shocking stories in the *New York Age,* Wells could see that whites had given her only "a meager hearing, and the press was dumb."[21]

The key to the door in the wall of white indifference lay not just outside the local white communities supportive of lynchers but outside the United States. The Scottish author Isabelle Fyvie Mayo, outraged by a terrible Texas lynching, offered to pay Wells's passage to England. In some ways Mayo's life paralleled Wells's. Wells had become a writer while teaching; Mayo had become a writer while pursuing secretarial work. Wells broke barriers to become a journalist. Mayo wrote that she had to break through "unnecessary limitations" to escape the "straight groove in which I had been reared." In fact, though, the similarities were mostly superficial. Mayo's parents did not work as servants; they employed them. The "groove" she had escaped was her own bourgeois upbringing. Mayo recalled that the escaped slave her father had employed as a handyman was driven to suicide by the horrors he had experienced. Her memory of the old man who called her "Missie" might have made her more sympathetic to the plight of lynching victims, but there were limits to her sensitivities. She warned her readers against toleration of "female 'easiness of virtue.'" Mothers of illegitimate children, she lectured, must be consigned to the factory or put to work washing clothes. Decent folk should not be exposed to someone "a-wrestling with unruly passions."[22]

Mayo thought that an American denouncing lynching in England would arouse public sentiment in America against extralegal violence. White Americans might ignore Wells's writings in America, but they would find it harder to resist an aroused English public. Americans looked to the English as particularly cultured. If the civilized British denounced lynchers as uncivilized, white southerners would be embarrassed. For Wells, arousing English indignation must have seemed an opportunity to set a higher legal standard against mob violence. If white judges could not be made to hew to the line of incorruptible law, perhaps a kind of higher law could be established in the popular culture—with the help of the English news media.

Wells sailed for England on April 5, 1893. In England and Scotland she gave lectures and received good notices in the press. When one English citizen asked why British citizens should take an interest in "the local police arrangements" in American towns, Wells penned a reply. "The pulpit and press of our own country remains silent," she wrote. "It is to the religious and moral sentiment of Great Britain we now turn. . . . Americans cannot and will not ignore the voice of a nation that is her superior in civilization."[23]

Wells's visit to England had resulted from an alliance between Mayo and Catherine Impey, an opponent of the caste system in India. It was Impey who had suggested Wells's name to Mayo. The alliance between Wells, Mayo, and Impey ended after Impey wrote a letter declaring her love for a member of a "darker race." In fact, the object of her desire felt no love for Impey and turned her letter over to a very shocked Mayo. When Wells would not join Mayo in repudiating Impey, Mayo withdrew her support. Wells went home.

This reversal did not end Wells's effort to enlist the British in her fight against lynching. In 1894 she returned to England. Whereas her first tour had aroused little press coverage in America, the second attracted all the attention she could have hoped for. By June 23, Wells could report that her lecturing and writing had aroused the South. Georgia's governor had denounced Wells, urging the English to get their facts from a more reputable source. The Memphis *Daily Commercial* attacked Wells's character. "From one end of the United States to the other," Wells wrote, press and pulpit were stung by the criticism of press and pulpit abroad."[24] Her campaign in England convinced at least some Americans to distance themselves from their earlier toleration of lynching. In her autobiography, Wells would credit English denunciations of American extralegal violence with also shaming American leaders into distancing themselves from lynching.

When whites counterattacked, they charged that Wells had not actually breached the walls that confined African Americans. Temperance leaders such as Frances Willard sought white Southerners' votes to achieve a constitutional amendment prohibiting alcohol, which was allowed in some southern communities. Her need for white votes may have influenced her position, which like lynching itself remained stubbornly provincial. Willard announced she favored literacy tests to prevent illiterate foreigners and blacks from voting. The ideas of the plantation Negro, Willard declared, "are bounded by the fence of his own field and the price of his own mule."[25] Willard even complained that the presence of blacks trapped white women and children. Menaced by brutal black men,

Willard insisted, white women dared not go beyond sight of their own rooflines.

Some feminists feared that Wells's marriage to F. L. Barnett in 1895 would confine her to the sight of her own roofline. Though Wells carried her babies with her when making speeches and lobbying Congress for a federal antilynching law, she did believe she had to put her family ahead of public works. Newspapers criticized her for deserting the cause, and Susan B. Anthony rebuked her for becoming a mother and housewife. At the same time, Wells helped found the Afro-American Council only to be maneuvered out of a leadership role in that organization.

Despite her family obligations, Wells continued her efforts against white racism. In this campaign, she confronted not just white opposition but black provincialism as well. On the Sunday after the 1908 Springfield, Illinois, race riot, she called on her Sunday school class to organize, passionately denouncing blacks' apathy. At first just three members of her church class responded, but Wells pushed ahead, organizing the Negro Fellowship League. In 1909, she again confronted local blacks' indifference after Cairo, Illinois, whites lynched Will "Frog" James for the murder of a white woman. In 1905 the Illinois legislature had enacted a strong law stipulating that when lynchers murdered a prisoner under a sheriff's care, the governor was required to remove that sheriff from office. After the James lynching, the governor of Illinois dutifully removed Sheriff Frank Davis from office. The law also allowed the ousted sheriff to make his case for reinstatement in a hearing before the governor. In Cairo, Wells found that many blacks had written letters to the governor asking that the sheriff be returned to office. Narrow political concerns controlled the thinking of local blacks. As one local African American explained to Wells, the ousted sheriff had been a friend to Cairo blacks and had hired black deputies. His replacement, a Democrat, had turned out all the black deputies. Wells argued that Cairo blacks endangered the lives of blacks all over Illinois by permitting such local concerns to determine their course. She declared that blacks must unite against lynchings in Illinois by repudiating the sheriff, and she succeeded in persuading some Cairo blacks to sign a petition. Traveling to Springfield, she made a powerful speech against the sheriff and countered the petitions he produced with her own resolutions. In the end, the governor agreed with her that Davis could not be reinstated because he had not properly protected his prisoner. Wells had once again triumphed over localism.

The Springfield riot also prompted formation of the National Association for the Advancement of Colored People (NAACP). With some reluctance, organizers called on Wells to lend her support to the association, although her fundamental approach to racial problems differed from its guiding principles. In a 1909 article that articulated the founders' ideas, W. E. B. Du Bois urged that the Negro "problem" not be segregated from other reform movements. Poverty and ignorance represented a "human problem," not a black problem, Du Bois declared. The solution lay in "human methods."[26] Years earlier Wells had been frustrated in her own attempts to surmount race. In her autobiography, she judged the NAACP harshly. It lasted longer than other such movements, she wrote, but fell short of its founders' expectations. Wells blamed the NAACP's troubles on the chair of its executive committee, a white woman named Mary White Ovington. Wells complained that Ovington had experience only in New York City and Brooklyn and lacked the ability to seize situations in a "truly big way."[27] Wells's daughter explained that her mother thought the leadership of the NAACP should be entirely black.

Ida B. Wells lived until 1936. She had broken through gender barriers to make herself an international spokesperson for her race and broken into a career not previously open to women. She defined her life by her ability to transcend geographic boundaries. The end of slavery allowed her to leave her plantation, but she escaped Memphis and the South through her own efforts. Her scheme to attack lynching in America by going to England represented a masterstroke, one that might not have appealed so strongly to someone who did not associate freedom with physical mobility. In England, Wells was able to speak to American whites in a way that she could not in the United States. But for all her work, she never breached the boundary of race. The anguish she expressed after her defeat before the Tennessee supreme court shows that she understood the tragic significance of the failure of incorruptible law. Without truly impartial law to referee relations between the races, all she could do was "gather my race in my arms and fly far away with them." Wells abandoned faith both in law and in a truly pluralistic United States, instead concentrating on survival strategies in a hopelessly brutal, segregated society.

Notes

1. *State v Caesar,* 31 NC 414 (1849).

2. Hubert Howe Bancroft, *Popular Tribunals,* 2 vols. (San Francisco: History Company, 1887), 1:9.

3. Miriam DeCosta-Willis, *The Memphis Diary of Ida B. Wells* (Boston: Beacon Press, 1995), 42.

4. Ibid., 183–87.

5. Ibid., 141; Mildred I. Thompson, *Ida B. Wells-Barnett: An Explora-*

tory Study of an American Black Woman, 1893–1930 (Brooklyn: Carlson Press, 1990), 15.

6. *An Act to Protect All Citizens in Their Constitutional and Legal Rights*, U.S. *Statutes at Large* 18 (1875): 336.

7. Joseph H. Cartwright, *The Triumph of Jim Crow: Tennessee Race Relations in the 1880s* (Knoxville: University of Tennessee Press, 1976), 104–5.

8. *West Chester and Philadelphia Railroad Company v. Miles*, 55 PA 309 (1867).

9. *Slaughter-House Cases*, 83 US 71, 77 (1873).

10. *Civil Rights Cases*, 109 US 25 (1883).

11. 1881 Tennessee Acts 211; 1882 Tennessee Acts 12.

12. *Chesapeake, Ohio, and Southwestern Railroad Co. v. Ida B. Wells*, West Tennessee 312, 319 (Tennessee State Library and Archives, Nashville). Further quotes from the trial are from this court transcript.

13. *Chesapeake, Ohio & Southwestern Railroad Company v. Wells*, 85 Tennessee 613 (1887). All further quotations regarding the railroad's appeal are from this source.

14. DeCosta-Willis, *Memphis Diary*, 141.

15. Elizabeth Pleck, *Domestic Tyranny: The Making of Social Policy against Family Violence from Colonial Times to the Present* (New York: Oxford University Press, 1987), 53–54.

16. Ida B. Wells, *Crusade for Justice: The Autobiography of Ida B. Wells*, ed. Alfreda M. Duster (Chicago: University of Chicago Press, 1970), 64.

17. Ibid., 54–55.

18. Wells's article appeared in pamphlet form as *Southern Horrors: Lynch Law in All Its Phases*. See Trudier Harris, comp., *Selected Works of Ida B. Wells-Barnett* (New York: Oxford University Press, 1991), 17.

19. Alice Walker, "Advancing Luna—and Ida B. Wells," in *You Can't Keep a Good Woman Down* (San Diego: Harcourt, Brace, Jovanovich, 1981), 94.

20. Ida B. Wells, *Southern Horrors: Lynch Law in All Its Phases*, in Harris, *Selected Works of Ida B. Wells-Barnett*, 20–21.

21. Wells, *Crusade for Justice*, 86.

22. Isabelle Fyvie Mayo, *Recollections: Of What I Saw, What I Lived Through, and What I Learned, during More than Fifty Years of Social and Literary Experience* (London: J. Murray, 1910), 18, 71–115, 271–349.

23. Wells, *Crusade for Justice*, 100–101.

24. Ibid., 181–83.

25. Ibid., 207.

26. Charles Flint Kellogg, *NAACP: A History of the National Association for the Advancement of Colored People* (Baltimore, MD: Johns Hopkins University Press, 1967), 25.

27. Dorothy Sterling, afterword in DeCosta-Willis, *Memphis Diary*, 197; Wells, *Crusade for Justice*, 321–33.

Suggested Readings

Ida B. Wells wrote an autobiography that is in print and is the most important source for her life: *Crusade for Justice: The Autobiography of Ida B. Wells,* ed. Alfreda M. Duster (Chicago: University of Chicago Press, 1970). Wells's extant diaries have also been published: Miriam DeCosta-Willis, *The Memphis Diary of Ida B. Wells* (Boston: Beacon Press, 1995). For Wells's writings, see Trudier Harris, comp., *Selected Works of Ida B. Wells-Barnett* (New York: Oxford University Press, 1991), 20–21. In addition, see Mildred I. Thompson, *Ida B. Wells-Barnett: An Exploratory Study of an American Black Woman, 1893–1930* (Brooklyn: Carlson Press, 1990). Linda O. Murry has written Wells's biography: *To Keep Waters Troubled: The Life of Ida B. Wells* (New York: Oxford University Press, 1998). Gail Bederman has analyzed Wells's life in "'Civilization,' the Decline of Middle-Class Manliness, and Ida B. Wells's Antilynching Campaign (1892–94)," *Radical History Review* 52 (1992): 5–24, and also in *Manliness and Civilization: A Cultural History of Gender and Race in the United States, 1880–1917* (Chicago: University of Chicago Press, 1995). For Tennessee race relations generally for the 1880s, see Joseph H. Cartwright, *The Triumph of Jim Crow: Tennessee Race Relations in the 1880s* (Knoxville: University of Tennessee Press, 1976).

4

Mary Lease and the Sources of Populist Protest

Rebecca Edwards

Mary Lease faced more than her share of challenges. Her father died of dysentery in a Confederate prison when she was thirteen. She watched two of her own children die as infants and a grown son succumb to appendicitis. Her husband went bankrupt in the depression of the 1870s and failed again as a farmer in the 1880s. Lease was a central figure in the rise of Populist party power in Kansas yet suffered dismissal from office, sexual discrimination, and political abuse. At midlife she gained a divorce and started over again as a single woman in New York City, defying conventions of the time. Despite these setbacks, Mary Lease remained a fighter, refusing to compromise her ideals.

Rebecca Edwards, a historian of women and politics, devotes her chapter to this courageous and combative woman who became a symbol of the farmer protest on the Great Plains during the 1890s. Mary Lease's public career illustrates the range of political activities open to an energetic female before women could vote. She organized a female suffrage association, worked for the Woman's Christian Temperance Union, joined the local Knights of Labor, and spoke for the Kansas Farmers' Alliance, which sponsored the Populist political party. She campaigned for William Jennings Bryan, the Democratic candidate for president in 1896. She supported the birth control movement in New York City. But Lease will always be identified with populism. As Professor Edwards shows, life on the Great Plains was hard generally, but it was harder for women and even more so for one who entered the male domain of politics and supported the underdogs.

Rebecca Edwards received her Ph.D. from the University of Virginia in 1995. She is the author of *Angels in the Machinery: Gender in American Party Politics from the Civil War to the Progressive Era* (1997) and is now conducting research for a full-length biography of Mary Lease. She is assistant professor of history at Vassar College and lives in Poughkeepsie, New York.

In the 1890s Mary Lease was one of the most famous women in the United States, so well known that newspapers called her simply "Mrs. Lease of Kansas." The decade of her fame coincided with a deep economic depression, mass unemployment, and hundreds of strikes. By 1900, Americans were uneasily conscious of growing

divisions between rich and poor. Lease won her fame by speaking to
these issues with anger, humor, and eloquence. As a leader of the
Populist Party, she helped shape a movement of farmers, workers,
and reformers that challenged the political and economic status quo.
Today, Lease is largely forgotten, receiving only an occasional mention as the woman who urged American farmers to "raise less corn
and more hell."[1]

Historians have written a great deal about the Populists' ideas
and identities. For the most part they have described populism as a
movement of native-born, Protestant, Anglo-American farmers
whose cause failed because of the fraud and intimidation practiced
by southern Democrats and because the new party never won a following in the Midwest and Northeast. Yet although the Populist
party disappeared in a few years, it left an important legacy. Much
of its program won passage in the Progressive Era and New Deal,
having been taken up by other reformers. Before Mary Lease died in
1933, she witnessed federal regulation of banks and railroads, government aid to farmers, direct election of U.S. senators, and a
national progressive income tax, all of which the Populists had
proposed.

The Populists, then, have not been forgotten, but Mary Lease
has, perhaps because she remains an ambiguous figure. Her life
contradicts much of what we think we know about populism. Born
in Pennsylvania less than a year after her parents arrived from
Ireland, Lease was heir to her father's legacy of agricultural poverty. A Catholic by birth and education, she had become an agnostic by
1900, contradicting historians' picture of populism as an evangelical
Protestant crusade. Only briefly a farmer's wife, Lease gained an
eclectic political education from the Woman's Christian Temperance
Union, the women's suffrage movement, labor unions, and the Irish
nationalist cause. A champion of "equal rights for all, special privileges for none," she nonetheless made anti-Semitic remarks and
endorsed U.S. colonization of Latin America. When, in Lease's opinion, the Populists caved in to the Democratic party, she turned
against them. She then divorced her husband, moved to New York
City, and worked as a journalist, lawyer, and advocate of birth
control.

Perhaps Lease was an oddity, a woman whose background and
beliefs lay outside the mainstream of her movement. If so, she was
a very influential oddity. Her claim that she single-handedly
brought the Kansas Populists to power was only a slight exaggeration. She sat in Populist inner councils, played a pivotal role in two
national conventions, and conducted speaking tours across the
nation from Georgia to Minnesota and Montana to New York. Her
life tells us a great deal about the political and economic reshaping

of the United States between the Civil War and the New Deal. It also tells us a great deal about how these changes affected women and how women themselves became agents of change. Lease was that much-feared figure, an angry woman. She helped build up populism, and then in bitter disillusionment she helped destroy it, exiling herself from history's ranks of Populist heroes. She remains, today, a complicated figure: courageous, ambitious, immensely talented, alternately petty and visionary, a woman of small prejudices and great dreams.

Mary Lease, born Mary Clyens, experienced poverty and loss from her earliest childhood. Her parents came to the United States in 1849 from County Monaghan, Ireland, during the devastating potato famine that reduced Ireland's population by 2.5 million through emigration, starvation, and disease. Mary's two older sisters and one of her older brothers died in the famine, probably from cholera. Her father joined other tenant farmers in protesting British policies in Ireland; his absentee landlord finally got rid of this "objectionable" tenant by paying the family's passage to America. Mary was born a year after the Clyens' arrival in northwestern Pennsylvania. Her parents had barely scraped together enough money to buy a farm when her father and brother enlisted in the Civil War. Both died—her father of scurvy and dysentery in a Confederate prison camp—and Mary's mother was forced to sell the land. Only through the help of family friends did Mary receive an education at St. Elizabeth's Academy in nearby Allegany, New York.

Twenty-year-old Mary Clyens, like many Americans of the postwar period, decided that a better future lay in the West. She had been an excellent student, and in 1871 the nuns at St. Elizabeth's arranged a teaching post for her at Osage Mission in eastern Kansas. Saying good-bye to her younger brother and sister and her widowed mother, Mary boarded the train and apparently never looked back. After three years teaching in Kansas, where the ratio of men to women was high, Mary fulfilled the contemporary prophecy that an unmarried woman, once west of the Mississippi, would soon write home as a bride. Surrounded by her new friends in Osage Mission, she married Charles Lease in January 1873.

Charles owned a successful drugstore, sat on the board of a local bank, and a year after the wedding became the mayor of Osage Mission. The Leases had many friends, and Mary seemed destined for respectable small-town prosperity until, in May 1874, her fortunes came crashing down with those of her new husband. In the wake of a severe financial panic, Charles Lease lost his store under circumstances that left him not only bankrupt but under a cloud of suspicion. When the scandal broke, Mary was four months pregnant with their first child. Embarrassed both financially and socially, the couple moved to Denison, Texas, where Charles found work as a pharmacy clerk. They stayed nine years.

For Mary, the poverty of these years was a sad repetition of her mother's troubles. She probably knew little of her husband's business affairs when they first married, but his financial ruin and the subsequent disgrace and social ostracism must have made a deep impression on her. She later asserted that the key source of women's oppression was economic dependence on their husbands—a conviction surely born of personal experience. Other shocks were in store. Less than a year after moving to Denison, she received news of her mother's death in Pennsylvania. After the birth of Charles, her first child, she became pregnant five more times and watched two of her children die in infancy—an event not uncommon at the time. On her husband's meager salary, Mary struggled to raise the surviving children, Charles, Louisa, Grace, and Ben. Like her own mother she valued education, and she took in other families' laundry in order to pay for her children's school clothes and books. Publicly, at least, she never expressed bitterness or anger toward her husband for the crisis into which they had plunged, but the couple grew increasingly distant.

By 1884 the Leases had saved enough money to move back to Kansas and pursue Charles's old dream of farming in the dry lands west of Wichita. During the post-Civil War years, frontier "boosters" offered glowing descriptions of the future prosperity of farms on the Great Plains. Fresh from Union victory, the nation abounded in optimistic editors, politicians, businesspeople, and railroad managers, the latter of whom needed to sell lands granted to them by Congress to finance a flurry of railroad construction in the largely unsettled West. Even scientists joined in, arguing that settlement would create more and more rainfall because the crops and trees planted by pioneers would attract atmospheric moisture. This prediction was not true, of course, but "rain follows the plow" became a Plains axiom. A settlers' guide commissioned by the Missouri Pacific Railroad, and published in the year Mary Lease first arrived in Osage Mission, made extravagant claims about Kansas's climate and the certainty of its economic growth. "Every year there has been a noted increase in the fall of rain," the guide reported, "unquestionably brought about by the cultivation of the soil, and planting of forest trees and orchards."[2]

The Leases, along with thousands of other settlers, were shocked by the actual conditions in western Kansas. Staking a claim in Kingman County, Charles and Mary took the government up on its offer, under the Homestead Act of 1862, to provide 160 free acres to anyone who lived on the land for three consecutive years. Because the policy encouraged settlement on lands of marginal quality, free land was not necessarily the road to prosperity. Like many others, the Leases found that rain did not follow the plow. A 160-acre farm could provide a good living in Pennsylvania, but it was not large enough to sustain a family on the Plains, especially during periods of drought. The Leases soon resettled in Wichita, little better off financially than at the start of their marriage. Charles found a job as a pharmacy clerk, and Mary continued to take in laundry.

Driven by her hardships, Mary began as early as 1880 to seek a public role in movements for political and economic change. While still in Texas she joined a local chapter of the Woman's Christian Temperance Union (WCTU), the most successful women's organization of the 1870s and 1880s. Though prohibition of liquor may today seem a quixotic or narrow-minded goal, the WCTU construed it broadly. Refusing to trivialize the costs of alcoholism, WCTU leaders argued that thousands of women and children suffered neglect and abuse at the hands of drinking husbands and fathers. For Mary Lease, as for many women, temperance was a way to begin speaking tentatively about women's rights. The WCTU also addressed economic injustice. By the 1890s the WCTU's charismatic national president, Frances Willard of Illinois, described herself as a Christian Socialist and cited poverty as the chief cause of alcoholism. Mary Lease's ideas developed along the same lines.

Lease became immersed in a host of reform organizations after moving to Wichita. First, she organized a women's study club, whose members sought to cultivate their intellectual talents. In 1886 she cofounded the Wichita Equal Suffrage Association (WESA), which asserted women's right to vote. Suffrage was a radical demand, and WESA was subject to immediate ridicule in the columns of Wichita newspapers, all of whose editors were men. When these men poked fun at the "pants-wearing" women who wanted to vote, Lease riposted with witty poems and letters. She learned, however, that suffrage was an uphill battle and its supporters had to bear public insults, including claims that they were aggressive, "unwomanly," and bad mothers to boot.

By the late 1880s, Lease's interests expanded in other directions. She reclaimed her Irish-American identity, which she seems to have downplayed or even hidden during her early quest for respectability. Wichita had a large working-class Irish community, many of whom had arrived to work in railroad construction. Invited to address Irish social and political clubs, Lease began to give stirring speeches advocating the end of British colonial rule in Ireland as well as fair treatment for Irish tenant farmers. Around the same time, not coincidentally, she joined a local assembly of the largest and most inclusive labor union in the United States, the Knights of

Labor. In 1886 the Knights organized a massive strike against the Southwestern Railway System, operated by wealthy New York financier Jay Gould. At many points along Gould's railroads, including Wichita, local members of the Knights of Labor blocked trains and disabled engines. Though the governor of Kansas called in the National Guard to put down the strike, Lease had witnessed a vivid episode of collective protest against low wages, layoffs, and dangerous working conditions.

Three years later, well practiced in stump speaking and organizing, Lease also joined the Wichita branch of the Farmers' Alliance and Industrial Union, or "the Alliance," as it was widely known. At the time, the Alliance was sweeping across the South and the Great Plains in response to the problems of drought, low crop prices, and heavy farm debts. The Alliance sought allies among union members, including the Knights of Labor. These two groups saw themselves as sharing the same enemies, especially railroad owners such as Jay Gould, whom angry farmers accused of monopolizing key routes and overcharging farmers for the transport of crops to market. (Gould's Missouri Pacific, among others, had promised Kansans "rain would follow the plow.")

More broadly, Knights and Alliance members shared a common set of beliefs that historians have called "producerism." In the decades after the Civil War, railroads and large industrial corporations gained unprecedented power; farmers and laborers increasingly found their fate in the hands of faraway managers and shareholders. Influential thinkers such as Henry George, author of *Progress and Poverty*, identified the income from land rentals, bonds, and other investments as the cause of growing disparities between rich and poor. Lenders were growing rich on high interest rates, such thinkers argued, while borrowers were falling into hopeless debt. Thus, economic reformers began to draw a sharp distinction between bankers and bondholders on the one hand (viewed as parasites who lived on the labor of others) and farmers and the working class on the other. Both the Knights and the Alliance, along with organizations of international scope such as the Irish National League, spoke for the interests of "producers": men and women who did hard, physical work.

Lease's activities on behalf of temperance, women's suffrage, Irish nationalism, and farmers' and workers' rights thus were not as scattered as they might seem. The immigrant men and women who cheered Lease's speeches on behalf of Irish freedom were, in many cases, the same people she met in Knights of Labor meetings. They saw a connection between their parents' poverty in the Old World and labor exploitation in America. Many, like Lease, came from families experienced in protest, and they had emigrated from parts of Ireland where Ribbonmen and other secret societies organized to defend tenants' rights. In these movements, Irishwomen had long played an important role, so it was natural for Irish-American women to play prominent roles in both the Knights and Irish nationalist organizations.

In the meantime, many temperance leaders such as Frances Willard emphasized poverty and unemployment as causes of alcohol abuse, and the Knights and Farmers' Alliance promoted temperance among their members. Furthermore, male leaders of the Knights and the Alliance gave lectures, as Lease had done, to encourage women to join the movement. The strongest justification for women's entry into such public activities was the view, widespread at the time, that women were morally purer than men. Both the WCTU and many suffragists emphasized women's special role as mothers and wives, seeking to extend "housekeeping" and maternal love into the public sphere. Lease found this rhetoric to be powerful and applicable to the problems of poor laboring women and farm families. "After all our years of toil and privation, dangers and hardships upon the Western frontier," she told one WCTU audience, "monopoly is taking our homes from us by an infamous system of mortgage foreclosure. . . . Do you wonder the women are joining the Alliance? I wonder if there is a woman in all this broad land who can afford to stay out."[3]

Both the Knights and Farmers' Alliance were divided on the question of women's suffrage; conversely, not all WCTU members agreed on the importance of poverty and unemployment as causes of intemperance. In Wichita, however, Mary Lease found sympathetic allies on all sides, and many of her fellow organizers agreed on the need for a grand, unified movement that would work for economic and social reform. By the late 1880s, many activists were furiously debating whether a political party was the best vehicle for collective action. The WCTU had already helped to build up the Prohibitionist party, and its leaders were seeking alliances with other reform-minded groups. In 1888, at a Knights convention in Kansas City, Mary Lease argued vigorously that the union should make partisan endorsements and even run its own candidates. In the fall elections, like-minded Knights ran a fledgling campaign as the Kansas Union Labor party, on whose behalf Lease gave her first partisan speeches. By 1890 the Kansas Farmers' Alliance was also frustrated by the failure of its cooperative stores and other self-help measures, and its members declared their readiness for electoral politics. Thus Kansas populism was born, and Mary Lease with her multiple affiliations and her experience as a speaker and organizer found herself on center stage.

From the start, Populists sought to remedy America's problems through electoral means, challenging Republicans and Democrats with a new program of government activism. Opposing Republicans' constriction of the money supply (a policy beneficial to lenders), Populists called for currency expansion to stimulate credit and ease the burdens of borrowers. They also demanded government regulation—if not outright ownership—of the railroads and telegraphs, which made up the nation's basic infrastructure. At the local level, Populist editors and orators suggested a host of other measures to rescue farmers and industrial laborers from poverty and foreclosure. Like any movement embracing hundreds of thousands of people, populism contained tensions and contradictions; yet all Populists agreed that the "money power" (meaning Wall Street financiers and the politicians whose influence they bought) threatened the interests of hardworking Americans.

Populists' first testing ground was the Kansas election of 1890, a campaign in which Lease played a key role. Incensed at Republican senator John J. Ingalls—who ridiculed the Populists and told women their proper place was at home, not in politics—Lease went on the stump, giving an estimated 160 speeches in three months. Like her fellow Populists, Lease saw the new party as a movement not of farmers only but of all the producing classes. She excoriated bankers, corporate managers, and those who lived on income from their investments. In broader terms she spoke out against government and corporate policies that were rapidly making the rich richer while the poor stayed poor. "I hold to the theory," she said, "that if one man has not enough to eat three times a day and another man has $25 million, that last man has something that belongs to the first."[4]

Lease quickly emerged as one of her party's most effective orators. She had a low, powerful voice—described by listeners as resonant, masculine, or even hypnotic—along with a keen memory for statistics, a sense of humor, and the ability to think on her feet. In an era when political speeches were mass entertainment, she excelled at holding audiences' attention, often for two hours or more. "One of the best addresses, if not the best and most eloquent address I ever heard from a woman," a Nevada newspaperman wrote in his diary after hearing her speak. "Splendid style, voice and elocution." "She is the greatest natural orator of the female sex (or of either sex) that has appeared on earth," wrote another admirer.[5] Lease laced her speeches with quotations from Shakespeare and the Bible, and she learned to handle hecklers with scathing sarcasm or disarming wit.

Hailing "Our Queen Mary," the upstart Kansas Populists won five of the state's seven congressional districts and a majority of seats in the legislature. Because state legislatures elected U.S. senators until the Seventeenth Amendment, ratified in 1913, the new legislature promptly unseated John Ingalls and chose William

Peffer as the nation's first Populist senator. It was a stunning victory. The events of 1890 in Kansas brought national fame to the new party and to Lease, and they persuaded Alliance members and Knights in other parts of the country that electoral politics was worth a try.

Thus, there was hardly time to celebrate the Kansas victory as organizers hastened to build the movement nationwide. A proven orator, Lease spent little time in Kansas over the next two years. Leaving her four teenage children in Wichita with their father, she represented the party all over the nation. In February 1892, her speech in St. Louis provoked wild enthusiasm from a gathering of thousands. The following June, as the lone woman in the Kansas delegation, Lease participated in the Omaha convention that established a national People's party. She helped craft parts of the platform in committee, and she gave the seconding speech for James B. Weaver, the party's presidential nominee. In the famous Omaha Platform, the new party presented a bold program for reform. "The conditions which surround us best justify our cooperation," argued the platform's preamble.

> The fruits of the toil of millions are boldly stolen to build up colossal fortunes for a few, unprecedented in the history of mankind; and the possessors of these, in turn, despise the republic and endanger liberty. . . . We believe that the powers of government— in other words, of the people—should be expanded . . . as rapidly and as far as the good sense of an intelligent people and the teachings of experience shall justify, to the end that oppression, injustice, and poverty shall eventually cease in the land.[6]

The 1892 campaign was, in retrospect, the height of populism and of Mary Lease's fame. By this time a member of the party's top inner circle, she accompanied Weaver and his wife on grueling campaign tours around the country. In August they spoke to huge audiences in the West with Lease making as many as eight speeches in a day. "A mortgaged home, an empty stomach and a ragged back know no party," she told a San Francisco audience, urging it to make the "nonpartisan" choice and vote for populism. "We will live to write the epitaphs of the old parties: 'Died of general debility, old age and chronic falsehoods.'"[7]

Populists' greatest difficulty lay, however, in capturing support beyond the West. This they failed to do. Though a Populist coalition emerged in Chicago, most urban workers in the Midwest and Northeast did not respond to appeals from a movement depicted as a "farmers' revolt." Eastern newspapers alternately ridiculed the party and warned that its leaders were anarchists and Communists. Both Republicans and Democrats, wherever they were entrenched at the state and local levels, commanded vastly greater funds and patronage than did the upstart party and were not averse to using it. Lease herself apparently received offers of bribes to work for the Republicans. Many Northeasterners apparently stayed loyal to the Grand Old Party (GOP) for other reasons: Republicans still took credit for preserving the Union in the Civil War, and they argued that their protective tariff policies sheltered workers in the textile and other industries from low-wage competitors overseas.

The South was the site of populism's most tragic failures. Before 1892, thousands of southern farmers had built a strong Farmers' Alliance ranging from North Carolina to Texas, including a segregated but active Colored Farmers' Alliance. Yet this activism never translated into Populist strength. Black Southerners' voting rights were increasingly restricted through poll taxes and disfranchisement laws, and white farmers were reluctant to abandon the Democrats, who pronounced themselves the champions of (white) "home rule" for the South and of resistance to federal intrusion. Those Southerners who became Populists often did so at great risk. Weaver and Lease vividly experienced southern Democrats' fear and hatred when they arrived in Georgia in September 1892. In Macon, only a few miles from the place where Lease's father had died in a Confederate prison camp, she and Weaver were hooted down and pelted with rotten vegetables and eggs. At Albany, the speakers and their entourage hid in their hotel, unsure for hours whether the angry crowd outside intended to lynch them. Within a week Weaver and Lease had canceled the rest of their southern tour. In November, Democrats retained control of almost every southern state—by persuading Populist voters where they could and, where necessary, by using overt violence and fraud.

Weaver's defeat—though he won more than a million votes— was only the beginning of Mary Lease's troubles. Though Kansas Populists won many offices in 1892, including the governorship, they did so through ticket-splitting (or "fusion") arrangements with Democrats. To Lease, who spent less and less of her time in Kansas, such an alliance was a betrayal of populism. Democrats were the men she had encountered in Georgia, many of whom were former Confederates, and in her view they were responsible for killing her father.

Furthermore, Democrats in Kansas and elsewhere were staunch opponents of women's suffrage and prohibition, and Populists had to give up these goals in order to appease their new friends. For some Populists this apparent compromise was not a problem, since they had never supported such measures in the first place. But many others, Lease included, wanted the party to articulate a much broader vision. Outside the former Confederacy, in almost every state where they had held a convention in the early 1890s, Populists had adopted women's suffrage planks. Some had also made favorable mention of prohibition. Yet at the 1892 National Populist Convention these planks had been dropped, largely in deference to the party's more conservative southern wing. Lease observed the same Populist-Democratic fusion in her home state of Kansas: the men in power dismissed women's suffrage and prohibition as side issues at best or even as extremist, illegitimate demands. Small wonder that some Kansas Populists began bitterly denouncing the fusionists, claiming they were no longer Populists at all. Those who favored fusion responded, with some justification, that unless the new party allied itself with Democrats, it could not win; with fusion, it had elected a Populist governor.

For Lease, the biggest affront was the division of appointments after the 1892 state campaign. She let it be known that she was interested in Kansas's second U.S. Senate seat, which the new legislature would fill. Lease's candidacy created a nationwide sensation: in only two states (Wyoming and Colorado) were women allowed to vote for national offices, and the idea of a woman senator was entirely new. To many progressive-minded onlookers, this issue was a test of the party's true colors. Women's suffrage leader Susan B. Anthony offered a public endorsement. James Weaver and other Populists also wrote letters of support, stating that the Constitution clearly allowed women to serve in Congress. But Kansas's new governor and legislators had no desire to appoint either a woman or a "mid-roader," a Populist who avoided fusion with either the Democrats or the Republicans. Their victory had been at best a shaky one, and they calculated that Lease's strongest supporters among the citizenry of Kansas were Alliance women, who had no future votes with which to retaliate if they were displeased. Lease was shunted aside and offered a lesser appointment as state superintendent of charities. No American woman had ever held such a prominent office, and the new governor, Lorenzo Lewelling, no doubt thought he was making a suitable offer. Lease, who rightly considered herself one of her party's most valuable assets, took a different view.

She nonetheless accepted the post Lewelling offered and for a year oversaw the state's asylums for orphans, the mentally retarded, and elderly veterans. With little experience in such work, Lease attended national conferences and listened to the advice of experts, but at the same time she continued to jockey for power within the Kansas party. When Lewelling tried to appoint two Democrats to the Board of Charities as part of the new fusion agreement, Lease protested vigorously and even criticized the governor in her interviews with reporters. Populists who supported Lewelling began to criticize her for disloyalty; many mid-roaders hailed her as a hero. Facing division within Populist ranks, Lewelling dismissed Lease from her post in December 1893. Lease fought an expensive legal battle for reinstatement, but she lost.

By 1895, Lease was also worn down by opponents' attacks. As a woman who spoke for new, radical ideas, she was an outsider to the world of politics, and from the first she received treatment as such. Republican and Democratic editors and politicians branded her as ugly, loud, aggressive, and "unwomanly"—terms of abuse that activist women of all political persuasions have faced. After Kansas's 1892 inauguration ceremony, *Harper's Weekly* ignored Lease's speech for the occasion, reporting instead that she was too flat-chested to wear a ballgown. Some opposition newspapers hinted that Lease "prostituted" her talents; one snidely remarked that her voice was the only thing marketable about her. As Kansas Populists split between fusionists and mid-roaders, some Populists joined in such attacks. Lease claimed in 1894 that Governor Lewelling, when Lease had begun to expose corruption in his administration, had threatened to buy evidence purporting to prove that she and James Weaver had slept together during their 1892 campaign tour. As a poor woman, Lease was particularly vulnerable to such charges, in part because her use of words such as "hell" (even though she was quoting from the Bible) shocked many a respectable citizen.

Angry and isolated, Lease found herself cut off from many former allies as the Populist party fell apart. She first tried to reestablish her influence by publishing a book, *The Problem of Civilization Solved,* which appeared in 1895. It was a rambling work that foreshadowed the logic of the most extreme imperialists in the next decade. Lease argued that European-American farmers needed new land and resources in order to prosper; their future lay in Central and South America, and "enterprising white men from the North" should "colonize the valley of the Amazon and the tropical plateaux."[8] How they would acquire this land remained unclear; Lease repeatedly denounced war and helped found the National Peace Society. In contrast, she praised the U.S. Army for its wars against the Sioux and Cheyenne on the northern plains, and she later gave her wholehearted endorsement to imperialism. With her muddled thinking and overt racial condescension, Lease was lucky that her book was largely ignored.

In 1896, she recommitted herself to stump-speaking tours in one of the most important presidential elections in U.S. history. Democrats nominated William Jennings Bryan for president on a platform that borrowed a few planks from the Populists, most notably in advocating currency expansion. Despite strenuous objections from Lease and others, the Populist national convention seconded Bryan's nomination, adopting a fusion strategy again. Lease spent most of the autumn in New York and Minnesota, speaking for Bryan but noting in an occasional aside that Bryan's platform offered only the barest of reform measures. By the time the Republican candidate, William McKinley, won the White House in November, Lease was declaring herself a Socialist. She was one of the first prominent Populists to do so, and many other Populists (including Eugene Debs, later a famous Socialist candidate for the U.S. presidency) soon followed her lead.

In the wake of McKinley's election the Populist party fragmented and fell into decline. Bitter about the effects of fusion, Lease probably also agreed with former Colorado governor Davis Waite, another Populist who had exhausted himself for the cause. "I have done traveling 1000 miles to make a single speech," Waite wrote Ignatius Donnelly in 1896, "or attempting to fill spasmodic appointments with spasmodic speeches. I want some organization, to make a regular daily series of appointments, provide halls & pay actual living & travel expenses from day to day."[9] The Populist leadership, presiding over a shrinking party, could not offer even these shreds of support.

At the age of forty-eight, so financially desperate that on one occasion her luggage was repossessed, Lease decided to leave Kansas and start a new life. She secured an amicable divorce from Charles and moved with her children to New York City. Having studied law and passed the bar in Wichita during the 1880s, she established a part-time legal practice in New York's Lower East Side, largely serving the immigrant poor. She also taught evening classes on history and literature for the New York Board of Education, and she lectured occasionally on literary, economic, and political topics. In the 1910s she joined a group of reformers working for women's reproductive rights—no doubt recollecting her harsh experiences as a frontier wife and mother. At the end of her life, looking back Lease considered her efforts on behalf the National Birth Control League, headquartered in New York, among her most important works of public service.

After 1900, Lease never quite found another political home. As early as 1896 she had identified herself as a Socialist, and she became a friend of American Socialist party leader Eugene Debs, for whose ideas and candidacies she spoke on many occasions. At the same time, Lease was painfully aware of the difficult position of third parties, which had meager campaign funds and no patronage posts to distribute and whose enemies increasingly sought to exclude them from the ballot altogether. Lease retained a fierce hatred of Democrats, based on her father's death and her own touring experiences in Georgia, and she remained hopeful that

Republicans would take up new reforms. She admired Theodore Roosevelt, and when he made his Progressive party presidential bid in 1912, she made a series of speeches on his behalf. In a typical move, she afterward sued the campaign for not paying her as much as they had promised—reminding male party leaders, as always, that they could not take her services for granted.

In 1905, Lease suffered another personal tragedy when her beloved oldest son, Charles, died suddenly of appendicitis. In her last years, however, she found the financial security she had sought for so long and proudly watched her three surviving children graduate from college, fulfilling the dream of her own mother, Mary Clyens, that her American grandchildren be well educated. Louisa, Grace, and Ben settled comfortably in Brooklyn. Ben, ironically, became a stockbroker; Louisa married a writer; and Grace followed her mother into politics, becoming a district organizer for the Republicans. In 1932 Mary Lease purchased a farm in Sullivan County, New York, along the Delaware River, where she spent the final year of her life.

Before she died, Lease witnessed the implementation of many policies she had espoused even though Progressive Era economic reforms fell far short of what Populists had dreamed of, leaving the "money power" more entrenched than reformers had hoped. Lease lived to see national women's suffrage, and she watched a one-time Populist ally, Rebecca Felton, become the first woman to sit in the U.S. Senate, albeit if only briefly to serve out her deceased husband's term.

Lease died in 1933 at the age of eighty-three. William Allen White, an old foe who had grown more sympathetic to some of Lease's views, wrote upon her death that "as a voice calling the people to action she has never had a superior in Kansas politics. . . . She was an honest, competent woman who felt deeply and wielded great power unselfishly."[10] Lease did, indeed, seek public solutions to private problems, impoverishing herself in the 1890s by working for measures that would aid millions of Americans rather than only herself. In her long life she experienced many reversals of fortune. Poverty and the deaths of three children were griefs she shared with millions of women; other sufferings—including the countless attacks on her as a public speaker, in which she heard herself called everything from a harlot to a harpy—she shared with only a few. Her restless search for reform continued despite it all.

In her private life, Lease continually reinvented herself. She remained open to new ideas and willing to start again from scratch in the face of bankruptcy, a failed marriage, public scorn, and the loss of those close to her, from the death of her father when she was thirteen to that of her oldest son when she was fifty-five. In her public life she displayed the same willingness to start over when the causes she worked for crumbled to dust and had to be resurrected or reshaped under new names. "Keep your eye fixed upon the mark," she once remarked, "and don't flinch when you pull the trigger."[11] Not all her views were admirable, but they were bold and often ahead of her time, and throughout her career she kept a sustained focus on inequities of class and gender. Her eloquence moved tens of thousands of listeners to share—whether for a few moments, a few years, or a lifetime—a vision of a future America in which citizens would demand that their government guarantee equality to women and justice to the poor.

Notes

1. Lease once told a reporter that she never made this comment but that she "let it stand, because she thought it was a right good piece of advice." O. Gene Clanton, "Intolerant Populist? The Disaffection of Mary Elizabeth Lease," *Kansas Historical Quarterly* 34 (1968): 190, n. 2.

2. *Facts and Figures about Kansas: An Emigrants' and Settlers' Guide* (Lawrence, KS: Blackburn, 1870), 24–25.

3. Joan Jensen, ed., *With These Hands* (Old Westbury, NY: Feminist Press, 1981), 158–59.

4. Dorothy Rose Blumberg, "Mary Elizabeth Lease: Populist Orator: A Profile," *Kansas History* 1 (1978): 14.

5. Walter Van Tilburg Clark, ed., *The Journals of Alfred Doten, 1849–1903,* 3 vols. (Reno: University of Nevada Press, 1973), 3:1825; Ignatius Donnelly, *Representative,* September 8, 1897.

6. John D. Hicks, *The Populist Revolt: A History of the Farmers' Alliance and the People's Party* (Minneapolis: University of Minnesota Press, 1931), 439–41.

7. Blumberg, "Mary Elizabeth Lease," 14.

8. Mary Elizabeth Lease, *The Problem of Civilization Solved* (Chicago: Laird and Lee, 1895), 176, 178.

9. Davis Waite to Ignatius Donnelly, August 20, 1900, Donnelly Papers, Minnesota Historical Society, Minneapolis.

10. William Allen White, *Forty Years on Main Street* (New York: Farrar and Rinehart, 1937), 227.

11. *Wichita Independent,* March 23, 1889.

Suggested Readings

Robert McMath's *American Populism: A Social History* (New York: Hill and Wang, 1993) is an excellent account of populism's origins, platforms, and fate. In his introduction, McMath reviews four influential works on populism that are very much worth reading in their own right: John Hicks's classic *The Populist Revolt* (Minneapolis: University of Minnesota Press, 1939); C. Vann Woodward's *Tom Watson, Agrarian Rebel* (New York: Oxford University Press, 1938); Richard Hofstadter's *The Age of Reform* (New York: Knopf, 1955), which is highly critical of populism; and Lawrence Goodwyn's *Democratic Promises: The Populist Moment in America* (New York: Oxford University Press, 1976), a controversial account of the Populists' "movement culture." McMath also analyzes producerism as espoused by the Knights of Labor, Farmers' Alliance, and other movements for economic reform, and he provides a good bibliography. Michael Lewis Goldberg's *An Army of Women: Gender in Kansas Politics* (Baltimore: Johns Hopkins University Press, 1997) places Mary Lease in state and gender context.

For broader overviews of women in politics see Mary Jo Buhle, *Women and American Socialism* (Urbana: University of Illinois Press, 1981); Ruth Bordin, *Woman and Temperance* (Philadelphia: Temple University Press, 1981); and Rebecca Edwards, *Angels in the Machinery: Gender in American Party Politics from the Civil War to the Progressive Era* (New York: Oxford University Press, 1997). The views of representative farm women who joined Lease's crusade appear in Marion K. Barthelme, ed., *Women in the Texas Populist Movement: Letters to the Southern Mercury* (College Station, TX; Texas A&M University Press, 1997).

On the settlement of western Kansas see Craig Miner's *West of Wichita* (Lawrence: University Press of Kansas, 1986). For women's experiences on the Great Plains see Glenda Riley, *The Female Frontier* (Lawrence: University Press of Kansas, 1988); and Joanna L. Stratton, ed., *Pioneer Women: Voices from the Kansas Frontier* (New York: Simon and Schuster, 1981).

5

Richard Olney and the Pullman Strike

Ballard C. Campbell

Richard Olney's fame and fortune were intimately tied to railroads. An attorney who counseled railroad executives and sat on corporation boards, Olney developed a reputation for thorough and prudent legal advice. These qualities appealed to Grover Cleveland, who appointed him attorney general of the United States in the president's second administration. Ballard Campbell, a political and business historian, examines Olney's career, which illustrates the role that railroad attorneys played during the Gilded Age. One assignment was to advise management on labor relations. Disagreements between workers and rail managers flared frequently during the late nineteenth century as trainmen sought better conditions and pay and managers strained to keep costs down.

Olney went to Washington shortly before the depression of 1893 began. This was also the year that Eugene Debs, a former trainman, attempted to organize rail workers into a single, nationwide union. As this process occurred, employees at the Pullman Palace Car Company Factory near Chicago walked off their jobs. When Debs's fledgling American Railroad Union lent its support, a local dispute escalated into a massive work stoppage. The Pullman strike thrust Olney and Debs into the national spotlight and locked the two men in a struggle over power and principle. Professor Campbell examines the crisis from the perspective of rail managers, trainmen, and national officials. He concludes that the strike enhanced the power of the presidency, weakened organized labor, and fragmented the Democratic party.

Ballard C. Campbell is professor of history at Northeastern University in Boston and holds a Ph.D. from the University of Wisconsin, Madison. He is the author of *The Growth of American Government: Governance from the Cleveland Era to the Present* (1995) and *Representative Democracy: Public Policy and Midwestern Legislatures in the Late Nineteenth Century* (1980). He is associate editor of the *American National Biography* (1999).

Richard Olney lived during the golden age of American railroads. The spread of rail transportation had an enormous impact on the United States during the last half of the nineteenth century. Railroads affected how Americans made their living, where they located their homes, how they shopped and what they bought, and how far and frequently they traveled. Two million men worked for railroad companies at their peak employment, and thousands more invested their money in them. Olney did both, tying his career and his social status to the fortunes of the railroad. Although railroads enabled Olney and many other Americans to achieve economic success, they also produced bitter conflicts between workers and managers. Occasionally this tension burst into violence, as occurred in the Pullman strike of 1894. Olney was attorney general of the United States at the time the crisis erupted, presenting him and President Cleveland with a complex legal and political challenge.

Olney was born on September 15, 1835, in Oxford, Massachusetts, a small community south of Worcester, an emerging industrial city located forty miles west of Boston. His father managed a woolen company and a bank, businesses that Richard's grandfather had started in Oxford. After a common school education and attendance at a private academy, Richard went to Brown University, graduated in 1856, and then entered Harvard Law School. After passing the bar exam in 1859, he secured a position in the office of Benjamin F. Thomas, a prominent attorney in Boston. Shortly after entering the firm, Richard married Thomas's daughter Agnes. The couple's first daughter was born in 1861 and their second in 1865, the boundary years of the Civil War. Olney avoided military service by hiring a substitute, a practice that was legal.

Civil War Boston was dominated by Brahmins, the city's social and commercial elite. Entrance into this charmed circle occurred by birth or marriage, thus excluding Olney. Instead of brooding over this impediment, he doubled his efforts to get ahead. Specializing in wills and trusts early in his career, he became known for his thoroughness and capacity to master technicalities. By the 1870s these talents had earned him an income sufficient to begin construction of a rambling summerhouse in Falmouth, Massachusetts. Olney returned to his Cape Cod retreat every summer thereafter. In the mid-1870s he also attempted to combine politics with the law, but successive defeats for the state house, senate, and office of attorney general convinced him that his brisk temperament and methodical approach to matters was better suited to serving clients as a private attorney.

Although he did not hobnob with Boston's Brahmins, Olney mimicked their lifestyle as he moved up the income scale. As his fortunes rose he built a four-story town house on Commonwealth Avenue in Boston. The residence faced the Back Bay Fens (the park near the Boston Red Sox's Fenway Park), was wired for electricity, and had an elevator. Servants helped with everyday chores such as the evening meal, for which the Olneys dressed formally. Like some others of his class in the Victorian era, Richard lorded over his servants and family in a patriarchal fashion.

Drawing up wills and trusts gave Olney a taste of success, but routine legal work could not propel him into the moneyed class. Work for railroads allowed him to rise to this next level. Born at the dawn of rail transportation in New England, Richard was five when the Norwich and Worcester Railroad came to Oxford. During his teens, rail lines linked Worcester to Boston and Providence and extended to New York, Albany, and Portland. Whereas it had taken Abigail Adams, wife of the second president, a week to travel by horse and coach from Quincy (a Boston suburb) to New York City in 1797 during a rainy spring, steam locomotives covered the same distance in a little over eight hours on the eve of the Civil War. When Olney began his legal career a rail network was spreading across New England and had already ventured into America's midwestern heartland.

In both prosperous years and difficult times, railroads offered numerous opportunities for aspiring lawyers. The misfortunes of the Eastern Railroad gave Olney his first big break. The Eastern ran between Boston and Portland, Maine, a route whose popularity attracted other companies, including the Boston and Maine. Competition from the B&M enticed Eastern owners to overexpand, a decision that saddled the company with a large debt. A slump in business after the panic of 1873 undermined the company's ability to pay the interest on its loans. Two years later the company went bankrupt. The Eastern hired Olney to salvage some of the company's value for its investors. He helped to reorganize the company and became the new firm's general counsel (chief legal adviser) and one of its directors. He transferred these positions to the Boston and Maine when it leased the Eastern in 1884. Six years later he wrote the legislation that merged the Eastern into the B&M. By 1890, Olney was a key figure in the largest railroad corporation in northern New England. Equally fortuitous, his work caught the eye of Bostonians with interests in railroads in the Midwest.

Railroads grew quickly after the Civil War. Their expansion coincided with the settlement of the Great Plains and the far West, as well as with the emergence of the Midwest as a diversified region of farms, factories, and cities. By reducing transportation costs, railroads promoted commercial development among many kinds of businesses and lowered the prices that consumers paid. Local promoters flooded state legislatures between the 1840s and 1870s with requests to charter rail companies. Citizens in town after town argued that their economic future depended on acquiring rail connections. These proponents saw railroads as steel highways that joined producers, wholesalers, processors, and consumers in expanding economic networks.

Investors saw profits in this development. One of the most perceptive was John Murray Forbes, a Boston merchant and capitalist who gravitated to railroading in the mid-1840s. In the early 1850s Forbes and his partners acquired control of a short line in northern Illinois that ran into Chicago. By 1865 the Forbes group had nurtured the company—renamed the Chicago, Burlington, and Quincy (C, B&Q)—into an enterprise that linked Chicago with the Mississippi River and controlled lines in Iowa and Missouri. Forbes and his young assistant, Charles Perkins, built the Burlington by purchasing local railroad companies and laying additional track. Under their leadership the Burlington grew during the 1870s and 1880s into one of the major carriers in the Midwest, serving the grain belts of Illinois, Iowa, Missouri, and Nebraska and providing a strategic connection for through traffic from the far West to Chicago, the great commercial depot in the nation's heartland.

Unlike the swashbuckling raiders who speculated in railroad stocks, Forbes and Perkins proceeded cautiously. They worked to build a stable business based on reliable transport for farmers' commodities and prudent management of the corporation's finances. Competition, however, forced deviations from this conservative strategy. One challenge came from other midwestern railroads (such as the Rock Island Line and the Chicago and North Western) that served Chicago's broad western hinterland. From time to time the Burlington split territories and pooled revenues with these rivals, based on the philosophy of live and let live. A second rivalry came from the great transcontinental lines that pushed east from the Rocky Mountains. Jay Gould, whose Union Pacific was the first of the cross-country railways to reach the Pacific Coast, entertained aspirations to build or buy his way into Chicago. In the late 1870s, Gould attempted to dislodge the Burlington's foothold in Iowa and Nebraska and muscle his way into the Windy City. To protect the Burlington's turf, Perkins believed that it had to open its own corridor to the west. By 1890 the C, B&Q had reached Denver and ranged as far south as St. Louis and as far north as St. Paul.

Enlarging the Burlington into a regional system required large sums of capital to finance construction and to purchase existing routes. Railroad executives preferred to issue new stock to raise these funds. Many investors viewed stocks as too risky, however, and favored bonds, which paid interest regularly. Between 1874 and 1890 the Burlington tripled its stock issues and quadrupled its bond debt. These financial obligations put pressure on the railroad to meet the carrier's fixed costs, which consisted of the interest on bonds and dividend payments on stock. The task of a rail superintendent was to keep traffic flowing so that the line collected enough revenue to meet operating expenses (labor and fuel) and cover the fixed costs. Missed dividends or interest payments not only tarnished a firm's reputation, which made raising additional capital more costly, but also threatened to spark an investor revolt, which could topple a company's management team. Bankruptcy could reduce stocks to worthlessness and put the railroad in the hands of court-appointed "receivers." Numerous railroads had met this fate during the depression of the 1870s, and the 1890s brought on more bankruptcies.

Confronted with these pressures, managers approached the complex task of rate-setting with care. One challenge arose from other railroads that plied similar "through" routes. Competition on these long-distance runs drove rates down. To compensate for revenue shortfalls, railroads often charged more per mile on the local, noncompetitive branch routes. The discrepancies between long-haul and short-haul charges led to angry allegations that railroads discriminated against customers in certain localities. The general decline of railroad rates in the late nineteenth century further complicated pricing because it forced railroads to increase the volume of freight carried in order to maintain a constant revenue intake. Moreover, some economic factors, such as depressions, lay beyond the control of railroad managers.

One step that managers could take to improve chances for profitability was to hire capable associates, including lawyers. The latter could persuade legislators to charter railroad corporations and to block proposals of their rivals. Lawyers also examined charters— legal documents written by state legislators that authorized a corporation to carry out a specific activity—for loopholes that allowed corporations more strategic flexibility. They lobbied legislators to kill proposed regulations, and they read the fine print in private contracts between companies and sued (or threatened to sue) firms that violated the terms of a deal.

Richard Olney excelled at these tasks. In 1886 the Burlington hired him to oppose legislation in Congress that proposed to regulate railroads. Olney failed to stop the enactment, in part because of building sentiment for national controls after the Supreme Court's *Wabash* decision. This 1886 ruling prohibited state governments from regulating railroads whose routes crossed state boundaries (that is, were involved in interstate commerce). Since no national statute was on the books, railroads that engaged in interstate commerce operated in a regulatory void. The 1887 Interstate Commerce Act filled this gap. The law disallowed various practices such as the pooling of freight or division of revenues among several carriers and charging more for short than long hauls, but authority to regulate rates remained unclear. The statute assigned enforcement responsibility to the Interstate Commerce Commission, the federal government's first "independent" regulatory commission.

After Congress created the commission, Olney advised Perkins, Burlington's president, to get along with the agency, which Olney predicted would become pro-railroad over time. Perkins remained skeptical and urged repeal of the law, in part because he considered pooling a necessary part of the railroad business. In his thinking, pools helped railroads to remain solvent and thus competitive; the alternative was consolidation and less competition. Perkins also realized that the states still could regulate rates of lines that operated within their borders, and he asked Olney to help with this threat. In 1889 the Burlington appointed Olney its chief counsel and voted him a seat on the board of directors at a salary of $10,000 (about $170,000 in 1999). At the time the Burlington was protesting an Iowa rate regulation.

Olney began work for the Burlington at a stormy time in its relations with its employees. Running a railroad required many hands to perform a variety of different tasks. The best positions paid well compared to other industrial employment and were avidly sought. These jobs formed a pecking order in terms of wages and status. At the top were locomotive engineers and conductors on passenger trains and master mechanics in the shops. Below them were firemen, brakemen, and assistant mechanics. At the bottom were trackmen, station hands, and common laborers. Regardless of their assignments, trainmen faced slack periods when their services were not needed, a circumstance that caused their incomes to fluctuate unpredictably. When they were called the work was long—ten- to fifteen-hour days were not unusual—and often dangerous. Before the introduction of air brakes, for example, brakemen walked on top of moving cars in all kinds of weather to reach brake controls, which they turned manually. They also inserted by hand linking pins that coupled one car to another. Not surprisingly, brakemen suffered a high rate of accidents and fatalities. A trainman who was missing several fingers took a visible sign of his railroad experience into a job interview.

The nature of their work bred a close camaraderie among railroaders, who carried these bonds over to labor organizations called brotherhoods. Engineers formed the first brotherhood in 1863, the conductors followed in 1868, and workers in other railroad occupations followed in later decades. Although the brotherhoods were largely social in nature, they did press for better pay and working conditions. The engineers and firemen on the Burlington, for example, walked off their jobs in 1888 over the method of calculating wages. Charles Perkins believed it was wise to treat his men fairly, but he stood his ground against the brotherhoods. When strikers persuaded trainmen on other lines not to handle C, B&Q cars, Perkins turned to the courts for help. Compliant federal judges issued orders called injunctions that instructed workers to cease their boycott. This judicial intervention, plus the refusal of Burlington's conductors, brakemen, and switchmen to join the walkout, doomed it to failure.

The Burlington strike had a profound effect on Eugene Debs, the man destined to be Olney's chief protagonist. Debs was born and raised in Terre Haute, Indiana, where he went to work as a young man as a fireman on the Vandalia Railroad. He gave up railroading after his layoff during the depression of the 1870s but he continued his association with trainmen, first as the secretary of their local brotherhood and then as an official with the group's national organization. Initially, Debs conceived of the brotherhood as a group that helped its members improve their moral character, guiding them to become "honest and upright citizens." The Burlington strike shocked him out of this old-fashioned outlook, which was common before industrialization transformed relations between workers and employers. After 1888, Debs questioned the idea that workers were part of an economic community in which cooperation and unity reigned. He came to see railroads as part of the world of corporations, whose interests differed from those of labor. He also realized that the divisions of trainmen into separate brotherhoods worked against their interest and advantaged managers. The way to improve workers' conditions, he concluded, was to build a single union that united all railroaders. Debs resigned as secretary-treasurer of the Firemen's Brotherhood and began to organize the American Railway Union in 1893.

This was the year that Grover Cleveland returned to the White House after an absence of four years. Looking to fill the position of attorney general with someone whose legal and political outlook paralleled his own, Cleveland received a recommendation from William C. Whitney, a New York financier and transportation entrepreneur. Olney, Whitney said, possessed the right credentials. He was a widely respected attorney who had headed the Boston Bar Association and been offered a seat on Massachusett's top court. Besides his numerous legal contacts, Olney had advised railroad managers and directors of big businesses for years. He had experience working with both state legislators and members of Congress and the Interstate Commerce Commission in Washington. Moreover, he shared Cleveland's philosophy of conservatism that emphasized a government that kept costs low, cooperated with private enterprise, and ran an honest administration. Despite the honor of Cleveland's invitation to join the cabinet, Olney hesitated.

He would have to give up his $50,000-per-year legal practice (about $870,000 in 1999) for a post that paid only $8,000. But encouragement from his business associates, including Charles Perkins and John Forbes, persuaded him to join the administration. They saw it in their interest to have Olney hold the nation's top legal position. Olney performed as expected, offering advice to his business colleagues from Washington and pocketing his annual fee from the Burlington during his first year and a half as attorney general.

Three months into the Cleveland presidency a financial panic struck Wall Street. The bankruptcy of the Philadelphia and Reading Railroad in February had weakened the stock market, where share values plummeted in May. The Dow Jones index of stocks (composed mainly of railroad issues) declined by a third in the first half of 1893. Olney attributed the panic to "reckless speculation . . . official dishonesty . . . [and] the mad rush to be quickly rich."[1] Debs saw the downturn as a premeditated "bankers' panic."[2] Many banks did not survive the depression, which also dragged numerous railroads into bankruptcy. By mid-1894 the courts had placed 124 bankrupt carriers in the hands of temporary managers known as receivers. Railroads that escaped this fate saw their incomes dwindle. The Burlington's response to sagging revenue was to cut wages, lay off workers, and postpone purchases of new equipment.

The panic precipitated a prolonged economic depression that spelled hard times for workers. Joblessness averaged 20 percent of the workforce in 1893 and idled perhaps half of all workers in some cities during the winter of 1893–94. In an era before government provided unemployment compensation, depressions cast idled workers into difficult predicaments. Few workers had accumulated much savings or owned a home. Many men abandoned their families and set to "tramping" to find work. Disappointed job seekers sometimes turned to alcohol and violence. Some workers reacted to cuts in wages and reductions in hours by striking. In the West unemployed men hijacked several trains and ran them east until the "bandits" were apprehended by the U.S. Army.

Hard times drifted into Pullman, Illinois. This town was the brainchild of George M. Pullman, who accumulated a fortune by building specialty railroad cars such as his famed "sleepers." Rather than sell his sleeping and dining cars, Pullman leased and maintained them, an arrangement that led to an ongoing business relationship with numerous railroads. Acting on the belief that adequate housing and a pleasing environment would make his workers more reliable and loyal, Pullman constructed a model community twelve miles south of Chicago. Possessing its own water and sewer systems, farm, stores, and recreational facilities, the town was virtually self-contained. It also was run by Pullman's iron hand with rules that barred union organizers and leases that permitted easy eviction of tenants.

Like other entrepreneurs, Pullman saw his business fall off in 1893. As orders for sleepers dropped, Pullman laid off workers and cut the wages of those remaining on his payroll. But he did not reduce the housing rents charged to his workers or trim the salaries of his executives. These affronts and lingering grievances toward Pullman's labor practices attracted some workers to the American Railway Union (ARU). When company officials refused to meet with an employee grievance committee in May 1894, workers walked off their jobs and Pullman closed his factory.

Debs realized that the timing for a major strike was not right. His union was new and relatively untested, and an army of unemployed workers formed a pool of potential strikebreakers. At first he offered only moral support for the strikers. Visiting Pullman, he denounced its owner as "a greater felon than a poor thief" and vowed that the ARU, which was scheduled to convene in Chicago, would "show him to the world as an oppressor of labor."[3] Once assembled, ARU delegates rallied behind Pullman workers, voting to refrain from handling trains that included Pullman cars. By means of this selective (secondary) boycott, the ARU hoped to force George Pullman into negotiations with his employees. Olney viewed these events with alarm, as did his business friends. One of these acquaintances was George Pullman, who sat with Olney as a member of the Boston and Maine Railroad's board of directors.

The depression threw several problems into Olney's lap. Soon after he settled into his office on Lafayette Square, located several blocks from the Capitol, the slump in business triggered the eruption of local strikes around the country, train hijackings, and marches of men toward Washington. Coxey's Army, the most publicized of these groups, turned out to be a small, ragtag band of unemployed souls who supported Jacob Coxey's petition to Congress for public works projects. Coxey had conceived the idea as a way of putting idle men to work. Olney saw this "petition in boots" as part of a broad attack of labor on "the whole organized order of things."[4] He put the entourage under the surveillance of plainclothes officers. Washington police prevented Coxey from delivering his oration, arrested him for walking on the grass, and charged him with violating a law that prohibited the display of banners on the Capitol grounds. The visionary "general" spent twenty days in jail.

The western hijackings required a more intricate solution. The fact that railroads served as an arm of the U.S. government by carrying the mail and that many western railroads were operating under federally appointed managers (receivers), gave Olney certain legal footholds. He authorized district attorneys around the country to request that federal judges issue injunctions that prohibited interference with particular railroads. He then cited a violation of an injunction as grounds for ordering the U.S. Army to protect a company's trains once federal marshals affirmed that the company was not up to the task. Although he had to proceed carefully in view of President Cleveland's cautious position on use of the military in civilian matters, Olney had prepared his weapons for a showdown with Debs.

Olney had help from the railroads in this confrontation. Executives of the twenty-four railroads with terminals in Chicago had organized the General Managers Association to deal with common labor problems. Like George Pullman, the Chicago executives refused to negotiate with the ARU. Viewing the Pullman boycott as an opportunity to crush the union, the rail managers required that Pullman sleepers be attached to trains that hauled mail cars and that employees who refused to handle such combinations be fired. As this scenario unfolded, dismissed workers retaliated by striking. As traffic ground to a halt around Chicago in early July 1894, railroad managers cited the tie-up as grounds for the attorney general to enjoin the ARU from interfering with the mail.

Olney was a willing accomplice in this scheme. He accepted the railroads' contention that trains pulling sleepers qualified as the normal and customary complement of cars. He appointed Edwin Walker, a railroad attorney, as a special Justice Department agent for Chicago and instructed him to request a sweeping injunction aimed at Debs and ARU organizations in Chicago. Because this restraining order forbade virtually any union participation in the strike, violation of the injunction was a certainty. It is not unreasonable to presume that personal economic interest motivated Olney's behavior in these events. The Burlington was among the Chicago lines that resolved to face down the trainmen's union, and the company still paid Olney a retainer. Yet his conflict with Debs also flowed from ideological objections to labor unions. This feeling was widely shared by members of the business community, numerous judges, and the middle classes, many of whom saw the Pullman strike as illegal and thought that the attorney general ought to stop it.

A showdown between government and protesters was a virtual certainty because ARU officials could not control the actions of workers across the nation. Many individuals who took to the streets were not railroad employees. Some in these crowds used the opportunity to vent anger at corporations and capitalists and, perhaps, at their own bad luck during the depression. Moreover, Olney spread his net broadly. He instructed U.S. district attorneys at various locations in the Midwest and Far West to request injunctions similar to the Chicago order. With the pretext in hand for introducing federal troops into labor hot spots, Olney turned to convincing the president that the situation was a crisis that demanded military intervention. Despite his cautious nature, Cleveland needed little persuasion that the authority of the federal government should be upheld and that the lines of commerce, including mail service, should be kept open. "If it takes the entire army and navy . . . to deliver a postal card in Chicago," the president asserted, "that card will be delivered."[5] On the Fourth of July, 1894, soldiers of the U.S. Army took up positions in Chicago.

The appearance of soldiers in the streets threw fuel on a volatile situation that burst into a full-fledged riot. Mobs in Chicago destroyed large amounts of railroad property over the next several days. On July 7 the Illinois militia fired into a crowd, killing four. In all, thirteen deaths occurred during the days of violence in Chicago, although none were attributed to a U.S. soldier. The Windy City was turned into an armed camp with fourteen thousand police, Illinois militiamen, deputy sheriffs, federal troops, and deputy federal marshals patrolling the streets and rail yards. Many of these men were railroad workers assigned by their employers to serve as deputy federal marshals. Similar scenarios unfolded at other locations in the nation. At its peak the strike spread to twenty-seven states and shut down two-thirds of the country's railroads.

While armed officials restored peace in the streets, the federal injunction muzzled strike leaders. Police used the court order to arrest Debs and his assistants, who were coordinating the work stoppage. Debs had sent thousands of telegrams to worker groups around the country, issuing optimistic pronouncements, pleading for unity, and challenging workers to "proclaim your manhood." Federal officials raided ARU headquarters and seized its records, including Debs's correspondence. Olney later disavowed the confiscation, but the damage had been done. With the union leadership silenced and behind bars, the strike collapsed.

Business leaders and much of the general public hailed the administration's hard line on strikers. Given the hysterical tone that some newspapers exhibited, one can understand why people felt anxious during the crisis. The *Washington Post* asserted, "War of the bloodiest kind in Chicago is imminent." Federal officials, the article alleged, had learned that "the anarchists and socialist element, made up largely of the unemployed, were preparing to blow up . . . the federal building."[6] *Harper's Weekly* contended that "the rebellion" challenged the survival of the nation.[7] Olney himself announced on the eve of the troop deployment, "We have been brought to the ragged edge of anarchy" by workers who defied the government.[8] The statement probably represented his hyperbolic characterization of aggressive labor tactics more than a serious prediction of impending revolution. Nonetheless, one can imagine the remark unsettling some citizens. Many in the country no doubt believed that signs of a general labor uprising had already surfaced. The Great Railway Strike of 1877 and the incident in Haymarket Square, where Chicago police had shot and killed several people following the explosion of a bomb at a labor meeting in 1886, were the most publicized instances of numerous violent encounters in prior years. Against the background of this stress and public apprehension, Olney and Cleveland signaled to the nation that they would apply the force necessary to ensure civic order.

Olney reinforced this point by personally participating in court proceedings against Debs and his associates for their role in the strike. Late in 1894 the federal district court in Chicago found Debs guilty of contempt of court for violating the injunction and sentenced him to six months in the McHenry County Jail in Illinois. Clarence Darrow, a railroad attorney who became a noted advocate of social justice, defended Debs, arguing that his client was the victim of a conspiracy by Chicago railroads that sought to cut wages and smash the trainmen's union. Olney responded that federal intervention was justified because the railroads assisted in the delivery of the mail, which was a legitimate function of the government. He added that the Interstate Commerce Act permitted the government to prohibit interference with interstate rail transportation. Railroads, Olney argued, were "national highways," thus equating them to public utilities. Defending federal actions, he claimed that state governments had been slow to respond to the crisis and were ineffective when they had.

The case was appealed to the Supreme Court, which ruled unanimously against Debs (*In Re Debs*). Explaining the court's decision, Justice David Brewer endorsed Olney's argument and carried his logic one step further: "The strong arm of the national government may be put forth to brush away all obstructions to the freedom of interstate commerce," he wrote. "If the emergency arises," he continued, "the army of the Nation . . . [is] at the service of the Nation to compel obedience to its laws."[9] This statement was a bold assertion of power at a time when most people believed that the authority of the federal government should be limited. The idea that constraints on political power protected liberty had long been a staple of American ideology. During the Gilded Age business had drawn on the axiom as a legal defense against regulation by all levels of government. The Democratic party had traditionally championed reliance on state and local government as the surest strategy for preserving the principles of American politics. But in this instance the court saw a threat to civic harmony of sufficient magnitude to warrant national involvement. Olney and Cleveland, who can be accurately labeled conservatives, had boldly expanded the power of the national government. In the process they had overruled the objections of several governors, including John Altgeld of Illinois, whom Olney branded a prolabor radical. With Olney's prodding, Cleveland had established an important precedent for the president in initiating intervention into labor disputes.

The Pullman strike was one of several extraordinary upheavals in the Gilded Age. Compounding tensions brought on by the depression, the strike helped to shift American politics and labor relations in some new directions. Debs emerged from jail a changed man. After receiving a hero's welcome from supporters upon his release from jail, he abandoned union work, having lost faith in strikes to extract concessions from corporations. He turned to politics instead, following a path that led him to socialism. In 1900 Debs became the candidate of the Social Democratic party for the presidency, the first of five nominations by Socialists. Nor did the town of Pullman survive. In 1898 the Illinois supreme court ruled that George Pullman had exceeded his authority in building the community and ordered the property sold. The strike also undermined the Democratic party, which suffered huge losses in the election of 1894. Over the next two years most party activists repudiated Cleveland, in part because of his benign approach to the depression and his anti-union position. In 1896, Democrats embraced William Jennings Bryan as the party's presidential nominee and a silver-inflated money supply to cure the depression. Bryan lost to William McKinley, and Democrats did not regain the White House until Woodrow Wilson's victory in 1912.

The Burlington and Charles Perkins charted new paths after 1894. Perkins realized that the Burlington was a prime target for takeover because the line was profitable and because it occupied a strategic position between Chicago and the western transcontinental railroads. He witnessed how the depression had swept weaker carriers into the hands of more powerful lines. He resigned Burlington's presidency in 1901 but retained sufficient control to influence the company's fate. Preferring Jim Hill of the Great Northern among Burlington's suitors, Perkins held out for his price. A deal was reached at a meeting in 1901 in Boston, where Hill was accompanied by his investment banker, the famed J. P. Morgan; Olney assisted the Perkins group. Shortly after the merger, the Great Northern and the Union Pacific formed a combination called the Northern Securities Company. Heeding outcries against monopoly, President Theodore Roosevelt authorized the Justice Department to launch an antimonopoly prosecution of Northern Securities. "Malefactors of great wealth," Roosevelt charged, referring to the

Wall Street financiers who arranged corporate consolidations, threatened to bring on the "tyranny of a plutocracy." The U.S. Supreme Court disallowed the merger in 1904.

The fate of many railroad workers who joined the Pullman boycott was blacklisting, the practice whereby employers refused to hire former strikers. While railroad executives took a hard line on strikers and ARU members, politicians slowly gravitated to the conclusion that the promotion of industrial harmony was in the public interest. The Pullman Strike Commission, which investigated the conflict, drafted an arbitration bill that Olney revised substantially before its submission to Congress. Enacted in 1898 as the Erdman Act, the measure was weak but did outlaw "yellowdog contracts," which required workers to promise not to join labor unions. A quarter-century elapsed before Congress recognized unions as legal bargaining agents for railroad workers.

Even Olney softened his position on unions. Despite his ties to business, he was sympathetic to the difficulties workers faced. His response to the Pullman strike grew out of his attitude toward labor unions, whose legitimacy he questioned, especially when they used coercive methods to extract concessions from corporations. He regarded secondary boycotts and most strikes, which challenged the prerogatives of property owners, as illegal. These positions differed little from the outlooks of most corporate executives, White House officials, and perhaps the majority of the middle class in the Gilded Age. Nevertheless, as the memory of the Pullman strike faded, many people came to accept unions as part of modern industrial relations. Olney's thinking moved in this direction too.

Union leaders denounced Olney for breaking the Pullman strike. President Cleveland, of a different mind, promoted him to secretary of state when the position became vacant in 1895. The most memorable event in Olney's two-year stewardship of this department was his bellicose warning to Britain, which was locked in a dispute with Venezuela over a boundary in South America. A conflict between Spain and the United States over a rebellion against Spanish colonial rule in Cuba was just reaching a crisis stage when the Cleveland administration departed Washington in March 1897. Thirteen months later the country was at war. By then Olney had returned to Boston and the life he had led before his sojourn in the capital. He resumed his work as a director of the Burlington, the B&M, and other railroads and acquired new corporate clients, including AT&T and General Electric.

Never a fan of William Jennings Bryan, he held his nose and voted for the "commoner" in 1900, perhaps because he harbored his own presidential ambitions. A small boomlet promoting Olney for president died a stillbirth in 1904. Apparently undeterred, he continued with his usual routine of lawyering in a one-man firm in downtown Boston, exercising vigorously every day, summering on the Cape, lording over his household, and donating time and some of his substantial wealth to nonprofit organizations. An admirer of President Woodrow Wilson and in accord with much of progressive reform, Olney nonetheless refused Wilson's offers to become ambassador to England and a federal trade commissioner. He explained that he had retired and that his health was faltering. He died of cancer in 1917 at the age of eighty-one and was interred in Mount Auburn Cemetery in Cambridge, the resting place of many famous Boston Brahmins.

Notes

1. Gerald G. Eggert, *Richard Olney: Evolution of a Statesman* (University Park: Pennsylvania State University Press, 1974), 67.
2. Nick Salvatore, *Eugene V. Debs: Citizen and Socialist* (Urbana: University of Illinois Press, 1982), 143.
3. Almont Lindsey, *The Pullman Strike* (Chicago: University of Chicago Press, 1942), 124.
4. Eggert, *Olney*, 132.
5. Allan Nevins, *Grover Cleveland: A Study in Courage* (New York: Dodd, Mead, 1932), 628.
6. Lindsey, *Pullman Strike*, 311.
7. Ibid., 312.
8. Eggert, *Olney*, 142.
9. Stanley I. Kutler, ed., *The Supreme Court and the Constitution: Readings in American Constitutional History* (New York: W. W. Norton, 1977), 295.

Suggestions for Further Reading

Gerald G. Eggert, *Richard Olney: Evolution of a Statesman* (University Park: Pennsylvania State University Press, 1974), examines Olney's life and career. John F. Stover's *American Railroads* (Chicago: University of Chicago Press, 1961) provides an overview of the subject. More detailed treatments of railroads are Edward C. Kirkland, *Men, Cities, and Transportation: A Study in New England History, 1820–1900* (Cambridge, MA: Harvard University Press, 1968); Richard C. Overton, *Burlington Route: A History of the Burlington Lines* (New York: Alfred A. Knopf, 1965); and Walter Licht, *Working for the Railroad: The Organization of Work in the Nineteenth Century* (Princeton, NJ: Princeton University Press, 1983). Charles Hoffman, *The Depression of the Nineties* (Westport, CT: Greenwood Press, 1970), reviews the economic downturn. Nick Salvatore, *Eugene V. Debs: Citizen and Socialist* (Urbana: University of Illinois Press, 1982), offers a modern interpretation of the man. Almont Lindsey, *The Pullman Strike* (Chicago: University of Chicago Press, 1942), is the standard account of the conflict.

6

Mary Harris Jones
Immigrant and Labor Activist

Donna R. Gabaccia

Millions of immigrants streamed into the United States after the Civil War. They headed for the factories and sweatshops in the Northeast; the forests and pastures of the upper Midwest and Pacific Northwest; the fields of the Great Plains; and the mines in Appalachia, the Ohio River valley, and the mountains of the Far West. Many of these newcomers not only lacked job skills but also encountered employers intent on keeping wages down and unions away. Anti-union sentiment was especially fierce among mine owners, many of whom were small operators struggling to survive amid stiff competition. The operators employed a tough breed of men whose work underground in the coal and mineral shafts was the most dangerous in industrial America. These conditions sparked repeated conflicts at mining sites across the country.

Mary Harris Jones, the "miners' angel," could be found at many of these confrontations. Donna Gabaccia, a social historian, sketches the career of this tough-skinned and tenderhearted woman who was known around the mining camps as "Mother Jones." Officially a union organizer, she described herself as simply a hell-raiser. She was a courageous one too, as she demonstrated by braving all kinds of weather, dodging bullets, and spending time in jail as she urged workers to stand up to the bosses and demand justice. Neither a theoretician nor a mainstream reformer, Mother Jones brought a unique brand of talk and action to her fight against the economic inequalities that divided workers and employers. She also acted from a female working-class tradition of protest, which Professor Gabaccia sees as having succumbed to historical change. Mother Jones epitomized this older role, using earthy language to berate capitalists, belittle timid workers, and rally the women to support their men. Her voice had an Irish lilt, but her tongue was sharp as a razor.

Donna R. Gabaccia is the Charles H. Stone Professor of American History at the University of North Carolina at Charlotte. A graduate of Mount Holyoke College and the University of Michigan, she is the author of several books on Italian migration and labor and on immigrant life in the United States. Recent publications include *From the Other Side: Women and Gender in Immigrant Life, 1820–1980* (1994) and *We Are What We Eat: Ethnic Food and the Making of Americans* (1998).

"**M**other" Mary Harris Jones summed up her life as a labor activist in characteristically rude fashion when she abruptly interrupted a college professor who had called her a humanitarian at a public meeting: "Get it right. I am not a humanitarian. I am a hell-raiser."[1]

Jones was already sixty—or close to it (she insisted her birthday was May Day, 1830)—when she first gained public notoriety. A labor agitator who tramped through the West Virginia coal fields in high boots and black silk, Jones is remembered today largely because she shocked and puzzled almost every observer of her day—as she has puzzled historians ever since. Like many immigrant women, past and present, Jones ignored American ideals of womanly behavior. By the Victorian standards of her day, she seemed anything but motherly. "I do not belong in the church or the parlor or the club-room," she boasted. "I belong on the firing line."[2]

Jones was Irish and herself an immigrant at a time when most U.S. industrial workers were either foreigners or the children of immigrants. She differed in other ways from the "huddled masses" of silent and largely unskilled toilers who crowded into the United States from eastern and southern Europe between 1880 and 1914. She spoke English and had graduated from normal school, and unlike most immigrant women, she was only intermittently connected to women's industries such as canning, textiles, or garments or to paid domestic work. She certainly did not consider herself bound by this "woman's sphere," and her occasional involvement was not as a worker but as a protester. She most enjoyed working with America's coal and metal miners and their families, who dubbed her "the miners' angel."

She did seem angelic, even to opponents. White-haired and always dressed primly, Jones looked like the perfect old-fashioned grandmother, the very epitome of sweet, respectable motherhood as Victorian Americans imagined it—until she opened her mouth. Then, the combination of her very conventional appearance and her preference for blunt language confused those she met. Jones was a beer-drinking radical, proud of her ability to talk tough to men and women of all walks of life. She relished both conflict and danger, and she locked horns fearlessly with capitalists, labor bureaucrats, society ladies, and suffragists with considerable gusto. What she had to say she said in language no American lady used.

Industrial workers—whether native or foreign born—adored her. Unlike middle-class Americans, they had no trouble seeing Jones, with her heartfelt concern for working men, women, and children alike, as both womanly and motherly. Jones herself was proud of the many men and women of American mining who called her Mother. She organized some of her most controversial—and noisiest—protests with miners' wives, and she regularly excoriated a society that condemned workers' children to ignorance, poverty, and hard labor. Apparently working-class men and women understood Jones when she scorned the conventions of sentimental motherhood and domestic respectability as well as the sisterhood of middle-class "new women" who had graduated from college, supported suffrage, or become involved in social service professions. Unlike native-born women, the motherly woman idealized by America's immigrant and working class was physically tough, fearless, and outspoken.

How and why "Mother" Mary Harris Jones became such a popular hell-raiser as an elderly woman remains a matter of speculation, since almost everything about her first sixty years is mysterious. Jones provided little detail about her early life even when critics accused her of having been a prostitute. Born in Cork, Ireland, sometime between 1830 and 1843 (probably in 1836), she followed her migrant Irish father (who had earlier worked in the United States and become a citizen) to Toronto. There she grew up as a railroad laborer's daughter, nevertheless gaining a good public education. (Her brother also received an education as a priest and later became dean of the Archdiocese of Toronto.)

As a teacher in Michigan in 1859, Mary Harris quickly discovered—she later claimed—that she did not enjoy "bossing" little children. By 1861, she was married and living with her ironworker husband, George Jones, in Memphis. After the Civil War, Jones lost both her husband—whom she later praised as a staunch union man—and her four children in an 1867 yellow fever epidemic. She then worked for a time as a seamstress for wealthy families on Prairie Avenue in Chicago, but she was burned out of her shop during the great fire of 1871. Sometime thereafter she seems to have become involved in the early activities of the Knights of Labor, and in the 1880s she may have met Terence Powderly, Grand Master Workman of that organization. Powderly became a lifelong friend and supporter despite vast political differences between the two. (He disapproved of the strike as a tool of working-class organization, whereas Jones devoted most of the rest of her life to workers on strike.)

Jones's own (and possibly ghostwritten) memoirs, published very late in her life, and a few late-life interviews tell us what little we know about her life as a struggling widow. Her account establishes that she was familiar with some of the most violent and dramatic occurrences of Gilded Age labor history—including the "great insurrection" of railroad workers in 1877 and the Haymarket Affair of 1886. But Jones had little specific to relate about her participation in either event. Still, it is clear that she viewed labor history and her life as a connected series of dramatic moments when workers struggled collectively and passionately against their exploiters. Jones did not even mention in interviews or in her memoirs the founding of the American Federation of Labor or its founder, Samuel Gompers. She showed little interest in the fate of unions or workers' parties, although she belonged to the United Mine Workers and the Socialist party and numbered among the founders of the IWW (Industrial Workers of the World). Over the years, Jones repeatedly expressed impatience with unions that sought accommodation with capitalism and with theoreticians of the Socialist party. At heart she remained, as she said, "a social revolutionist."[3]

After 1890, we can trace Jones's life in better detail in the public record. After working in and around the coal mines and cotton mills of Birmingham, Alabama, in the early 1890s, she met Eugene V. Debs and—like him—soon became a Socialist and a contributor to the Socialist journal *Appeal to Reason*. In 1897 she found her voice as an agitator in a coal miners' strike called by the newly founded United Mine Workers, and she eventually became a "walking delegate" (organizer) for that union. She reported regularly to its president, John Mitchell. Thereafter, Jones did most of her hell-raising among striking miners. In eastern coal mines, she served as organizer, fund-raiser, stump speaker, public spokesperson, and nurse. Jones knew how to attract attention to the miners' cause both with her own fiery personality and with carefully staged public spectacles that highlighted the hardships of working-class life. Today, we might praise her genius for self-promotion and public relations.

From 1890 until World War I, Jones pleased miners when she insisted on sharing their hardships. She slept on bare floors and walked endless miles through inclement weather, often having eaten but little. She truly seemed one of them in a way that many other organizers did not. Jones used the sharp contrast between her sex, age, and apparent fragility and her enormous physical stamina and courage to inspire miners to greater commitment and sacrifice for their own cause. During these years, she tramped and lectured in the coal districts of West Virginia, Pennsylvania, Illinois, and Indiana and among the metal and coal miners of Michigan, Minnesota, Colorado, and Arizona. Hers became a life of ceaseless travel, considerable physical discomfort, and not infrequent danger. "My address is like my shoes," she boasted, "it travels with me." On another occasion, she confirmed, "I live wherever there is a bunch of workers fighting the robbers."[4] Several times, her West Virginia organizing campaigns occurred during periods of genuine warfare between the armed guards of the mine owners ("the damned Pennsylvania Coal and Iron Police") and desperate miners. Miners' desperation in West Virginia stemmed from court injunctions that prohibited them from meeting or picketing anywhere on the vast tracts of land owned by the mines. Jones suffered incarceration in 1897 and again in 1902 in the East. In 1913, during violent Colorado confrontations between state militia and strikers, she was put under military arrest for months even though no charges were brought against her. She was released around the time of the Ludlow Massacre (in 1914, gun-toting thugs and troops burned a strikers' tent colony in Ludlow, Colorado, killing two hiding women and eleven children). Jones arrived in Denver to observe the arrival of federal troops to restore order. With clenched fist, she addressed a crowd of miners screaming both from anguish at their recent losses and from the pleasure of seeing her free again.

As important as the miners were to Jones, she did not limit her activities to them even during turn-of-the-century years when she worked most closely with them. For a time in the 1890s she lived and worked in textile mills in the South, and there she developed a lifelong and virulent opposition to child labor—the subject of her first publication in the *International Socialist Review*. In 1903, she led a march (her "army," she called it) of child laborers and strikers from mills near Philadelphia northward to President Roosevelt's summer home at Oyster Bay, Long Island, seeking legislation that would outlaw child labor.

Through her work with miners, Jones also developed a strong interest in the problem of workers from Mexico. While in the Southwest in 1907, she learned of the capture on U.S. soil of Manuel Sarabia (then leader of forces seeking to overthrow Mexican dictator Porfirio Díaz). She subsequently became an ardent advocate of the Mexican Revolution, raising money for Mexican revolutionaries imprisoned in the United States. She traveled to labor meetings in Mexico, where workers knew her as Madre Juanita, and in 1923 addressed the Third Congress of the Pan-American Federation of Labor.

Perhaps more than any other labor activist of the Gilded Age and Progressive Era, Mother Mary Jones represents the tensions and conflicting pulls of class, gender, and ethnicity in American society. She examined all these tensions in her characteristically blunt language. In doing so, she left us with some of the best available illustrations of what it meant to be foreign, female, and a working-class moralist in a world dominated by middle-class, Victorian ideals of female propriety.

Mother Jones's words were often harsh, but her voice was unusually sweet. More than one observer attributed her gift for words to her Irish origins and noted an Irish lilt to her voice, which although low and calm, carried well even when she spoke outside to large or rowdy crowds in dangerous circumstances. Clearly, Jones possessed great personal charm; a charismatic speaker, she could move audiences to action. But her charisma was not limited to the stump. She also possessed a rare skill for establishing personal rapport with most anyone she met. Judges, industrialists, and soldiers often remembered her, even after sharp confrontations, with considerable fondness. John D. Rockefeller, the owner of vast mineral wealth in Colorado and Jones's nemesis during labor struggles there and during their conflicting testimony to the Commission on Industrial Relations in 1915, wired her greetings for her hundredth birthday. For her part, Jones could acknowledge Rockefeller as a good son, a religious man, and a "damn good sport." But she also insisted she had won a moral victory over him. "I've licked him several times, but now we've made peace—this telegram rather squares things," she informed visitors.[5] To say a nice word about an industrialist as a fellow human being was no violation of Jones's firmly held convictions.

Those convictions were as simple as they were unwavering. They, too, help explain her popularity with working men and women of the Gilded Age and Progressive Era. To Jones, capitalism was evil and immoral. Like many radicals with roots in the rural and communal villages of Europe and America, she saw modern capitalism sundering the social ties that nurtured humanity rather than emancipating workers from the tyranny of those families and communities. Indeed, to Jones, wage work under capitalism was a new form of slavery in which the rich exploited the poor. Only tenacious solidarity among this new class of slaves could end the power of capital and allow justice to flourish. Wherever she went, Jones preached solidarity and action. "I belong to a class who have been robbed, exploited, and plundered down through many long centuries, and because I belong to that class I have an instinct to go and help break the chains," she wrote.[6]

Capitalists' power rested, Jones argued, on their control of government; economic inequality rendered democracy a travesty, and—in her eyes—workers had not yet found a way to use democracy to topple capitalist political influence. Like many of her generation, Jones viewed class conflict as a modern expression of the kinds of revolts Irish and Americans had organized against the tyranny of the British Empire. Jones proudly claimed Irish rebels and martyrs among her forebears. She often labeled capitalists as the King Georges, monarchs, or czars of their day. Although she sometimes urged workers to political action, more often she seemed to assume that only revolt could produce change, just as it had in the American Revolution. She repeatedly compared striking workers to the revolutionaries of 1776.

In addition to using the language of republican anticolonialism, Jones possessed an almost religious—some might say millenarian—

faith in the justice and inevitability of workers' eventual triumph. She was generally impatient with the Catholic (and other) churches for promising workers only pie in the sky while leaving them to suffer privation on earth. But Jones also firmly believed that economic justice was the foundation of Christianity and that God was on her side. Like most other Irish and German immigrants, however, she regularly expressed her disgust for Puritan or Protestant expressions of American religiosity, notably the temperance and prohibition movements. At least once, she invited a striking worker to "have a drink on Jesus," and she often pleaded for sympathy for prostitutes whose ruin originated in poverty, not in any moral weakness on their part.

Although firm in her beliefs, Jones was no theoretician. She always stated her fundamental principles in the heat of dramatic moments of conflict and struggle. She was entirely consistent only in interpreting every event, every person, and every organization of her times through the prism of class. Did it help the poor? Then she approved. Did it divide or weaken workers? Then she was against it whether it was an injunction, the Catholic Church, a politician, a fight among leftist theoreticians, or a campaign to raise funds for a new house for John Mitchell.

Since Jones never viewed class struggle theoretically, she might argue for violence in one setting and against it in another—depending on her own sense of what was good for workers at that particular time and place. Her ethical judgments were as thoroughly situational as her appeal was personal. She cared not at all for consistency or even abstract truth as others defined it. In both respects, she has seemed erratic to those who have tried to interpret her life. Yet in all her utterances, Jones always declared herself of the working class, proud of it, and impatient for a world where the poor would suffer less than they did in Gilded Age America.

Mother Jones always expressed solidarity with workers as a woman, as a sister, and—most often—as a mother. She did not resent her name, Mother, and it was not imposed on her. She believed that mothers possessed great power within their families and in their communities. Modern feminists might call Jones a maternalist and a communitarian rather than an egalitarian or "liberal" feminist. She used the pungent language of enduring, working-class womanhood and the language of European peasants and artisans transplanted to the United States.

Mother Jones was no lady but neither was she a downtrodden victim of poverty or patriarchy, and she let neither upper-class men and women nor her working-class "sons" or "sisters" forget that fact. Given her loyalties to the poor, it was scarcely surprising that Jones lambasted the captains of industry, or "robber barons," along with their political representatives, at every opportunity. She called them "bloodsucking leeches" and pirates and labeled the guards, sheriffs, and state militia who protected their property "dogs," "curs," and "human bloodhounds."[7] She especially despised the ethics of mine owners, who mourned the death of a mule that cost $200 but scarcely noted human deaths, since workers cost them only their wages and could be replaced in an instant. Jones attacked capitalist manhood directly, and often with considerable deprecatory and ribald humor. Like the early modern rebels who tarred and feathered rich men and British agents during the American Revolution, Jones sought to humiliate her male capitalist enemies, not just defeat them. Thus, in 1912, she urged striking miners to stop being so respectful of West Virginia governor William E. Glasscock ("a goddamned dirty coward") and to initiate his public humiliation by calling him henceforth "Crystal Peter."[8]

Jones's frequent, and particularly vehement, attacks on the genteel mothers of the upper classes revealed her deep disrespect for American gender ideology. That ideology made respectable women responsible for caring for the poor and for easing their suffering through charitable work with them. Jones laughed at the notion. "While the wives of you streetcar men are wondering where the next meal is coming from, the wives of your masters are strutting about with their dresses cut to here ('Mother' Jones indicated a point near her waist line) and their hands loaded with diamonds. These diamonds are the blood of your little children whom they have robbed and starved."[9] Jones told workers that instead of working for humanity and Christianity, ladies were at home "nursing [their] poodle dogs." According to Jones the lady "lived off the blood of women and children, she decorated her neck and hands with the blood of innocent children." One of Jones's favorite stories was of J. P. Morgan's daughter, who worked for the welfare department of the National Civic Federation. According to Jones, this lady accosted an Irish machinist—who had brought along a large piece of bologna to accompany the soup she distributed for free—and told him, "Oh, my dear man, don't eat that, it will give you indigestion." The stalwart worker, reported Jones, snapped back that "the trouble with me is I never get enough to digest—indigestion, hell."[10] Jones saw no hope in workers finding either charity or justice from the hands of rich men or women, no matter how respectable or charitable.

More surprising was the wrath Jones could also turn on the men of the labor movement—whether humble strikers or union presidents. Although older than many of them, Jones in most respects resembled her brothers in the early labor movement. Like her, most were either immigrants (like Samuel Gompers) or they were the sons of the Irish and German immigrant workers who had arrived in the United States in large numbers between 1845 and 1860. Toward John Mitchell, president of the United Mine Workers, Jones assumed the stance of equal partner in the early years of the century, but she did so as his mother, not his brother, as union fraternalism demanded. Jones began letters to Mitchell with "Dear Comrade" and ended them with "Take care of your health, fraternally yours," or even "fraternally yours, Mother." Her letters were full of advice and firm reassurances for the younger man: "You have done just what you should have done," she noted on one occasion. Never did Jones hesitate to remind Mitchell of his dependence on her. "You know you need news. Send any request to me." Even in her occasional moments of self-effacement, Jones sent mixed messages, as when she wrote Mitchell, "I feel sometimes the burden is more than you can bear I only wish I could assume part of it. All I can do is to keep this old heart true to you in my humble way help you all I can." For his part, Mitchell usually addressed Jones sentimentally as "My Dear Mother" but signed his letters with an uncomfortable mixture of affection and formality, "With love and best wishes, I am, yours truly, John Mitchell, President UMWofA."[11]

Early in the century, when Jones was Mitchell's trusted assistant, she liked to remind him that she stood also in motherly judgment of him. "Let me say," she wrote him in 1901, "so long as you are the John Mitchell you are I'll be with you."[12] Well before Mitchell resigned as president of the UMW in 1908, he had felt Jones's wrath by withdrawing from the heart—and heat—of conflict between striking workers and mine owners. "Mitchell is in Boston," Jones complained in Colorado in 1903. "We are here in the field. A general cannot give orders unless he is in the field." Jones had little patience with union officials who were interested, she claimed, only in their "rotten salary," not in organizing and in strikes. These were not men but babies, she insisted: One might as well "send [such an organizer] home, put a mother hubbard on him and give him a nursing bottle." In her 1911 address to a UMW convention, Jones aired her disagreements with labor bureaucrats openly: "I am talking to you miners. I am not talking to officers—this organization is dear to me. It has been bought with the blood of men who are scarcely known today."[13] Jones valued men who risked their lives for a cause, as she believed she did, daily, in her organizing campaigns.

By 1911, Jones saw Mitchell as a traitor to labor's cause and as a man "her boys" should ostracize "like a mad dog."[14] The former UMW president was working with the National Civic Federation, a group of capitalists and labor leaders who sought to create industrial peace through collective bargaining and mediation. According to Jones, however, the federation was "strictly a capitalist machine."

Labor "never will progress; it cannot as long as they sit down and eat and drink and fill their stomachs and get their brains filled with champagne."[15] Jones remained a revolutionary, convinced there could be no cooperation between male "robber barons" and their "slaves." The labor leaders who abandoned revolt were no longer her "boys" or "brothers"; they were not really men at all. "Mother" had spoken.

Jones directed her motherly blend of inspirational, supportive, and reassuring words and actions, together with her equally harsh judgments, even more starkly toward striking miners. In her speeches she usually began sympathetically with vivid images of the hardships miners endured in their workplaces and those they and their families suffered at home. Poverty meant illness, death, and hunger not just for miners but for their wives and children, Jones lamented. She saw this suffering as reason enough for men to organize, strike, and revolt. When positive appeals seemed insufficient to move men to action, however, Jones felt free to lecture her "boys"— with an imaginary switch always in hand for those who failed to obey. Confronting mine workers at the UMW convention of 1916 with the images of children killed in the Ludlow Massacre, Jones criticized them harshly for their failures. "It was not the Rockefellers that did it, it was not the Shaws, it was the working men of this nation; they are responsible for the death of those children. If you were not cowards you would be organized, you would pay your dues, you would carry on the campaign of education that would bring peace to the nation." In 1913, in the midst of the Colorado struggles, she had spoken to striking miners even more harshly: "What is the matter with you? Are you afraid? Do you fear your pitiful little bosses?"[16] Jones stood in judgment of her boys, challenging them to live up to her own high standards (and example) of moral courage and tenacity.

More than once Jones suggested that workers' wives and daughters would be braver strikers and more loyal union members than they were. Indeed, that is what she had said to the striking miners of Colorado after belittling their fears. "Are you great strong men, with so much latent power in you, afraid of your masters or the Baldwin-Felts thugs hired by your masters? I can't believe it. I can't believe you are so cowardly, and I tell you this, if you are, you are not fit to have women live with you."[17] On another occasion, while denouncing judges' use of law and injunction to break strikes, she announced, "You measly things—women are not responsible because they have no vote. You'd all better put on petticoats. If you like those bullets, vote to put them into your own bodies. Don't you think it's about time you began to shoot ballots instead of voting for capitalistic bullets?"[18] Jones reported with satisfaction that the men took her harsh criticisms to heart and committed themselves to greater hardships after such a lecture. That such words from a woman they called Mother could inspire working-class men reminds us how far workers' notions of motherly behavior departed from those of Victorian America.

Jones easily found ways—albeit controversial ones—to involve women of mining communities as full participants in strikes, even when they were not themselves wage earners. On occasion, Jones encouraged women to participate in union strike meetings: In 1902 she reported that when she called a union meeting in West Virginia, "the women had never come before. This time they came. They came and for the first time heard and understood. Instead of returning to work, the women took up the fight and for five months longer the struggle went on, when the company gave in and the fight was won. Women are fighters."[19] In West Virginia, Jones organized what were essentially auxiliaries to men's unions. But she also expected women's auxiliaries, as she told wives in an El Paso, Texas, streetcar workers' strike, to raise hell.

When Mother Jones and her female comrades raised hell, they cast aside all strictures of female respectability, creating a carnival-like atmosphere of a world turned upside down. Their public demonstrations hinted of revolutionary change to come and often terrified observers. In West Virginia mining communities, women armed themselves with brooms and pans and marched in fierce noisy parades to shame or scare off scabs or militiamen. Beating on their pans and singing patriotic songs, "an army of strong mining women makes a wonderfully spectacular picture," Jones later noted. They were spectacular precisely because they seemed capable of violent action—like the "fierce-eyed, red-haired woman with a scarlet shawl wrapped around her head" who particularly impressed observers as a potential revolutionary.[20] To a frightened young girl who watched a bullet whiz past Jones's head as she spoke to a group of strikers from a tree stump, Jones gave a few words of advice about proper womanly conduct: "Now don't you get scared."[21]

Throughout the United States in the early years of the twentieth century, working-class and immigrant women, along with their children, specialized in street protests that humiliated their enemies and made spectacles of themselves. In Texas, Mexican women strikers cut the hair of women scabs, branding them as traitors to their communities. In New York, Jewish housewives stormed and sacked the meat stores of shopkeepers who charged high prices for their kosher goods. In Lawrence, Massachusetts, immigrant wives and workers paraded the streets, attacking female scabs and pulling the pants off a policeman before dumping him into the river. The same women marched to the train station to send their children on long railroad journeys to supporters in other cities only to find them-selves attacked by local police. When Mother Jones led the striking children who worked in the textile mills of Philadelphia to Long Island, she took her charges for a visit to Coney Island and to enjoy a wild animal exhibition. When the show was over, Jones had sev-eral children enter the animals' cages and locked them in. She sought mainly to dramatize her point that unlike the pets of the rich, working-class children were slaves. As the animal show had just demonstrated, however, caged animals could roar and even attack if released from their bonds.

Jones called activist working-class women—not respectable American ladies—her sisters. She extended the term to any woman willing to cast aside respectability and to fight, and there were many of these. During one mining strike, Jones extended her gruff affection even to an older black woman who approached her to kiss the hem of her garment. Embarrassed but also nonplussed, Jones admonished the woman to embrace her "not in the dust, sister to me, but here on my breast, heart to heart."[22]

Jones was ambivalent about female wage earning; she believed women already carried heavy responsibilities without adding wage slavery. Despite her ambivalence, she organized female brewery workers in Wisconsin and was concerned about the problems of women in southern textile mills. But she never became intensely involved in the lives of the girl strikers who brought the largest number of immigrant women wage earners into the American labor movement in the first decades of the twentieth century. The strikes of these textile workers occurred under the radical and syndicalist IWW in Lowell, Massachusetts, and Paterson, New Jersey. At the time of these strikes, she was in Colorado and Arizona, where she worked as easily with foreign-born women in mining communities as she had with workers of Virginia's Appalachian mountains.

Jones did address striking immigrant garment workers in New York in 1909 and again in 1916, but these Jewish and Italian female workers never became either her girls or her sisters, perhaps because she refused to work with middle-class ladies as allies. In her speech to these strikers during their "great uprising" of 1909, Jones reiterated familiar themes. She reminded workers, "This is a fight" and urged them to "parade past the shops where you work and up the avenue where the swells who wear the waists [that the girls manufactured] live. They won't like to see you, they will be afraid of you."[23] In New York, however, these observations seemed misplaced. Jones's reference to "swells" reveal either her ignorance of or her indifference to the Women's Trade Union League (WTUL) of New York, which was heavily involved in the girl workers' strike. Organized by middle- and upper-class women reformers simultaneously interested in educating and uplifting and in organizing their "little sisters" of immigrant communities, the WTUL played a leading role in the "great uprising." Ladies called themselves allies of the girl strikers. They bailed them out of jail, gave them money, and provided them with the publicity they needed to gain a wider audience for their cause (which had been ignored by male unionists).

If she knew of this cross-class alliance, Jones would scarcely have approved. To her "the swells"—the female enemy—could only sabotage a battle workers had to fight for themselves. Jones was not completely wrong about the problems of cross-class cooperation based on a common sisterhood. Tensions between young class-conscious and militant immigrant Jewish and Irish activists and much older, middle-class American allies were sometimes quite intense in the WTUL. The "girls" were often Socialists and preferred collective bargaining and strikes to solve their problems. Their allies, including wealthy women such as Mrs. August Belmont, were more conservative and more enthusiastic about the passage of factory laws and other kinds of legislation to protect women workers' health and wages. More than one lady in the WTUL wanted to teach the girls respectable, genteel behavior more than picket-line deportment. Still, the cross-class alliance within WTUL contributed mightily to growing female membership in the International Ladies Garment Workers Union. Ironically, the ladies Jones hated were arguably more successful in producing women labor activists than Jones herself.

Jones's distrust of ladies encouraged her also to distance herself from the suffrage movement. In late life, Jones often portrayed herself as an antisuffragist, telling interviewers that women had no place in politics. Earlier, however, Jones's stance on suffrage had been more dismissive than negative: "You don't need a vote to raise hell! You need convictions and a voice!"[24] Jones had also regularly argued that women should participate in government. She raised the issue of women's enfranchisement repeatedly with striking men, suggesting that women could be their allies in a political struggle against the bosses. "Why is it they [men] cannot stand together at the ballot box? No bayonet, no injunction can interfere there. You pay Senators, Governors, Legislators, and then beg on your knees for them to pass a bill in labor's protection. You will never solve the problem until you let in the women. No nation is greater than its women."[25] Jones was, however, too class-conscious to believe that women's morality alone could make them such superior voters that they could save government from corruption or immorality. Nor could she ever consider an alliance with society ladies a sensible strategy for working-class women dedicated to improving the lot of their class. She acerbically, and accurately, noted that "women of

Colorado have had the vote for two generations and the working men and women are in slavery."[26]

Reluctant to interact with middle-class "allies" in strikes or in a suffrage movement, Jones had no chance to build a working women's movement for political change. She seemed not even to know of working-class women's own efforts to gain the vote or to use it in workers' interests. If she knew of the Wage-earners' Equity League, founded by Harriot Stanton Blatch, or its labor activist immigrant members, for example, she never mentioned it.

Jones was not alone among immigrant, working-class women in her ambivalence about suffrage. Russian-born Emma Goldman, the anarchist radical and feminist who may have been the second most hated woman in America (Jones, of course claimed first place), also mocked the idea that legal rights could advance the cause of working-class women. Far younger and far more interested in sexual and reproductive freedoms than was Jones, Goldman had just as little patience with Victorian gender ideology. But whereas Jones focused her ire on wealthy suffragists like Mrs. Belmont, Goldman more often ridiculed the lives of feminist "new women." Goldman saw the new women's commitment to professional careers, to celibacy, and to lifelong female friendships, or "Boston marriages," as little more than modern expressions of American Puritanism. Goldman doubted that either the vote or a job equaled emancipation, and she instead pursued heterosexual liberation and free speech in her own deeply unconventional life.

Although her interest in women's issues was limited, Jones remained interested in miners' issues and in close communication with mining union officials until her death. In the last decade of her life her travels diminished, recovery from illnesses took longer, and she increasingly sought rest in the homes of several old friends. Jones lived to what she claimed to be her hundredth birthday. At her birthday celebration, she impatiently and characteristically rejected the gift of a corsage of sweet peas with the complaint, "Hell, I never have worn these and I don't want to now." She died soon thereafter, on November 30, 1930.[27] Jones wanted to be (and was) buried in Virden, Ohio, alongside miners who had been killed in 1898 while trying to prevent strikebreakers from entering the mines they had worked. Her burial place is thus a perpetual symbol of her commitment to the men and the mining families that had been the focus of much of her life.

Even as a deeply unconventional woman, Mary Harris Jones could scarcely have viewed the world in which she lived through anything other than female eyes. With no children of her own, Mother Jones had made the miners her sons, and she had looked forward to a better world for the children of miners and their wives and for all of the working class, of which she felt a part. By the time Jones died, new understandings of womanhood, also focused on women's responsibilities to children and modern motherhood, helped the daughters of Jones's immigrant generation to find their own rapprochement with American notions of gentility, gender, and domesticity. Whatever their origins, American working-class women had lost a tradition of fierce public activism.

Notes

1. Dale Fetherling, *Mother Jones: The Miners' Angel* (Carbondale: Southern Illinois University Press, 1974), 10.

2. Philip S. Foner, *Mother Jones Speaks: Collected Writings and Speeches* (New York: Monad Press, 1983), 286.

3. Ibid., 24.

4. Fetherling, *Mother Jones,* 78; Foner, *Mother Jones Speaks,* 145.

5. Foner, *Mother Jones Speaks,* 203.

6. Ibid., 70.

7. Foner, *Mother Jones Speaks,* 163, 273, 289.

8. Fetherling, *Mother Jones,* 86-87.

9. Foner, *Mother Jones Speaks,* 286.

10. Ibid., 286, 169, 179.

11. Edward M. Steel, ed., *The Correspondence of Mother Jones* (Pittsburgh: University of Pittsburgh Press, 1985), 3, 9, 26, 33.

12. Ibid., 9.

13. Foner, *Mother Jones Speaks,* 107, 146, 147, 150.

14. Ibid., 150.

15. Fetherling, *Mother Jones,* 84.

16. Foner, *Mother Jones Speaks,* 274, 237.

17. Ibid., 237.

18. Ibid., 97–98.

19. Ibid., 92–93.

20. Priscilla Long, *Mother Jones, Woman Organizer, and Her Relations with Miners' Wives, Working Women, and the Suffrage Movement* (Boston: South End Press, 1976), 14.

21. Foner, *Mother Jones Speaks,* 45.

22. Ibid., 27.

23. Ibid., 136–37.

24. Mother Jones, *The Autobiography of Mother Jones* (Chicago: Charles H. Kerr, 1925; reprint ed., 1972), 234–35.

25. Foner, *Mother Jones Speaks,* 92.

26. Fetherling, *Mother Jones,* 164.

27. Ibid., 202.

Suggested Readings

Dale Fetherling, *Mother Jones: The Miners' Angel* (Carbondale: Southern Illinois University Press, 1974), is still the best starting place for an overall account of Jones's life. In an important collection of documents, Philip S. Foner, *Mother Jones Speaks: Collected Writings and Speeches* (New York: Monad Press, 1983), convincingly defends Jones's reputation as a committed Socialist and feminist. Mother Jones, *The Autobiography of Mother Jones* (Chicago: Charles H. Kerr, 1925; reprint ed., 1972), is sporadic and incomplete in its coverage of her life and is riddled with errors yet is nevertheless essential reading.

Edward M. Steel, ed., *The Correspondence of Mother Jones* (Pittsburgh: University of Pittsburgh Press, 1985), is an important collection of primary sources about Mother Jones. Edward M. Steel, "Mother Jones in the Fairmont Field, 1902," *Journal of American History* 57 (1970): 290–307, offers an account of Jones's early interactions with mining communities and the personal relationships she developed there.

Donna Gabaccia, *From the Other Side: Women and Gender in Immigrant Life in the United States, 1820–1990* (Bloomington: Indiana University Press, 1994), gives an overview of what foreign-born women gained and lost by becoming American. Alice Kessler-Harris, "Where Are the Organized Women Workers?" *Feminist Studies* 3 (1975): 92–110, focuses on the problem women faced in finding support from organized male workers and their unions. Priscilla Long, *Mother Jones, Woman Organizer, and Her Relations with Miners' Wives, Working Women, and the Suffrage Movement* (Boston: South End Press, 1976), is the best example of how early feminist scholarship interpreted Jones's opposition to suffrage and her activism among men and women workers.

7

Francis G. Newlands, Water for the West, and Progressivism

William D. Rowley

As much as any feature, aridity differentiated the West from other regions of the United States. Access to water was the key to agricultural growth and urban development throughout much of the Far West and especially Nevada, situated in the dry Great Basin that lay between the Rockies and the ranges of the West Coast. Francis Newlands's political legacy rests primarily on his role in bringing water to his Nevada constituents. William D. Rowley, a historian of the West and its natural resources, profiles this complicated western politician.

Newlands was one of the driving forces behind the National Reclamation Act of 1902, which provided federal funds for irrigation projects. The law represented the opening wedge of an evolving public program of dams and aqueducts that transformed portions of the western desert into thriving gardens and dense residential communities—and generated an ongoing debate about attempts to circumvent nature. Newlands's support of irrigation was the centerpiece of his ambitious blueprint to stimulate economic activity through federal developmental programs. As Rowley explains in this chapter, Newlands represented a variant of western progressivism that was tied to traditional Democratic ideas on the one hand and sympathy for the activist outlook of the Roosevelt wing of the Republican party on the other. In describing this duality, Rowley illuminates the tensions that challenged politics and policymaking in the Progressive Era.

William D. Rowley holds the Grace A. Griffen Chair of History at the University of Nevada, Reno. His works *U.S. Forest Service Grazing and Rangelands: A History* (1985) and *Reclaiming the Arid West: The Career of Francis G. Newlands* (1996) reflect his interest in western resource conservation and use. He is editor of the *Nevada Historical Society Quarterly,* has served on the governing board of the Forest History Society, and is a member of the Executive Committee of the American Society for Environmental History.

No one gave more attention to the western water problem at the turn of the century than Francis G. Newlands, Nevada's leading political figure. Although his interest in water was paramount, his career also reflected many of the tenets of the emerging Progressive movement. As a U.S. representative from Nevada from 1893 to 1902 and a senator from 1903 until his death in 1917, he was a transitional figure from the Gilded Age to the Progressive Era. Early on, Newlands became a spokesman for the western wing of the Progressive movement, which championed federal aid for the reclamation of the desert West.

Like most of the West, Nevada was arid, but its aridity surpassed that of any other western state. A traveler's eye easily detected its barrenness—its few and feeble rivers and the sterile alkali sands of its playas surrounded by miles of gray sagebrush desert. Its snow-topped mountains cast dark, forbidding shadows over the landscape. Travel brochures advised rail passengers to pull down the window shades and sleep while traveling across Nevada's endless miles. If ever there was a land in need of human ingenuity and improvement, it was Nevada. Newlands saw himself as the instrument of this improvement and water was the key to a better future for Nevada as well as the entire arid West. Newlands sought to attach his mission to the doctrines of Progressive uplift, efficiency, and justice in American society—all of which echoed the ideas of the "new nationalism" outlined in Herbert Croly's 1909 book *The Promise of American Life*.

Most nineteenth-century wealth in the West grew out of the exploitation of natural resources, but without water, Nevada's prospects for developing agricultural and grazing lands, forests, hydropower, and fisheries were severely limited. The state was rich only in minerals—a resource that provided the foundation for its statehood in 1864 after the discovery and development of the great Comstock lode in 1859.

Newlands grew up in genteel poverty, although his parents imparted decidedly middle-class values to their children. James and Jesse Newlands had emigrated from Scotland, where James was a medical doctor trained at the University of Edinburgh. The family settled in Troy, New York, but soon departed for St. Louis, where James sought the "water cure" for alcoholism. The treatment having apparently been successful, James took his family to Natchez, Mississippi. It was there in 1848 that Francis Griffith Newlands, the fourth of five children, was born. A relapse induced James to move the family again, this time up the Mississippi to Quincy, Illinois. The change in environment failed to rehabilitate him, and he died in 1851 at the age of forty-four, leaving Jesse an impoverished widow with five children.

Jesse's subsequent marriage to a local man of some means appeared to resolve her financial dilemma until the depression of 1857, which destroyed her husband's livelihood. The family relocated to Chicago and then to Washington, DC, where Jesse's husband found work as a minor political appointee at the outset of the Civil War. Barely into his teens, Francis Newlands became fascinated with the affairs of government in this national capital aswirl over wartime events. Pushed by his mother's determination, he set out for Yale College as a youngster of fourteen. Two years later a lack of money forced him back to the family household and into a low-paying clerk's job in the postal department. Yet he was able to attend a local law school and at the end of the 1860s gained admission to the bar. In 1870, now a young man of middling height and reddish blond hair that later gave way to baldness, Newlands decided to seek his fortune on the other side of the continent.

Arriving in San Francisco with only seventy-five dollars in his pocket, Newlands relied on talent and youthful energy to make his way in a city he later called "the Paris of America."[1] Besides being young and attractive, he had a good education and fine manners—what in that day was termed "good breeding." Soon he was moving in the highest circles of San Francisco's parvenu society. In November 1874, Newlands married Clara A. Sharon, the daughter of wealthy Comstock magnate William Sharon, the principal representative of the "bank crowd" (the Bank of California) on the Comstock mines in Nevada. From that date onward Newlands became identified with perhaps the largest fortune on the Pacific Coast—the Sharon estate.

His new circumstances fueled political ambition. But first he served as a robber baron's apprentice under the direction of his father-in-law, who was hated by many because of his sharp business practices on the Comstock and in California. Newlands became consumed with advancing and guarding the fortunes of the estate in its private ventures and dealings with local government in California. Frequent diagnoses of nervous exhaustion or neurasthenia, accompanied the development of his career and forced him to vacation in Europe. The ultimate strain came when he participated in the defense of the Sharon estate in a divorce proceeding. One Sara Althea Hill claimed that she had been Sharon's common-law wife and was entitled to a divorce settlement at the expense of the estate. The press portrayed Newlands as manipulating great and crass wealth against the just demands of a wronged woman. The tawdry nature of this "wretched case" and his friendship with Judge Stephen J. Field, who stood for the privileges of corporate wealth, especially the railroad, damaged his political prospects in California. By 1886 the ambitions of George Hearst to be a U.S. senator had ultimately shut Newlands out of the Democratic nomination for a U.S. Senate seat. By this time both Newlands's father-in-law and his first wife had died, leaving him a widower with three small daughters and the responsibility of managing the huge Sharon estate.

From 1886 to 1888, Newlands cast about trying to decide what to do with his life. In 1888, after seven years as a widower, he married Edith McAllister, of a prominent San Francisco family, whom he had met on holiday in England. At the relatively young age of forty, he had a new life before him. He could have retired and lived out a comfortable existence as a patron of the arts and world traveler with his new wife. Instead, he threw himself into the fray of Nevada politics, abandoning the Eden of California for an arid state suffering from an interminable mining depression. The Comstock had failed by 1880. Newlands saw the ephemeral nature of mining wealth and concluded that the boom-and-bust cycles of Nevada's mining economy could not possibly sustain a society of progress. He adopted water as the vehicle of his political career in the state.

One of the West Coast's wealthiest men arriving in a state with a population of less than fifty thousand caused a stir in Nevada and comment in San Francisco. Newspapers saw the move as politically inspired. In Nevada, Newlands would be a big fish in a small pond who could easily capture a U.S. Senate seat. Newspaper editors in Nevada strained at the bit to grab campaign money they hoped would be spread liberally. Nevada was known not only as a "rotten borough" where the wealthy could buy their way into prominent offices but more particularly as a "pocket borough" of California, meaning that wealthy Californians and certainly corporations, especially the railroad, could have their way. All of this speculation may have had an element of truth, but an additional reason for Newlands's move to Nevada was the "wretched" Sharon divorce case. With Newlands in Nevada, the diversity of state citizenship of the parties to the case placed it in federal court, where Newlands and his advisers believed the estate had a better chance of winning than in state courts. (To Newlands's satisfaction, both state and federal courts eventually ruled in the estate's favor.) In addition to being tainted by his involvement in the Sharon case, Newlands had in general served in California as a representative of great wealth. He had defended the Sharon-owned Spring Valley Water Company against the designs of local government—the city of San Francisco—that wanted to control and even lower water rates on the company's monopolistic water service to the city.

Nevada was, however, also a Sharon domain. Newland's former father-in-law had made a fortune in Nevada's Comstock years by trampling on many and gaining a reputation as a ruthless robber baron. Further, Sharon had used some of this vast wealth to buy a U.S. Senate seat. He was notoriously negligent of senatorial duties, preferring to use his time in the nation's capital buying up properties in suburban Washington, DC, for future development.

This background paints a somewhat sordid picture of New-lands's entrance into Nevada politics. However, it should not obscure his sincere interest in Nevada's water issues and ultimate-ly his attention to regional and national water questions. Fully aware of Sharon's past, Newlands declared he was not seeking "a mere Sharon sojourn" in the state; his move to Nevada offered a fresh opportunity "to pursue my career," which meant, by all accounts, to seek a U.S. Senate seat. He seized the opportunity to address Nevada's ills by presenting a program of water resource development at a time when no one in the state expected a political candidate of great wealth to have a legislative program.

One of Newlands's closest Nevada political advisers told him that only money turned the wheels of Nevada politics. Newlands rejected this approach. He sought legitimacy as a public figure that money alone could not achieve; and he was stingy. He had not made the Sharon fortune. He was its manager. The wealth he was now surrounded by enabled him to satisfy the middle-class values he espoused—respectability in thought and action. He wanted to con-serve the Sharon fortune and also redeem the reputation of the Sharon heritage in Nevada by working for the improvement of the state. Most Nevadans dismissed his rhetoric as platitude.

What was wrong with Nevada? And for that matter what was wrong with the West? Just about everything as far as Newlands was concerned. Soon after his arrival he pursued a series of proposals to attract immigrants to Nevada and to develop water storage on the Truckee River for irrigation development in the western part of the state. Community improvement projects were essential to the polit-ical style Newlands intended to follow. Nevada cried out for im-provements, suffering from a poverty of both natural and human resources. No one recognized this more than the outsider Newlands.

He looked forward to the decade of the 1890s for progress and change but was sorely disappointed. A national depression from 1893 to 1897 exacerbated Nevada's decline. Economically prostrate, the state was quickly mesmerized by the crusade for silver money. Nevadans believed the free coinage of silver at sixteen to one (16 parts silver to 1 part gold in a dollar) was the panacea for all their woes: the acceptance of a silver money supply would raise the price of the white metal, stimulating mining investment and prospecting with the promise of new Comstocks in Nevada's deserts. All of this hoopla sqelched Newlands's water development plans. Finally, in 1892, the political realities in Nevada dictated that he settle for the office of U.S. representative from Nevada. Many regarded his term in this capacity as his political apprenticeship for the Senate seat that finally opened for him in 1903.

The making of a Nevada "progressive" required many compro-mises. After the word became popular as denoting a political leader who embraced a modern future, Newlands traced his progressive label to his stand for programs of uplift and progress in Nevada through utilizing water resources and combating the railroad lobby. In the process, however, he resorted to the use of "the sack" to advance his objectives: editors and others often found on their desks a sack full of money in return for supporting Newlands and for printing statements reflecting his ideas on the issues of the day. Newlands was politically flexible. He became a Republican in Nevada, whereas he had been a Democrat in California. When a state Silver party emerged to monopolize politics, he quickly transformed into a Silverite, although he did not believe Silverite economics to be sound. By 1900 he had returned to the Democratic party. These flip-flops caused his critics to dub him "anything Newlands."

The end of the decade cleared the decks for the Newlands political agenda in Nevada. Supporters of silver coinage were defeated in the national elections of 1896 and again in 1900. The issue remained a lost cause in Nevada, although politicians regularly offered paeans. Newlands saw silver as a bothersome diversion from the true reforms that had to be made in Nevada—namely watering its deserts. After 1900 the resurgence of the mining economy in south-central Nevada did indeed threaten to divert attention away from water, and although the mines revived the state's economy, the gain was not sufficient to encourage hope of community or state aid for irrigation. With the depression passed, Newlands looked to the federal government. Also, since many believed that the irrigable areas had already been developed by private enterprise—the much-favored Truckee Meadows in and around Reno had been ditched, and the Truckee River had been diverted by the early 1880s—Newlands's best hope to expand irrigation into more marginal lands resided in federal aid.

The possibilities were immense. Already Newlands, William E. Smythe, and George Maxwell were trying to sell irrigation to the nation by linking it with the back-to-the-land movement. Maxwell organized the National Irrigation Association in anticipation of national reclamation legislation.[2] Proponents claimed that irrigation would open new acreage for immigrants from the city to establish homes and escape the poverty of city life. People living on the land renewed the vision of a Jeffersonian yeoman democracy in rural America—all made possible by the reclamation of arid lands. Smythe began the editorship of *Irrigation Age* in 1891, was instrumental in promoting annual irrigation congresses, and authored *Conquest of Arid America* in 1901. The message was loud and clear. Reclaiming arid America was the salvation of American democracy.

Smythe's publications covered not just irrigation and the construction of arid-land farms but also the broader questions of water resources in the West. Certainly water was scarce in the region, but constructive activities could conserve the available supply. For example, government could protect forests and other watersheds as well as build dams and reservoirs. Smythe and others drew a direct connection between water for irrigators and protection of the forested watershed, ultimately through the establishment of national forests. Western resource issues thus pointed directly to the emerging conservation movement. Conservationism was fundamental to progressivism in the West, and Newlands made reclamation the highest form of conservationism.

By 1900 a strong campaign for federal reclamation of the arid West was under way with Newlands campaigning tirelessly for national aid. Eastern and midwestern members of Congress opposed the development of additional agricultural lands in the West, arguing that agricultural markets were already saturated. Newlands countered these criticisms by turning to government scientists and engineers in the U.S. Geological Survey (USGS). Frederick H. Newell, hydrologist for the USGS, spoke expansively of dam building and the construction of water-delivery systems for irrigation in the West. In the spirit of the emerging progressive, Newlands called on experts to testify on impending legislation. By 1900, Newlands and Newell had drafted a bill for national aid to irrigation, to be funded by revenues from the sale of public lands in western states. The financing deflected criticism that the program was a raid on the public treasury on behalf of a particular region. Additionally, Westerners argued that the Homestead Act (1862), granting 160 acres of free land to heads of families, benefited the Midwest but was impractical in the arid West. The only way to make the Homestead Act effective in the arid West was to couple it with a national reclamation program. To their eastern and coastal state colleagues, western members of Congress made the stinging point that long-standing appropriations for the improvement of harbors and rivers rarely benefited the arid states. These pork-barrel appropriations faced Western opposition, and maybe a presidential veto, if Congress did not permit a reclamation bill to pass.

As the nation became transcontinental and also imperial after the Spanish-American War, the federal government assumed a greater role in the lives of American citizens. Newlands wanted that role to include funding and administration of the reclamation program. Others wanted a more administratively conservative, state-based program with grants from the federal government. For example, Senator Francis Warren of Wyoming, another spokesman for western irrigation, supported the state-based approach, which also provided opportunities for private developers. A charge surfaced that Newlands opposed state management of irrigation development because of his disappointment with his own state and its lack of administrative ability. Newlands refuted this claim, stressing the facts of western geography: western state boundaries did not encompass entire river systems; state lines were arbitrary and geographically illogical. He pointed to the map that showed the flow of western rivers with their sources in one state and their main bodies in other states. Thus, adequate control over water necessitated a national approach. Newlands's national viewpoint, which President Theodore Roosevelt shared, rejected John Wesley Powell's recommendation to redraw western state boundaries around naturally defined watersheds embracing entire river systems. State boundaries were here to stay. They could not easily be erased to facilitate water-resources development.

A national government "dealing with the entire public domain regardless of state lines, is better equipped to carry out a comprehensive plan than the state," said Newlands. Washington also possessed the experts to carry out these projects. For years the national government had been training scientists in the USGS, characterized by Newlands as "a corps unsurpassed in the world so far as regards education, scientific knowledge and practical experience." It "would be a blunder amounting to a crime to substitute for the accumulated experience and intelligence and comprehensive work of this corps the inexperience of individual states and territories operating under the most embarrassing limitations."[3]

Newlands introduced his bill in the House, where it was referred to the Committee on Arid Lands in early 1901. The legislation would not make its way out of committee in that year. "Uncle Joe" Cannon, the powerful chair of the House Appropriations Committee and future Speaker, effectively killed it by announcing: "I will not vote, as I am now informed, to pay by grant from the Federal Treasury, for the irrigation of 600,000,000 acres of land. It would be maladministration; it would be a great draft upon the Treasury; it would breed great scandal in the public service and destroy the manhood of the very constituents that the gentleman represents."[4]

Newlands did not concede the point and continued to lobby for the bill among all in Washington who would listen. He hosted a large dinner at the New Willard Hotel in late December 1901, bringing together supporters of national irrigation and opponents whose minds he hoped to change. Guests included Secretary of Agriculture James Wilson; George H. Maxwell, executive chair of the National Irrigation Association; Gifford Pinchot, head of the Forestry Bureau in the Department of Agriculture; and Charles D. Walcott, director of the USGS, who urged a compromise to resolve the dispute over national or state control of an irrigation program.

Theodore Roosevelt had been elevated to the presidency, succeeding President McKinley, who had been assassinated in September 1901. Roosevelt's western policies on conservation were largely shaped by Gifford Pinchot. By December, Roosevelt had pledged the Republican party's support of national irrigation. The year 1902 seemed to be emerging as the banner year for Newlands's vision of a federal program. Newlands's and especially President Roosevelt's opposition to a state-based program appeared to be the decisive factor in winning national control of irrigation. Newlands emphasized that a national approach simply continued the government's policy of administering the public domain as a great trust for development of the country. National supervision could ensure the planned development of entire watersheds or river basins, a project beyond the power of states. For Newlands, developing a river system meant securing the highest beneficial use of the water by building dams or harnessing its hydropower, preventing torrential floods, and storing water to ensure constant flows. Still, the bill vacillated on the issue of whether the national government or the states would control western water policy. The eventual compromise on this issue laid the foundation for much confusion.[5]

Under the 1902 National Reclamation Act the federal government, via the new Reclamation Service, would construct reservoirs and mainline irrigation delivery ditches. The sales of public lands in the West would create a revolving fund to finance the projects. Newlands liked to point out that more Democrats voted for the bill than Republicans, implying that the Democratic party was the greater champion of western interests. In the West both parties vied for the credit of passing the act. Much to Newlands's chagrin, President Roosevelt took credit for the law in his presidential campaign of 1904.

The new initiative represented reform, as did the 160-acre limitation on farms in the new projects, a provision designed to frustrate that old bugaboo in American society—monopoly. Water historian Donald Pisani asserts that "most westerners saw it mainly as a benefits program, a way to stimulate local economic development. Supporting the construction of irrigation projects was no different from supporting the construction of state prisons or hospitals; each expanded the economic horizon."[6] Thus, the Democratic party could be painted as the party fighting against the prevailing "system that embraced monopoly, business abuses all supported by the dominant Republican party."[7] But it was also the president's dynamic leadership in the Republican party that made reclamation possible.

The division between the parties was not as clear cut as Newlands portrayed. As the party out of power, the Democratic party tried to appeal to those who felt government was less than responsive to their needs—labor, small farmers, and those who felt passed by in the transition from agriculture to a modern industrial society.[8] In some respects the party was particularly well situated historically to become a critic of the new industrial society. After all, the Democrats were the party of states' rights and agrarian interests, not the party of the industrial Northeast, whose loyalty the Republicans had won in the Civil War and after.

But Democrats were ill-equipped for national leadership in America's new industrial order. In many respects the party was hobbled by its own history. The same policy of states' rights that appealed to labor and small farmers opposed a modern and growing national government capable of overseeing a multiracial, industrial society. The party's racial policies were anything but modern compared with those of Republicans, who had encouraged black political participation—albeit, perhaps, out of partisan motives. On racial issues Newlands was an unreconstructed Democrat. He believed African Americans should be removed from the political process by repealing the Fifteenth Amendment, arguing that a modern democracy should be composed of homogeneous peoples. Racial diversity only complicated democracy, making the modern state inefficient and unworkable. Newlands believed that his racial views and his water policies were forward looking and progressive. In fact, his position on race was not unusual for a West Coast progressive, many of whom worked actively for the exclusion of Asians from the country.

Although Newlands was well aware that the Democratic party had to be pulled reluctantly into the twentieth century, he failed to see that his perspective on racial issues reflected the most provincial and backward-looking views. After the passage of the Reclamation Act he increasingly regarded himself as a centralizer and a modernizer. As such he was an oddity in the Democratic party, which was widely regarded as a collection of rural southern hicks and non-English-speaking immigrants in cities dominated by corrupt politicians. Newlands frequently referred to the triumph of nationalizing irrigation and went on to suggest that most other problems facing the nation could be solved with nationally based programs. In this category he included "the race problem." He hoped that reclamation would promote a new outlook on Democrats in western states—of a party capable of utilizing the powers of the federal government to develop the region's water resources.

Reclamation was only one part of the federal government's attempt to deal with natural resource questions in the West. Presi-

dent Roosevelt adopted what he called "my policy," or more accurately, the policies of the conservation movement as framed by
Gifford Pinchot, first chief of the new U.S. Forest Service. These policies involved greater government presence in the western public-
land states. The creation of huge national forests on the remaining
public domain in the West meant regulations on the use of resources
—on timber cutting, on grazing, on the development of dam sites. A
spirit of utilitarianism pervaded the new resource bureaucracies.
They emphasized "wise use" under the management of a government agency, stressing efficiency and protection of resources for
renewable use in the future. Conservationists Newlands, Pinchot,
and Roosevelt believed the emphasis on use would overcome local
opposition to regulations. They denied an intention to turn the
forests into a vast national park reserve for preservation, as Sierra
Club founder John Muir once advocated.

Unfortunately for Newlands's nationalizing vision, the Democratic party in many western states opposed Roosevelt's national
conservation policies while still occasionally doting on the lost cause
of silver money. Resistance to nationalizing conservation was consistent with the Democratic party's longtime stance against the
growth of federal power and national interference in local affairs.
Newlands hoped that his party's opposition to conservation regulations would not extend to reclamation and his comprehensive plans
for river development, including flood control and hydroelectric
power. His outlook was closer to the Republican Roosevelt's on these
issues. He believed the national government could accomplish far
more than state government or business on public projects such as
the construction of dams and the Panama Canal.

He took the position that largeness was a factor in American
life. Water for the West could be accomplished only by a stronger,
larger federal government capable of fielding expert agencies such
as the U.S. Reclamation Service. As business continued to grow and
consolidate, labor unions sprang to life to protect the interests of
workers against huge conglomerates. It was futile to oppose the
growth of corporate business or powerful labor unions. Newlands's
reform ideas reached far beyond regional reclamation to national
incorporation laws, conservation, foreign affairs, labor, racial issues,
and children's welfare. All except foreign affairs called for greater
involvement by the federal government. Regarding the expansion of
American power overseas, he wished (as he put it) that the government would stop irritating foreign lands and get on with the business of irrigating domestic lands.[9]

At home the federal government needed overarching authority
to regulate the activities of corporations in the interest of all the
people. The general declaration of the 1890 Sherman Antitrust Act

that "all combinations in restraint of trade" were illegal was unacceptable and confusing to business, declared Newlands. Clearly, as Roosevelt asserted in agreement with the Supreme Court, there were "good trusts and bad trusts." The regulation of these large entities, not their disruption or breakup, should be the goal of government. Newlands advocated national incorporation for businesses rather than charters of incorporation in the individual states. He successfully advocated a federal trade commission (1914) to oversee the activities of the business community instead of subjecting it to capricious suits under the Sherman Antitrust Act. He also welcomed the passage of the Clayton Act, which clarified aspects of the Sherman Antitrust Act, and endorsed the idea that labor organizations were not illegal combinations. All these views were inherently endorsements of increased activity and authority on the part of the national government, a step that Newlands saw as the mark of a modern, centralized state. He was one of the few liberal nationalists in the Democratic party at the beginning of the century. *Town and Country* magazine in 1916 said he had "truly a national record." "Although a Democrat by inheritance, instinct and training Senator Newlands is also a nationalist." His views made him much more of a "New Nationalist Republican" than an old-time Democrat, except on questions of race.

Newlands would have been surprised at the development of inclusive racial attitudes and laws by the end of the twentieth century. He was, however, generally concerned with the progressive agenda of protecting the weaker members of society—women, children, injured workers, and the arid-lands farmer. Like many other progressives, he endorsed morality legislation to protect society from its own weaknesses. Antigambling laws, antiprostitution measures, and efforts to end Reno's notorious reputation as the divorce capital of the nation received his support. None of these efforts, including his endorsement of women's suffrage, won him friends among Reno's saloon crowd. Although Newlands's proposals for racial exclusion in American politics were not shocking to many of his fellow progressives, the leadership in both parties did not take him seriously. Democrats refused to include Newlands's proposal for the repeal of the Fifteenth Amendment in its 1912 platform.

Newlands attached himself to an activist tradition in his support for water projects for the West; he then expanded this activist principle to almost all the challenges facing America at the beginning of the century. His progressive career falls directly into the Hamiltonian tradition of American government. It was this tradition that Herbert Croly endorsed in *The Promise of American Life,* where he espoused a "New Nationalist" brand of progressivism. It championed national power to meet the problems of a modern state and, ironically, to achieve the Jeffersonian ends of greater individual freedom. Theodore Roosevelt adopted these views in 1911 as he moved toward his campaign to recapture the presidency in 1912. In the presidential election of that year the Democratic candidate, Woodrow Wilson, proclaimed a Democratic brand of progressivism in the "New Freedom" masterminded by Louis Brandeis. This Democratic version was a commitment not to national regulatory powers but rather to free competition as the key to keeping opportunity open in America. Predictably, Newlands regarded most aspects of the New Freedom as unacceptable and even radical, especially its free-trade and antitariff proposals. The New Freedom smacked of laissez-faire economics, free trade, and favoritism for competition rather than government-orchestrated cooperation in the business community, ideas analogous to the "business associationalism" that became popular in the 1920s.

Newlands opposed the Wilson administration's movement toward lower tariffs, especially on wool and sugar, and its attempts to break up conglomerates by an aggressive enforcement of the Sherman Antitrust Act, and he eventually felt vindicated as the administration reversed itself on its business policies during World War I. The New Freedom Democrats were forced to accept business conglomerates and cooperation in order to produce for the war effort. The organization of American business on a large scale during the war reflected a quest for efficiency and the new realities of American economic life. It confirmed Newland's vision of the future of Progressive America.

At the same time, Newlands pursued his "enlarged policy" to expand the original Reclamation Act to a general river-utilization act. He regarded this new approach as the fruition of work begun in the creation of the Inland Waterways Commission in the Roosevelt administration. When the commission closed its work during the Taft administration, Newlands proposed a permanent commission to oversee, plan, authorize, and implement river development for irrigation, dam building, flood control, navigation, forest and soil conservation, and hydroelectric power.

Few believed that during the wartime crisis such an ambitious program could be adopted. Surprisingly, the Newlands Waterways Amendment to the River and Harbors Bill passed in summer 1917. It provided for an oversight commission to achieve the objectives of Newlands's river-regulation bill. A press release by the Department of Commerce in September 1917 said that in the amendment Congress had created a "cohesive constructive, and continuing national policy of developing and using the now wasted forces of nature for the promotion of agriculture, soil conservation, forestry, and transportation." This amendment was the fulfillment of New-lands's progressive vision.

He saw the work of the Inland Waterways Commission as essential to linking the nation in a vast web of production, distribution, and efficient use of natural resources. Waterway transportation, he believed, was the remedy for an overburdened railway system. The implications of the internal combustion engine for the building of roads and interstate highways were only beginning to be understood.

With Newlands's death at the end of 1917, the Waterways Amendment lost its spokesman and was repealed by the Water Power Act of 1920. Unlike the Reclamation Act, Newlands's Enlarged Development Act became a failed vision at the end of two Democratic administrations.[10]

Federal arid-land reclamation, which Newlands and others had set in motion during the Progressive Era, continued. Even private lands within the projects received water from federally constructed systems after 1911. By the 1920s new dams and projects dotted the West under the auspices of the Reclamation Service, which became the Bureau of Reclamation in 1923. Project settlers were contractually obligated to pay back the cost of the water projects (without interest) to the federal government, but in many instances the repayment schedules faltered. Postponements, cancellations, and interest-free provisions all suggested subsidization by government and not the sound business partnership between water users and the federal government that Newlands had envisioned.

Many of the economic problems on the projects stemmed from the prolonged agricultural depression in the 1920s. Critics also pointed to the minuscule number of acres reclaimed compared to the grand predictions of over a million. When the depression of the 1930s brought President Franklin D. Roosevelt and the Democratic party to power, national lawmakers during the New Deal initiated more water and dam projects in the West as part of a publicly funded economic recovery program. Boulder Dam, Grand Coulee Dam, and Shasta Dam, as well as the Reclamation Bureau's assumption of the enormous California Central Valley Project, became monuments to big-government efforts to achieve an irrigated West.[11]

The water-for-the-West crusade that started out early in the twentieth century as a scheme to place farmers on arid lands was now far more. Building aqueducts and engineering large structures to withstand stress were technical triumphs in the spirit of spanning the continent with iron rails in the nineteenth century. In the twentieth century improvement projects in the West took a predictable twist toward overcoming the region's aridity. The Bureau of Reclamation saw its work as halting the waste of water in the West with methods such as flood control and expanding the utilization of water resources to obtain more power and even to create recreation areas—all of which Newlands had envisioned in his idea of total river resource development. The building of a water infrastructure (dams, hydropower, water-delivery systems, flood control) had by the 1930s won the bureau a new constituency in the region and had laid the foundation for a modern West with its agribusiness and glittering oasis cities.

It is precisely the wider developments in the latter part of the twentieth century that *new* critics of the western "hydraulic society" decry. Marc Reisner in his polemical work *Cadillac Desert: The American West and Its Disappearing Water* (1986) suggested that water for the West, far from being a progressive dream come true, has resulted in the expansion of a subsidized water bureaucracy (the Bureau of Reclamation) that has destroyed rivers and offered subsidies to agribusiness and below-cost electricity to gambling cities. The American taxpayer has been hoodwinked into paying the bill for the development of a region mainly for the benefit of monopolistic agriculture and urban real estate developers. This book is an updated version of "muckraking" that originally became popular in journalism during the Progressive Era.

Others point to the environmental damage of harnessing rivers for purely utilitarian purposes. Philip Fradkin's work on the Colorado River with its condemnatory title, *A River No More*, bemoans the damming of this once-wild river. Like Reisner, he points out the crimes of the built environment against the natural environment and criticizes those who profit from these transgressions. Richard White's 1995 essay on the Columbia River describes its conversion into "the organic machine," much to the detriment of all the organisms, especially the salmon, that once depended on the river for its life cycles. Others see not only an environmental and economic tragedy in the overdevelopment of water resources but also a sinister conspiracy to concentrate power in the hands of an economic and political elite in the West. This society built on the development of water projects is a far cry from the small-farmer democracy and community that William E. Smythe saw in his work *The Conquest of Arid America* and a later work, *Constructive Democracy* (1905, financed by Newlands), in which he saw the flourishing and revitalizing of American democracy in the arid-land settlements. Donald Worster in his *Rivers of Empire* (1984) generally condemns irrigated societies and certainly "the hydraulic society" of the American West not only for living out of harmony with nature but also for the destruction of local communities and the removal of power to urban corporations, the agribusiness elite, and water development bureaucracies in the region.

No doubt Senator Newlands and other western progressives who supported reclamation at the beginning of the century would be surprised and dismayed by all of these criticisms. The controversies speak to the continuing debate around attempts to improve upon and tame nature in the West.

Notes

1. Francis G. Newlands, letter to the editor, *Evening Bulletin*, March 25, 26, 1887.

2. Donald J. Pisani, *From Family Farm to Agribusiness: The Irrigation Crusade in California and the West, 1850–1931* (Berkeley: University of California Press, 1984), 77, 291.

3. William D. Rowley, *Reclaiming the Arid West: The Career of Francis G. Newlands* (Bloomington: Indiana University Press, 1996), 100–101.

4. *Congressional Record*, 56th Cong., 2d sess., February 19, 1901, 34, pt. 3:2666.

5. Donald Pisani, *To Reclaim a Divided West: Water, Law and Public Policy, 1848–1902* (Albuquerque: University of New Mexico Press, 1992), 316. See the suggested readings for Pisani's comments on this compromise.

6. Ibid., 324.

7. Rowley, *Reclaiming the Arid West*, 110.

8. David Sarasohn, *The Party of Reform: Democrats in the Progressive Era* (Jackson: University Press of Mississippi, 1989).

9. Rowley, *Reclaiming the Arid West*, 115.

10. Department of Commerce Press Release, September 19, 1917, RG 1115, Records of the Bureau of Reclamation (Records of the National Reclamation Association), box 25, file "Special Correspondence with Presidents, Senators, etc." National Archives, Washington, DC.

11. Pisani, *From Family Farm to Agribusiness*, 352.

Suggested Readings

Philip L. Fradkin, *A River No More: The Colorado River and the West* (New York: A. E. Knopf, 1981), is an example of the emerging literature critical of engineered rivers. Marc Reisner, *Cadillac Desert: The American West and Its Disappearing Water* (New York: Viking Press, 1986), is a strident denunciation of western water projects. Richard White, *The Organic Machine* (New York: Hill and Wang, 1995), discusses the disheartening damming and harnessing of the River of the West—the Columbia. Donald J. Pisani, *From Family Farm to Agribusiness: The Irrigation Crusade in California and the West, 1850–1931* (Berkeley: University of California Press, 1984) notes the feeble nature of federal reclamation accomplishments in California until the Bureau of Reclamation assumed control of the Central Valley Project but sees reclamation as a part of society's increasing reliance on government initiative as it undergoes modernization. Donald J. Pisani, *To Reclaim a Divided West: Water, Law and Public Policy, 1848–1902* (Albuquerque: University of New Mexico Press, 1992), asserts that national reclamation failed to wrest from the states control over water and laid the foundation for conflict among government agencies over water development projects. In this vein, he rejects the arguments that national reclamation led to either centralization or efficiency, arguing that western irrigation rather supported local power and traditions.

In contrast to Pisani, Donald Worster, *Rivers of Empire: Water, Aridity, and the Growth of the American West* (New York: Pantheon Books, 1985), argues that "hydraulic societies" are centralized and authoritarian and that the American West is a good example of this development. William D. Rowley, *Reclaiming the Arid West: The Career of Francis G. Newlands* (Bloomington: Indiana University Press, 1996), places Newlands in the context of the Progressive movement and notes that reclamation was only a part of his larger reform agenda for America at the beginning of the century. David Sarasohn, *The Party of Reform: Democrats in the Progressive Era* (Jackson: University Press of Mississippi, 1989), probably overdraws the picture of the Democratic party as the champion of reform. For background on the San Francisco of Newlands's time see David Lavender's *Nothing Seemed Impossible: William C. Ralston and Early San Francisco* (Palo Alto, CA: American West, 1975). It is an epic biography and an update of Cecil G. Tilton, *William Chapman Ralston: Courageous Builders* (Boston: Christopher, 1935). Two insightful books that deal with questions of modernization and the expansion of government's administrative ability in the Progressive Era are Martin J. Sklar, *The United States as a Developing Country: Studies in U.S. History in the Progressive Era and 1920s* (New York: Cambridge University Press, 1992); and Stephen Skowronek, *Building a New American State: The Expansion of National Administrative Capacities, 1877–1920* (Cambridge, England: Cambridge University Press, 1982).

8

Clelia Duel Mosher and the Change in Women's Sexuality

Kathleen R. Parker

Attitudes toward sex in the Victorian era were restrictive and biased against women. The conventional understanding about the physiology of female sexuality during the latter decades of the nineteenth century had little scientific foundation and relied heavily on rigid stereotypes of how nature programmed gender roles. Women were understood to be innately passive and emotional; men were presumed to be naturally assertive and cerebral. Clelia Duel Mosher challenged these myths and helped to lay the groundwork for systematic research into women's sexuality.

Kathleen Parker traces the career of this educator and reformer who dedicated her life to combating misconceptions that limited women's activities. Mosher worked to overcome the presumption that women were unsuited for advanced education and that menstruation was a sickness requiring bed rest. Her interest in female sexuality led her to question the attitudes and marital practices of middle-class women between 1892 and 1920. Her findings from this pioneering survey rebutted the belief that women engaged in sexual relations only for reproduction. Mosher also found that although new views about marital intimacy had emerged, women still retained older, idealized images about marriage. Professor Parker sees Mosher's own bittersweet life as mirroring this subtle mixture of tradition and modernity in middle-class marriages.

Kathleen R. Parker holds a Ph.D. in American studies from Michigan State University and is assistant professor of history at Waynesburg College in Waynesburg, Pennsylvania, where she is codirector of the Gender Studies Program. Her research focuses on issues of sexuality and sex-crime law in the modern United States. Her publications include "'To Protect the Chastity of Children Under Sixteen': Statutory Rape Prosecutions in a Midwest County Circuit Court, 1850–1950," in *Michigan Historical Review* (Spring 1994).

In the years 1880 to 1920, urban middle-class women campaigned for the vote, worked in settlement houses, called for temperance laws, stood in picket lines with their working-class sisters, and lobbied to raise the age of consent regarding cases of statutory rape. Confronting the human troubles that marked an industrializing and

119

urbanizing society, they employed various styles of voluntary activism that demonstrated new avenues of personal choice and social commitment for women outside the traditional domestic sphere. Among these "new women," a small but growing number established themselves in the professions. One of these women was Clelia Duel Mosher, who sought in her lifelong work as a physician, scientist, and educator to dismantle the biological and sexual beliefs that limited women's achievements. Her studies to prove the constricting effects of Victorian clothing and disprove the common perception that menstruation was disabling contributed to a new stream of scholarship that questioned women's assumed physical weaknesses. The unique aspect of her work was her survey of sexual attitudes and practices administered to forty-five married middle-class women during the years 1892 to 1920. Although the survey itself was not published in her lifetime, her challenge to existing gender definitions accompanied rising expectations for women and men in higher education, family mobility, consumerism, and reform.

Clelia Mosher was born on December 16, 1863, in Albany, New York, into a family for which medicine was a traditional occupation. Her father, four uncles, and a distant cousin, Eliza Mosher, were all physicians. Clelia hoped to study medicine too, a goal that was possible only for daughters whose families believed in women's education. Her father had supported her early schooling at Albany Female Academy, but he worried that the demands of college life would threaten her health. Her only sister, Esther, had died, and Clelia had been weakened by childhood tuberculosis. To compensate for discouraging her educational ambitions, her father converted the small family greenhouse into a laboratory, financed her lessons in botany and horticulture, and built a small store from which she could sell her flowers. Clelia's floral business became the means to obtain the education she desired. Within a few years, she saved two thousand dollars, a sum sufficient to pay her way through college. At the age of twenty-five, she announced to her parents her intention to enroll at Wellesley College in Massachusetts. Her father accepted her decision and helped his independent daughter prepare for college by letting her study medicine with him.

Clelia arrived at Wellesley in 1889, when 36 percent of college students were women. The first year of study left her near physical collapse from overwork but it led her to an important decision. Inspired by Wellesley professor Mary Roberts Smith, Mosher committed her life to the women's movement. For her this resolve would mean using medical science to free women from culture-driven health limitations. Mosher followed Smith first to the University of Wisconsin in her junior year and then to Stanford University, where she graduated with a biology major in 1893.

As a student, Mosher questioned prevailing assumptions about women's health. Male physicians had relied on their observations of unhealthy women to make conclusions about all women. What seemed rather peculiar to Mosher, for example, was the common belief that women breathed costally (only with the upper chest) and men breathed diaphragmatically (a deeper breathing that involves the entire diaphragm). Upheld in all the nineteenth-century textbooks, women's shallow breathing was assumed to be an innate characteristic that served to justify their "natural" incapacity for heavy exertion. Such an idea seemed preposterous in light of the physical tasks performed by ordinary women in their households and by poorer women in industry, agriculture, and domestic service. Acting on Smith's suggestion to study healthy women, Mosher determined to expose the myth behind the so-called scientific truth of women's costal breathing.

Upon graduation Mosher accepted a position at Stanford as an assistant in the girls' gymnasium. She began examining the breathing of female students and pregnant girls at the nearby Pacific Rescue Home. Using an elaborate measuring device of her own making, she measured the upper-body circumferences of eighty-eight subjects, male and female, at three sites: under the arms, at the ninth rib, and at the waist. Each site was measured at repose, at expansion in quiet breathing, at fullest expiration, and at fullest inspiration. The process took several hours for each subject, evidence of her precise and thorough research methods. In all cases, she found that the presence of clothing decreased the measure of chest expansion. By 1894, she was able to offer her findings for her master's degree. What she had learned was corroborated two years later at Harvard University, namely that women's more shallow breathing was not due to any inherent sex differences but rather to the societally imposed requirement that women wear a corset. As a constrictive undergarment, the corset altered the bone structure of a woman's rib cage and confined her lung capacity to a small portion of the natural chest cavity.

From these findings, Mosher came to suspect that the incapacitating "sickness" routinely associated with menstruation—referred to then as "functional periodicity"—was at least partly a result of fashion. Corsets and voluminous skirts put downward pressure on all the abdominal organs and hindered their functioning. She measured the clothing of ninety-eight Stanford women students enrolled in her physical culture classes and found that the average circumference of their skirts was 13.5 feet. More impassioned than others who were making similar arguments, Mosher urged her students to abandon their corsets and heavy skirts. If they would wear sensible clothing, they could eliminate their monthly seven-day confinements in bed. Mosher's own dress reflected her belief in functional simplicity. As fashions came and went, she was well known among colleagues and students for her unchanging attire: a loose black shirtwaist dress, starched collar, four-in-hand tie, and untrimmed round hat. She was, noted one student, "quite a sight."[1]

Mosher's interest in debunking the assumed disability menstruation imposed on women is better understood given the ideas that shaped contemporary thinking. As women sought new opportunities to participate in the commercializing world of the late nineteenth century, keepers of tradition warned them against violating the dictates of their biology. Doctors and psychologists believed that a woman's uterus controlled both her physical and mental life, making her naturally weak, submissive, uncreative, emotional, intuitive, and inferior in comparison to men. The implications of this view, as one-time Harvard physician Dr. Edward Clarke had argued in his 1873 book *Sex Education; or, a Fair Chance for Girls*, were that women should not expend their energies on education. Mental exertion would impair the proper functioning of their reproductive organs. Clarke's ideas were buttressed in the 1870s by a dominant strain of Darwinian thinking, holding that orderly evolution toward advanced civilization depended on the proper maintenance of sex differences. In 1871, Charles Darwin had written in *The Descent of Man* that men could attain higher eminence than women in anything requiring "deep thought, reason, or imagination." Women's "greater tenderness" was characteristic of a lower state of civilization." Noted British economist Herbert Spencer agreed with Darwin but saw women's "intuitive capacity to empathize" in positive terms; it made them "especially well fitted for their parenting role."[2] In support of these ideas, Clarke University's G. Stanley Hall believed that male strength must be preserved to ensure optimum evolution of the human race. Hall feared that coeducation would lead girls to assimilate boys' ways and boys to assimilate girls' ways, threatening boys' understanding of a thoroughly masculine identity. By the 1890s, ideas about men and women were polarized: men were believed to be competitive, adventurous, and predisposed to excitement and to exhibit "mental variability"; women were assumed to be nurturing, passive, uncreative, tranquil, and lacking in sustained mental application.[3] It was this view of sex differences that Clarke, Hall, and others feared would be lost if women became educated.

Mosher's theory regarding "functional periodicity" challenged this kind of biological determinism. By 1896, her study had led her to examine 400 women and keep records of 3,350 menstrual cycles. Twenty years earlier, Dr. Mary Putnam Jacobi's award-winning book *The Question of Rest for Women During Menstruation* had concluded that there was no need for bed rest during menstruation. Mosher believed her study would result in similar conclusions that would carry more scientific weight, since Jacobi had based her observations on 286 responses obtained from a mail-in questionnaire. By contrast, Mosher interviewed her subjects personally and conducted follow-up discussions with them over a longer period.

As the extent of her study expanded, she decided to pursue her dream of medical training in order to properly interpret her data. With characteristic self-confidence, she applied only to Johns Hopkins School of Medicine, believing it offered the best medical training in the country. The school had been open for just three years and was prepared to admit both male and female students because a group of local women benefactors had raised an endowment of $500,000 on the condition that the school be open to women. Dr. Jacobi hailed this enrollment policy as an important precedent. Nineteen women's medical colleges had been established between 1850 and 1895, but Johns Hopkins was the first of its academic standing to admit both male and female students. After she completed the precondition of an additional course in physics, Mosher enrolled in 1899 as one of thirteen women in a class of forty-one students. Later she would write that at Johns Hopkins, she found a climate of support for women students and for her interest in women's physiology.

Mosher was fortunate to study under Dr. Howard Atwood Kelly, a leading figure in gynecological surgical methods and, by all accounts, an "extraordinary operator." When Mosher graduated in 1900, Kelly offered her a one-year position as a gynecological assistant in his sanatorium, which she accepted. She believed her work had come to Dr. Kelly's notice because of the attention it was getting from Dr. George Englemann, a noted Boston gynecologist. Englemann had collected records on menstruation from college and university teachers around the country. He had earlier sought access to Mosher's records while she was still a senior at Stanford, and now he pressured Kelly to "put the screws on Miss Mosher and see that she is heard from—and send me her data." When Kelly passed Englemann's letter on to Mosher, she chose to protect her research and did not respond. Englemann persisted by contacting her directly, allowing that if she wanted to utilize her records for "any especial purpose," she should at least give him the "general results." In a carefully worded letter of response, Mosher told Englemann that she was extending her Stanford studies, implying that her results were not yet complete. Privately, she wrote with indignation, "For what purpose would one spend all one's leisure and all the money to pay expenses of an extensive investigation of a subject if it was not to be used?" Very soon after this incident, in 1901, her research was published as her own work in the *Johns Hopkins Medical Bulletin*. Her findings contradicted those of

Englemann, who believed that education and labor had caused "great harm to the female nervous system."[4]

Kelly was apparently pleased with Mosher's performance as his assistant. At the end of the one-year appointment, he offered to train her as a gynecological surgeon, adding the warning that no male physician would likely be willing to work under her. Apparently she declined his offer not for this reason but because she preferred to work independently. She returned to California to begin a private practice in Palo Alto. There she would also be near her friend, Mary Roberts Smith. This decision proved to be an important turning point in her life. Her private practice was never more than a meager success. Her clients were mostly the chronic patients referred to her by established physicians, and her income was never adequate in this period to meet her needs. Records of her own medicinal recipes and her visits with patients suggest she devoted a good deal of attention to the science of healing. When she was offered in 1910 a chance to teach personal hygiene at Stanford and serve as medical adviser to women students, she eagerly accepted. From this position, she would be able to resume her research on menstruation. This work, she believed, would "make a great difference in women's lives . . . helping to give every woman her birth right of health."[5]

During these years she pursued her research and developed a series of exercises designed to strengthen abdominal muscles and "equalize circulation" among all the organs. These exercises, known through her several published articles as "moshers," were adopted by "physical culture" departments in other schools to prevent the kind of "congestion" that Mosher believed contributed to menstrual discomfort. In test studies, students who carried out the prescribed exercises reported experiencing less menstrual pain than had been customary for them before. Such testimony provided a valuable basis for challenging the restrictions of tradition. In a 1915 speech before a national officers' convention of the Young Women's Christian Association (YWCA), Mosher urged women to appreciate their physiological capabilities. Published as a small book, *The Relation of Health to the Woman Movement,* her speech concluded: "What we need are women no less fine and womanly, but with beautiful, perfect bodies, a suitable receptacle for their equally beautiful souls, who look sanely out on life with steady nerves and clear vision."[6]

Clelia Mosher gained national prominence in her lifetime for her work on breathing and menstruation, especially for her abdominal exercises. It is her survey on sexual attitudes and practices, however, that has uniquely captured the interest of historians, offering in a treasury of private, subjective responses, a fascinating glimpse of marital intimacy, childbirth, and the psychosexual health concerns of women at the turn of the century. The story behind the survey begins in 1892, while Clelia Mosher was still a twenty-eight-year-old biology student at the University of Wisconsin. Her mentor, Mary Roberts Smith, asked her to speak to the Mothers Club, made up mostly of the wives of university faculty, in Madison. Smith and Mosher collaborated in formulating a series of twenty-five health- and sex-related questions, to which Mosher initially compiled the responses of seven club women (one of whom was Smith herself). Over the next twenty-eight years (until 1920), a total of forty-five women responded to the survey. Their responses, which Mosher recorded in her own hand, constitute the only late-nineteenth- to early-twentieth-century document we have that was designed from the outset to elicit personal sexual information in a systematic way.

The limitations of the survey's historical value are that the respondents were few in number and did not represent a balanced cross section of women. All the respondents were white, married, well educated, and existing economically and culturally within a middle- to upper-middle-class frame of reference. It appears not to have been within the realm of appropriateness or possibility for Mosher to conduct the study otherwise. At the time only 2 percent of women graduated from college, and 40 to 60 percent of women college graduates did not marry. Thirty-four of Mosher's respondents had attended college or normal school (at Vassar, Smith, Cornell, Stanford, Indiana, Iowa State, and the University of California), twenty-seven had worked as teachers prior to marriage, and all were married to men who held college degrees. Moreover, at a time when major cities were teeming with immigrants, all of the respondents were born in the United States. All of them lived and went to school in the North or in California; not one was from the South.

In spite of these limitations, both the nature of the survey questions and the responses to them, collectively and individually, teach us much about turn-of-the-century normative sexual expectations. Each survey respondent was first asked general questions about her family history, her years of marriage, and her health. Then she was asked more specific questions about the condition and duration of her menstrual flow, how much she had known about sexual physiology before marriage, whether she slept with her husband and why, and how many times she had conceived and whether conception had been by choice. The most intimate questions came last. Each respondent was asked to describe her sex life with her husband: habits of sexual intercourse, whether she experienced orgasm, what she believed the purposes of intercourse to be, whether she used any means of birth control, and what she considered an ideal habit of intercourse to be.

Particularly significant to this era are the questions pertaining to sexual intercourse. They explore the distinction between intercourse for reproduction and intercourse for pleasure, both for the man and for the woman. Throughout much of the nineteenth century, the popular assumption was that men's desires for sex were boundless but that respectable women were "passionless." Thus, sexual intercourse for a woman was understood as a matter of duty, endured to please one's husband and to produce children. This survey posed the possibility that intercourse might be "agreeable" for the woman, which suggests that a less proscribed view of women's sexuality existed. By asking whether women "always" had a "venereal orgasm," Mosher conveyed the presumption that they would have them at least some of the time and that it was acceptable for them to admit it.

Late-nineteenth-century medical opinion was divided on the question of women's ability to experience sexual passion. From 1857 until its last printing in 1894, William Acton's widely quoted book *The Functions and Disorders of the Reproductive Organs* argued that women were "not troubled with sexual feelings of any kind." Their indifference to sex was "pre-ordained." In contrast, Orson S. Fowler, a phrenologist, wrote in 1870: "That female passion exists is as obvious as that the sun shines." The practice of coitus interruptus as a form of contraception, wrote Henry Chevasse, should be discouraged because it is "attended with disastrous consequences, most particularly to the female, whose nervous system suffers from ungratified excitement."[7]

The leader among those who believed that women were capable of sexual feelings was Dr. George Napheys, whose *Physical Life of Woman: Advice to the Maiden, Wife, and Mother* was published in 1869. With much scientific authority, Napheys proposed that women were divided into three groups: the first and smallest was made up of women who had no passion, the second and larger group was made up of those who had strong passion, and the third and largest group consisted of "the vast majority of women, in whom the sexual appetite is as moderate as all other appetites." The popularity of Napheys's work (there were sixty thousand copies in print in two years) suggests that it resonated well with the experiences of the literate middle-class women who constituted his readership.[8] They likely identified with those of moderate appetite. Poorer women, by contrast, were assumed to be promiscuous.

Remarkably, some doctors were so committed to an ideology of women's passionlessness that they performed cliterodectomies, or castrations, on their women patients to "cure" them of their feelings of sexual arousal. Intended to check a "growing incidence of female masturbation," these medical reactions were evidence that even respectable women had a natural sexual appetite.[9] Experts' more general acceptance of women's sexual capacity did not occur until after 1900. As early as 1912, William Robinson asserted in *Sex Problems of Today* that "every case of divorce has for its basis lack of sexual satisfaction." Charging men with the responsibility of arousing their wives' natural passions, Dr. Walter Robie wrote in 1921, "The husband should not rest easy, nor should his wife allow him to, until they have discovered the methods and positions which give her greatest pleasure and completest orgasm." Metaphorically, he added, "As dough is prepared for baking, so must a woman be prepared for sexual intercourse." The new premise, for both men and women, was that sex was to be playful and was to be mutually enjoyed by both parties.[10]

Among Mosher's earliest respondents, however, reluctance about intercourse seems to have outweighed enthusiasm for it. The women interviewed before 1900 were more likely to report that sex was not a necessity, especially for women; after 1900, the women were more accepting of the belief that sex was necessary for both men and women. One of these interviewees wrote that the "highest devotion is based upon it. . . . It is a very beautiful thing, and I am glad nature gave it to us." Representative of the thirty-four respondents who reported experiencing orgasm were admissions that the "absence of orgasm" is "disastrous, nerve wracking, and unbalancing"; the presence of orgasm "produces physical harmony."[11]

Mosher's later interviewees demonstrated this shift toward greater sexual pleasure for women; yet the qualifiers they offered suggest where the boundaries of such pleasure lay. One woman who found intercourse "agreeable" and "very nearly always" had an orgasm nonetheless wrote with some ambivalence that "the pleasure is sufficient to warrant it, provided people are extremely moderate and do not allow it to injure their health and degrade their best feelings toward each other." Her words imply that too frequent intercourse would be a detriment to well-being and might compromise the moral basis of the marital sexual relationship. Arguing for mutuality in the marital relation, respondents valued spirituality and a sense of affection in sexual intercourse over any reported physical arousal. One interviewee indicated that intercourse was "one of the highest manifestations of love, granted us by our Creator." Another stated that any "necessity" for intercourse was not physical, as with food and drink, but spiritual. She further elaborated, "My husband and I . . . believe in intercourse for its own sake . . . and spiritually miss it . . . when it does not occur because it is the highest, most sacred expression of our oneness."

Their desire for moderation, together with their insistence on the spiritual quality of intercourse, suggests that women wanted the intimacy of this relation to be treated with propriety. One woman interviewed in 1913 stated that although intercourse was a necessity to man and woman and served the purposes of both pleasure and reproduction, it could nonetheless be "loathsome" if a "pure woman [was] treated by her husband as he has treated the prostitute he had been to before marriage." Self-identified as a "pure woman" of middle-class social standing, she did not condone what she understood to be the more fluid sexual arrangements of the lower classes of women, especially prostitutes. Prostitution did indeed thrive in the nineteenth and early twentieth century—a result of the lack of viable employment opportunities for women and the double standard requiring "respectable" women to be completely chaste and excusing men their uncontrollable sexual urges.

A middle-class wife who in 1913 saw herself as a "pure woman" may have fully understood the economic and social realities that separated her from the prostitutes of the "red-light districts." She may have had sympathy for girls and women who had turned to prostitution. Nonetheless, she felt vulnerable because of the possibility of an unfaithful husband and the risks of venereal disease and the destruction of her family. Prince Morrow, a prominent New York physician, had powerfully articulated these apprehensions when he stated in 1899, "There is more venereal infection among virtuous wives than among professional prostitutes."[12] Doctors' concern over prostitution turned to alarm when gonorrhea was discovered in the 1890s to cause insanity among its carriers and blindness in infants born to infected mothers. Mosher would surely have been privy to intense discussions on these findings while at Johns Hopkins. Long thought to be little more serious than a common cold, gonorrhea (which was far more prevalent than syphilis) was now regarded as a deadly menace to society.

Campaigns to prevent premature sexual experience in adolescent girls, in the belief that it would lead to prostitution, brought on a flurry of state laws to raise the age of consent regarding statutory rape. By the early years of the twentieth century, psychiatrists had invented the category of the "hypersexual," providing a scientific justification for confining sexually active adolescent girls in state-funded "industrial schools." In the hysteria over ending prostitution, doctors gave up their campaign to "regulate" it, and social-purity reformers abandoned their opposition to sex education in the schools. Finally, the federal government enacted the Mann Act in 1911 for the prosecution of anyone who transported a white woman across state lines for purposes of prostitution. With such a fearful atmosphere of protection and condemnation separating respectable wives from women who were sexually active outside of marriage, it should not be surprising that Mosher's respondents, well into the twentieth century, distanced themselves from sexual excess and looked with favor on husbands who were neither sexually aggressive nor cavalier. Like women of her class, Mosher was repelled by public displays of affection. She held that women should be free to experience pleasure in sexual intercourse and believed that their ignorance of sexual matters before marriage was a prelude to sexual maladjustment in marriage. Nonetheless, like her respondents, she believed that sexual fulfillment should not be separated from morals.

Although early-twentieth-century thinking offered greater sexual autonomy to women, the belief that sexual anarchy was at hand contributed to a context in which later survey respondents idealized sex in spiritual terms. This idealization emerged as a new norm at the turn of the century and became a necessary condition of making a "pure" woman's enjoyment of sex morally acceptable, both to her and to society. It distinguished middle-class sexual experience from the alleged coarseness of sexual activity among the lower classes and prostitutes. A married middle-class woman could more readily admit to experiencing orgasms by the early twentieth century, but she would also believe that her physical pleasure was less important than the overall sense of metaphysical connection she shared with her husband. Imbuing sexual pleasure with piety, in other words, was a way to preserve the nineteenth-century ideal of women's moral superiority in a modern twentieth-century context.

The very real sexual pleasure reported by Mosher's respondents was nonetheless suffused with anxiety. Whereas their actual practice of intercourse was reported to be about one to two times a week, their reported "ideal habit" was considerably less often—about once a month. In short, they feared pregnancy. One woman articulated best what others hinted: "I heartily wish there were no accidental conceptions. I believe the world would take a most gigantic stride toward high ethical conditions if every child brought into the world were the product of pure love and conscious choice." This wish was no idle musing. In numerous heartfelt stories, respondents revealed the physical trauma and risk of death, either to themselves or to the infant, that pregnancy and childbirth occasioned. Even if the mother and newborn survived the birth process, the mother could sustain severe vaginal or urinary tract injuries that if surgery could not repair, left her an invalid for the rest of her life. Children's path to adulthood was fraught with health risks that today are mostly a dim memory: rickets from measles; diphtheria, scarlet fever, and tuberculosis; infections that never healed—and infants died from *cholera infantum*, spinal meningitis, prolonged labor, and intolerance to milk. In addition to health problems, numerous pregnancies brought financial strain. As families increasingly sought their livelihoods in urban environments, their children became less the economic asset they might have been on a farm and more of an economic burden, especially if they were to be educated. New ideas of child development required that parents give more attention to fewer children.

In spite of these compelling reasons to limit family size, suspicion of legalized birth control was widespread. Mainstream Americans feared it would give women an independence that would threaten the authority of men in the family. Feminists feared that birth control would free men to indulge their sexual passions both within and outside marriage. They called for a single standard that would hold men to the same high moral sexual ideal as women. Child-labor reformers derided the naïveté of birth control advocate Margaret Sanger, who argued that birth control would eliminate the exploitation of children. Doctors argued that legalizing contraceptive practice in the face of perceived working-class sexual promiscuity would bring about race suicide among the better classes. In the belief that reproduction was the only true purpose of intercourse, social-purity reformers aimed to protect for all women the high ideal of motherhood. They successfully pressured federal and state lawmakers to make illegal the printing, mailing, and disseminating of any "obscene material," including contraceptive devices or information. With the Comstock Law in 1873, the U.S. Post Office was empowered to intercept contraceptive devices and related information sent in the mail.

The irony was that the repression of birth control was a reaction against behavior patterns already in place. The average number of births among white women had dropped from 7.04 in 1800 to 3.56 in 1900, indicating that couples had long been exercising control over their fertility.[13] That two-thirds of Mosher's respondents confessed to using a variety of contraceptive methods and devices further illustrates this trend. Still, the societal suppression of birth control inhibited contraceptive practices. This suppression is apparent in the respondents' inconsistent use of unreliable methods, such as early withdrawal (which gave women no contraceptive power) and postcoital douching with hot, cold, or tepid water; alcohol; and sulfate of zinc (all of which were generally ineffective). One early interviewee, who reported that all three of her children were accidentally conceived, admitted to having used a douche only once. Another woman, married for twenty-seven years, reported having tried "a period of immunity" that "did not work." After giving birth to six children, only two of whom survived past childhood, she and her husband eventually resorted to sleeping in separate beds, by several accounts the most common way to sustain a habit of abstinence. A 1912 respondent recounted the sequencing of her five accidental conceptions (with one miscarriage); she and her husband tried unsuccessfully to limit their intercourse to the "two weeks [that are] supposed to be safe." The woman lamented that she "did not mean to have children for five years in order to study." These women and their husbands used birth control, but with much more restraint than the desire of both parties suggests would have been appropriate. Their contraceptive practice was reflective of societal misgivings about separating reproduction from intercourse.

In her introductory comments to the survey, Mosher wrote that the reported experiences of her respondents had given her "a priceless knowledge" that enabled her "to avoid prejudice in her work with women" as a physician and educator. She claimed that the "pressure of other routine work" prevented her from "arranging the work for publication." Since the number of survey participants was tiny relative to the sample size used in her studies of breathing and menstruation, it is likely she never intended to publish this work.[14] She received hundreds of letters from women who wrote of the positive effects of her abdominal exercises, but she would never know how readers might have benefited from the survey. Much of what Mosher's survey revealed would be corroborated in 1918 by Katherine Bement Davis. As was true for Mosher's later interviewees, Davis found that most of her 2,200 participants believed that love justified intercourse, that the use of contraceptives was acceptable, and that prior instruction in sexual matters would lead to a better adjustment in marriage for women. Davis's survey was more exploratory than Mosher's, asking about attitudes toward homosexuality, for instance. The Davis study would be followed in 1931 by Robert Latou Dickinson's book *A Thousand Marriages*. As a gynecologist who long advocated birth control, Dickinson wrote from his meticulous case records of 5,200 former patients. Alfred Kinsey's work would follow soon after World War II. Thus, in spite of its limitations, the Mosher survey stands as a lone pioneer in what would soon become a vital area of medical and social scientific investigation.

In her early life, Clelia Duel Mosher made important independent choices. Her decisions to get a college education, become a physician, and pursue and protect her research even as others attempted to take over her data are evidence of her intense claim to self-definition. Having chosen this course and having achieved so much, however, she later found herself searching for an involvement apart from the intellectual fulfillment of her work. In 1917, at the age of fifty-three, she initiated through an acquaintance a connection with the Red Cross in order to serve as a physician in France during World War I. In her journal she wrote that everything in her "cried out to do its part in this world catastrophe." From January 1918 through January 1919, she served as medical investigator for the Children's Bureau. Her assignment was to evacuate children from Paris. This experience left her profoundly moved by the devastation and human suffering she witnessed. She wrote to her mother, "It wrings this heart to see what the war has done to the people—especially the children—the helpless children and women! It makes me wish we could speed up the arrival of our American Army and bring this war to a victorious close."[15] She also came back from the war impressed with the competence of French women in replacing their men in all avenues of labor, even those requiring muscular strength. From these observations, she declared, albeit too broadly, that women were physically just as strong as men. She would present these ideas in 1924 at the International Conference of Women Physicians in England.

After the war, she seems to have gone through a period of personal difficulty. There were quarrels with the new Stanford administration, and her mother, who had come to live with her in California, was not well. She longed to give more time to her garden and to her failing mother, but resolved: "I must reap my intellectual harvest. I have something to contribute . . . something to give to the question of woman."[16] What followed was the publication in 1923 of her second book, *Woman's Physical Freedom*. This book achieved wider popularity than any of her previous writings. Within five years, it was in its sixth printing. In it, Mosher assured middle-aged women that any difficulties they might experience in menopause were due more to the social changes that accompany midlife than to the mental or emotional imbalance they supposed was to blame. She urged women whose children were now grown to fill their time with political, church, and community service. Such advice, so popular with women her age, belied her own solitary ways.

Mosher's uniqueness as a woman of great intellectual intensity isolated her from most of her contemporaries. At Stanford, she was one of only three women to become tenured before World War II. Her only close friend, Mary Roberts Smith, had left Stanford for San Francisco in 1904, remarried in 1906, and went on to teach at Mills College. Mosher was keenly aware of what she had missed in not marrying or having children. Her journal entries from 1915 to the mid-1920s make frequent mention of her loneliness, especially after the death of her mother in 1920. In 1915, after teaching at Stanford for five years, she conveyed in exquisitely delicate phrases the sensuous inner world within which her heart found expression. She looked out at her garden and wrote to an imaginary friend, "As I ate my breakfast in my booklined study I looked past the half opened daffodil and the violets, past your empty chair, through the open door to the miracle of beauty and awakening life which we call spring—realized suddenly why I have cared for you as no other friend. . . . I could see you with your hands full of the tiny golden poppies. . . . I know you will understand me when I say that the beauty of this perfect California spring almost hurts—I long for you to share the beauty of the spring with me—it would be too perfect."[17]

Mosher's unfulfilled longing for a close friend was in part a result of her own habit of mind. Whenever the possibility of collaboration presented itself, Mosher nearly always chose a path of singular action. She turned down the opportunity to work with Dr. Kelly at Johns Hopkins. While practicing medicine in California, she refused membership in the Women's Medical Club of the Pacific and did not join other women physicians in creating and serving the Children's Hospital. She declined an offer to join the prestigious Medical Women's Association, whose membership included better-known female physicians in the country, explaining that she had retired three years earlier.

Highly analytical and deeply introspective, she wrote at the age of fifty-two: "I am finding out gradually why I am so lonely. The only things I care about are things which use my brain. The women I meet are not much interested and I do not meet many men, so there is an intellectual solitude which is like the solitude of the desert—dangerous to one's sanity." Later she wrote, "Dear Friend who never was: I have given up ever finding you. I have tried out all my friends and they have not measured up to my dreams. . . . But I keep normal and wholesome by going ever alone in my land of dreams." She added, with a hint of intellectual disdain, "It would not take long to be as drab as most of my contemporaries were it not for this land of my dreams."[18] Aloof and single-minded, she seems to have felt that anyone who embodied less than the ideal of her imagination would disappoint her. She had closed many emotional doors in pursuit of her scholarship, even those that would have connected her with other professional women. Perhaps such women, whose similarly marginal positions had led them to form networks of support, reminded her of the kind of feminine vulnerability and dependency she had rejected. Claiming her research was her first priority, she seems to have used it to establish distance from a social arena in which she felt profoundly uncomfortable. For someone who so encouraged women's self-determination, this isolation was surely a high price to pay.

By her own account, her final years were happier. In her retirement she moved into a "dream house" of her own design and wrote of looking forward to her "solitary future, rich in the beauty of my surroundings."[19] Here she was able to draw on her relationships with former students, to whom she had always been devoted. They had once regarded her as an amusing oddity on campus. Now many of them visited her frequently, thanking her for her advice on "good citizenship, honesty in all situations, sensibility in dress and lifestyle, unselfishness, and the need for regular exercise."[20] In 1932, she began an autobiography entitled *The Autobiography of a Happy Old Woman*, which she dedicated "to my father, who believed in women when most men classified them with children and imbeciles."

Clelia Mosher's life in medicine, research, and teaching was the product of her feminism. When she died in 1940, she left behind a legacy of scholarship that challenged Victorian prescriptions for women. She proved that a woman's reproductive biology did not impose limits on her mental, physical, and sexual potential.

Notes

1. Kathryn Allamong Jacob, "The Mosher Report: The Sexual Habits of American Women, Examined Half a Century before Kinsey," *American Heritage* 32 (1981): 59. Elizabeth Brownlee Griego, "A Part and Yet Apart: Clelia Duel Mosher and Professional Women at the Turn-of-the-Century," (Ph.D. Diss., University of California, Berkeley, 1983), 161–63.

2. Griego, "A Part and Yet Apart," 47–49.

3. Rosalind Rosenberg, *Beyond Separate Spheres: Intellectual Roots of Modern Feminism* (New Haven, CT: Yale University Press, 1982), 42, 60–62, 68–72.

4. Griego, "A Part and Yet Apart," 130–31. Jacob, "The Mosher Report," 58.

5. Griego, "A Part and Yet Apart," 148.

6. Jacob, "The Mosher Report," 60.

7. Griego, "A Part and Yet Apart," 276–77.

8. Carl Degler, "What Ought to Be and What Was: Women's Sexuality in the Nineteenth Century," in *The American Family in Social Historical Perspective,* ed. Michael Gordon (New York: St. Martin's Press, 1978), 404–5.

9. G. J. Barker-Benfield, *The Horrors of the Half-Known Life: Male Attitudes toward Women and Sexuality in the Nineteenth Century* (New York: Harper and Row, 1976), 120–22.

10. Peter Laipson, "'Kiss without Shame, for She Desires It': Sexual Foreplay in American Marital Advice Literature, 1900–1925," *Journal of Social History* 29 (Spring 1996): 507–26.

11. All of the quotations attributable to the survey respondents are taken from Clelia Duel Mosher, *The Mosher Survey: Sexual Attitudes of Forty-Five Victorian Women,* ed. James MaHood and Kristine Wenburg (New York: Arno Press, 1980).

12. Allan F. Brandt, *No Magic Bullet: A Social History of Venereal*

Disease in the United States Since 1880 (New York: Oxford University Press, 1984), 14–18.

13. James Reed, *From Private Vice to Public Virtue: The Birth Control Movement and American Society since 1830* (New York: Basic Books, 1978), 3–5.

14. Mosher, *The Mosher Survey,* 3.

15. Griego, "A Part and Yet Apart," 217–18.

16. Jacob, "The Mosher Report," 60.

17. Griego, "A Part and Yet Apart," 345.

18. Jacob, "The Mosher Report," 64.

19. Ibid.

20. Griego, "A Part and Yet Apart," 152.

Suggested Readings

Analyses of the Mosher survey are found in Carl Degler, "What Ought to Be and What Was: Women's Sexuality in the Nineteenth Century," in *The American Family in Social Historical Perspective,* ed. Michael Gordon (New York: St. Martin's Press, 1978) 403–25; Kathryn Allamong Jacob, "The Mosher Report: The Sexual Habits of American Women, Examined Half a Century before Kinsey," *American Heritage* 32 (1981: 59); Carroll Smith-Rosenberg, "A Richer and Gentler Sex," *Social Research* 53, no. 2 (Summer 1986): 283–309. Rosalind Rosenberg discusses the influence of Darwin in *Beyond Separate Spheres: Intellectual Roots of Modern Feminism* (New Haven, CT: Yale University Press, 1982).

On the social-purity movement, see David Pivar, *Purity Crusade: Sexual Morality and Social Control, 1868–1900* (Westport, CT: Greenwood Press, 1973). On prostitution, see John C. Burnham, "The Progressive Era Revolution in American Attitudes toward Sex," *Journal of American History* 59, no. 4 (March 1973): 885–908. John D-Emilio and Estelle Freedman, *Intimate Matters: A History of Sexuality in America* (New York: Harper and Row, 1988), is a solid history of sexuality. On public responses to sexual change, see Barbara Epstein, "Family, Sexual Morality, and Popular Movements in Turn-of-the-Century America," in *Powers of Desire: The Politics of Sexuality,* ed. Ann Snitow, Christine Stansell, and Sharon Thompson (New York: Monthly Review Press, 1983), 117–30. Sheila M. Rothman, *Woman's Proper Place: A History of Changing Ideals and Practices, 1870 to the Present* (New York: Basic Books, 1978), offers an excellent overview of women in this period.

9

Christy Mathewson and the National Pastime

Steven A. Riess

Few activities are more reminiscent of childhood to many Americans than baseball. Most played for fun, others participated in organized competition, many watched, and some dreamed of going on to the major leagues. The few players who made it to the top in the 1910s performed in grand stadiums before tens of thousands of fans who roared approval when their team won the game. The next day the newspaper sports page dramatized the triumph and sometimes ran a picture of the hometown hero who had led his team to victory. Few experiences, real or imagined, topped the thrill of being involved in some way in the game.

Christy Mathewson not only lived the dream but also helped create it. "Matty" had all the ingredients of a sports hero: marvelous ability, a strong physique, affability, and respect for religious convention. He was the very embodiment of Christian manhood at a time when people worried about the feminization of middle-class men.

Mathewson appeared on the scene when professional baseball was hitting its stride as a commercial activity. Steven Riess, a sports historian, sketches the rise of the national pastime and how Christy Mathewson, longtime star of the New York Giants, helped promote it. Riess points out that the game not only symbolized popular democracy and sportsmanlike conduct but also was reflective of the changes in the nature of leisure.

Steven A. Riess is professor of history at Northeastern Illinois University. The former editor of the *Journal of Sport History*, he has written or edited seven books on sports, including *Touching Base: Professional Baseball and American Culture* (1980; rev. ed., 1999) and *City Games: The Evolution of American Urban Society and the Rise of Sports* (1989).

Baseball was the unchallenged national pastime in the early twentieth century, a status it had enjoyed even before the Civil War. Organized spectator sports had boomed in the late nineteenth century because of such social changes as urbanization and industrialization and the modernization, commercialization, and professionalization of sporting events. The principal spectator sports were baseball, boxing, horse racing, and college football. Yet except for baseball, professional sports were widely banned in the 1900s because of the dubious integrity of those involved; gambling, ethnic urban political "bosses," and organized crime were closely connected to sporting events.

The rules of baseball in 1900 were virtually identical to those today, and players generally used the same equipment. However, their small, lightly padded, pocketless gloves look primitive alongside modern gear, and the early major league years were known as the "dead ball era," so named because baseballs lacked a firm core and were kept in use the entire game (the balls became discolored and softened and thus became harder to hit). The resulting style of play differed from contemporary play. Managers stressed "inside baseball" (a strategy that employed sacrifices, place hitting, stealing, and the hit-and-run) and physically rough play to score one run at a time. Pitchers dominated the game and used spit, sandpaper ("emery ball"), or talcum powder ("shine ball") to make balls move unnaturally and befuddle batters. Runs were hard to come by, averaging fewer than seven a game. Home runs were so rare that the entire National League (NL) had only 101 in 1907.

Professional baseball was at an important turning point in 1900. The game had struggled in the 1890s because of inter-league wars, insufficient competition within the National League, syndicate baseball (owners controlling two teams at the same time), and the lingering effects of the depression of 1893. After the 1899 season, the NL dropped from twelve to eight teams, creating a glut of experienced, skilled players. Yet at this very time, baseball's popularity was about to boom with the establishment of a second major league, the American League (AL). The new organization was founded in 1900 and claimed major-league status the following year. The AL took advantage of the small number of teams in large cities, bickering among NL owners, and the availability of proven big leaguers to gain acceptance. Led by President Ban Johnson, the new AL raided the NL, hiring eighty-two contracted players, and filled its rosters with a majority of ballplayers with major-league experience. The new league was an immediate success and helped double big-league attendance between 1901 and 1909. The postseason World Series between the AL and NL champions, inaugurated in 1903, became an annual event beginning in 1905. There was also a national expansion of professional baseball with the number of minor leagues rising from thirteen in 1900 to forty-six in 1912. Growing public interest was reflected in the emergence of the sports page, dominated by baseball writers in the daily press; an explosion of coverage by popular periodicals and specialized baseball magazines; and the rise of sports literature for juvenile audiences.

Professional baseball's unsurpassed popularity was a result of several factors. The game was considered clean and uplifting, reflective of prevailing American values and beliefs. Old-stock native white Americans, who worried that the processes of industrialization, urbanization, bureaucratization, and immigration were creating a fractured society, turned to baseball to maintain their traditions, secure social integration, and acculturate newcomers into the core culture. It was widely accepted that baseball epitomized the nation's finest qualities; it was a democratic game of pastoral American origins and was run by selfless, community-minded businesspeople. The game was also fun to play and watch. Fans who had grown up playing the game could attend fast-paced, dramatic, well-played contests that took only about two hours. Spectators participated in such rituals as cheering for the home team, berating the umpire and the opposition, eating hot dogs, and drinking beer. Finally, professional baseball was thoroughly covered by the press, bringing the sport to the attention of the general public on a daily basis.

The prevailing broad-based Progressive ethos promoted order, traditional values, efficiency, and Americanization by looking back to an idealized past. Americans believed that in addition to promoting community, social democracy, and traditional agrarian values, baseball fostered better health, morality, and manliness. In the Progressive Era, manliness meant such qualities as courage, sexual discipline and general self-discipline, honor, physical prowess, rugged individualism, and virility. Many social critics in the late nineteenth century were afraid that middle-class American men were becoming "overcivilized," "sissies," and "stuffed shirts," losing their identity through the feminization of culture at home, at church, and in school. Service in the military or participation in vigorous sports, a "moral equivalent of war," were considered ways for middle-class young men to prove their manliness.

Baseball was said to exemplify democracy because people from different social backgrounds sat together at the ballpark, and players were recruited solely on merit , making the profession a valuable avenue of social mobility. Baseball supposedly fostered social integration by promoting acculturation and hometown pride, teaching cooperation and respect for authority (accepting umpire's decisions), and serving as a safety valve for social aggression. The game purportedly carried the values of small-town life into the cities yet also taught such modern values as teamwork and self-sacrifice. Playing baseball was considered second only to the public schools as a means to acculturate immigrant children, and all youngsters were said to learn to become good citizens by playing baseball and emulating manly ballplayers.

Much of the baseball creed was a myth. In reality, baseball was an urban game operated by politically prominent businesspeople. Spectators did not include people from all backgrounds because of the absence of Sunday baseball in the East, the late-afternoon starting time of games, and the cost of tickets. The game did not draw its players from across the social structure. And many of its heroes were flawed—for example, Ty Cobb, the greatest position player of the era, got along with no one and had a violent temper. However, sportswriters wrote little that was not positive about baseball, and fans were usually unaware of the character shortcomings of star players. The public was convinced that baseball's history and folklore were an expression of the core society's main values and goals. Middle-class white Anglo-Saxon Protestants (WASPs) were convinced by baseball's myths that traditional values still counted in a fast-paced, urbanizing society.

Major-league baseball did have at least one hero with few blemishes. He was Christy Mathewson, a pitcher with the New York Giants who won 373 games, the most won by any pitcher in National League history. In 1999, *Sporting News* rated him the seventh greatest player of all time. Matty was idolized nearly as much for his character, on and off the diamond, as for his outstanding play. He was a tall, handsome, muscular, college-educated Christian (believing in the harmonization of the mind, the body, and the spirit). He taught Sunday school and abstained from Sunday games; a good Baptist, he had promised his mother not to violate the Sabbath. He often spoke to youth organizations about fair play and clean living.

Mathewson was a hero because he had great athletic prowess, displayed ideal behavior, was moral and socially responsible, helped define individual and collective identity, and compensated for qualities apparently missing in many individuals and in society. He symbolized the continuing relevance of traditional values. American heroes up to then had mainly been politicians, military leaders, inventors, and business executives, with the exception of boxing champion John L. Sullivan, who had been a hero among the lower classes rather than to respectable, middle-class society. Sullivan epitomized the manliness of the male bachelor subculture that exalted physical violence, drinking to excess, gambling, and womanizing, traits that posed a threat to proper Victorians.

Christopher Mathewson was born on August 12, 1880, in Factoryville, a town of about 650 residents, in northeastern Pennsylvania. He was the eldest of five children; a sixth died in infancy. Of Scottish and Baptist heritage, his father was a gentleman farmer, the local postmaster, and a jack-of-all-trades. Matty played baseball as a child, and by age fifteen he was playing semipro ball, pitching for the town team for a dollar a game against players several years his senior. He attended Keystone Academy, a prep school his grandmother had founded, where he was an all-around athlete but was mainly known for his football prowess.

The summer after graduation, Matty played for Taunton, Massachusetts, in the New England League, for ninety dollars a month and began to learn his famous fadeaway pitch (screwball that moved away from left-handed batters). In fall 1898 he entered Bucknell College, where he was outstanding in every endeavor. He used his near photographic memory to help him gain all A's his freshman year; was president of the freshman class; participated in literary societies, the band, and glee club; and joined a fraternity. He was the star of the football team and also played baseball. In the summer following his sophomore year he played for Norfolk in the Virginia League for ninety dollars a month. He played superbly, winning twenty of his first twenty-two decisions, and became a hot prospect.

The New York Giants purchased Mathewson's minor-league contract for $1,500, and by July he was in the majors. He was, like most other players, white, middle-class, and American born and reared. But he came from a small town, whereas most professional ballplayers came from cities. He was also a college man, rare among nineteenth-century professional players, who had a negative image as rowdy, hard-drinking, gambling, working-class members of the bachelor subculture apparently interested only in immediate gratification. The prestige and wages of the occupation were on the rise in the early 1900s and began to attract men such as Mathewson, whose presence raised the game's status. One-fourth of all major leaguers in the 1900–1920 period had attended college. They represented a more Victorian and middle-class manliness based on hard work, saving money for the future, and sexual continence. They were not effete mollycoddles but vigorous athletes.

Mathewson's initiation to major-league baseball went poorly. He had a record of 0–3 (no wins, three losses) and was sent back to Norfolk. Disappointed, he considered returning to college. The Cincinnati Reds drafted him but then traded him back to the Giants for former star pitcher Amos Rusie.

The Giants were one of the worst-run franchises in baseball. They were owned by realtor Andrew Freedman, a prominent member of Tammany Hall and the city's powerful Democratic political machine. Freedman's political protection enabled him to run roughshod over other NL owners, and he used his clout to keep the American League out of New York. He was detested by his players, whom he paid low salaries and by fans for failing to produce winning teams. He fired managers virtually every season and regularly got into fights with the press.

Matty signed with the Giants in 1901 for $1,500 a year. He won his first eight decisions, including three shutouts (no runs for the opposing team), and pitched a no-hit shutout against the St. Louis Cardinals (the "Cards") on July 15, the first in the twentieth century. The Giants won only 52 games, but Matty's record was 20 wins against 17 losses. He pitched 336 innings, finishing 36 of 38 starts with an outstanding 1.99 earned run average (ERA—runs scored without errors per game). He received a raise to $3,500, well over the average player's $2,000 salary.

The Giants were still in turmoil in July 1902 when Freedman hired his third manager of the season, the feisty John J. McGraw, player-manager of the Baltimore Orioles. McGraw had just been suspended indefinitely by American League president Ban Johnson for goading and berating umpires. McGraw anticipated that Johnson was going to relocate the Orioles to New York and drop him, so he acted first. McGraw signed with the Giants for $11,000 a year for four years and total control over the team. He brought with him four players, including star pitcher Joe McGinnity and Roger Bresnahan, considered the best catcher in the majors; he then promptly released nine Giants. Matty and McGraw hit it off from the start, and after the young pitcher married hometown sweetheart Jane Stoughton in 1903, their families shared a large mid-Manhattan apartment. Matty and Jane had one son, Christy Junior, who became a military aviator and a colonel in the air force during World War II.

The conflict between the two major leagues was resolved in 1903. The AL and NL had previously competed for fans in Boston, Chicago, Philadelphia, and St. Louis as well as for players. The competition for players had escalated salaries and lowered profits. Early in 1903 the two major leagues signed a national agreement that recognized the AL, settled territorial rights and ownership of players, and classified the minor leagues for the purpose of drafting players. A national commission (the league presidents plus their designated chair, President August Herrmann of the NL Cincinnati Reds) was established to control organized baseball. The commission established the World Series in 1903 and took over scheduling for the leagues, creating the standard 154-game season in 1904.

The AL secured a New York franchise just before the 1903 season started. Freedman had sold the Giants to owner John Brush of the Cincinnati Reds for $200,000 in late 1902 but had continued to use his power to block the AL from New York. The new league did not secure a suitable site for a ball field until spring 1903, when Johnson awarded the old Baltimore franchise to politically influential Tammanyites William Devery, a former New York City police chief, and Frank Farrell, the city's leading gambler. They secured a field for their AL Highlanders at 168th Street, near the Giants' Polo Grounds.

Mathewson became a star in 1903, when he won 31 games and pitched 367 innings. Nicknamed "Big Six," possibly after a powerful horse-drawn fire engine used by the Big Six volunteer fire department, he at that time had only one weakness—poor control. Matty became part of the most formidable starting duo in baseball with "Iron Man" McGinnity, a former foundry worker renowned for pitching entire doubleheaders; in August 1903 he pitched three, winning six games. McGinnity pitched an incredible 434 innings by carefully pacing himself, a tactic Mathewson learned to emulate. After the season, pennant winners Pittsburgh (NL) and Boston (AL) played each other in the first World Series, won by Boston five games to four.

In 1904 the Giants fielded a very strong team built on pitching and recently acquired veterans such as outfielder Mike Donlin. They started strong, winning 53 of their first 71 games, and won easily, going 106–47, setting a major-league record for wins. Mathewson and McGinnity led the way, winning 33 and 35 games, respectively. They had to be very good because none of the starters hit over .300. Mathewson lost just 12 games with an ERA of 2.03. However, Giants manager McGraw still hated AL president Johnson, and new Giants owner Brush was angry because the Highlanders had moved into New York and cut into his profits. Brush and McGraw did not allow the Giants to play AL champion Boston in the World Series, a decision unpopular with the players, who lost out on the extra pay that came with the Series. As a result, several players went on tour (barnstorming) after the season, playing local semipro and town teams.

The Giants followed up with another pennant-winning season in 1905. Their rough-and-tumble style and use of "inside," or "scientific" baseball (sacrifice bunts, the hit-and-run, etc.) reminded fans of manager McGraw's old team, the 1890s Baltimore Orioles. The Giants became known for bench jockeying (name-calling), threatening umpires, and fighting. One week into the season when a baserunner was called out at home plate, McGraw disputed the umpire's decision and went berserk. The normally taciturn Mathewson got caught up in the moment and punched a boy selling lemonade who had run onto the field. After the game, which the Giants won 10–2, a portion of the crowd of twenty thousand threw rocks and bricks at the players, requiring police intervention. One month later, McGraw and rival Pittsburgh manager Fred Clarke almost got into a fight at the Polo Grounds after McGraw heckled Pirates owner Barney Dreyfuss for his influence on umpires and called him a welsher. The umpire threw McGraw out of the game; Mathewson was also thrown out after he posed in a boxing stance near the Pittsburgh bench. These incidents were an exceptions to Matty's customary good behavior on the field.

McGraw's 1905 pennant-winning Giants were a combination of speed and power. They stole 291 bases, led the NL with 39 homers, and had 5 pitchers with 15 or more wins. Mathewson went 31–8 with an ERA of 1.26 in 339 innings. He struck out 206 batters, walked just 64, and pitched his second no-hitter. He beat the Chicago Cubs 1–0, facing just twenty-eight batters, one over the minimum.

The NL had voted in 1905 to require its champion to play in the World Series. Owner Brush not only went along with the plan—he wanted the extra profits—but also introduced the "Brush rules," under which the Series would be conducted: a best-of-seven-game series with the players guaranteed 60 percent of the total gate (of which three-quarters went to the winner). The Giants were matched against Connie Mack's Philadelphia Athletics, a team that featured several former college players and an excellent pitching staff, including Albert "Chief" Bender, Eddie Plank, and the irrepressible Rube Waddell (unavailable to pitch because he had injured himself wrestling a teammate). That World Series was one of the most memorable with each of the games won by a shutout. Mathewson won the first game in Philadelphia 3–0 on a four-hitter, having started the Giants' winning rally by hitting a single. In New York, Bender won the next game 3-0. After a rainout, Mathewson pitched the third game in Philadelphia and won 9-0 with eight strikeouts. Then, back in New York, McGinnity outdueled Plank 1–0. Mathewson pitched the following day in front of twenty-five thousand loyal fans, winning 2–0. He had pitched three shutouts in six days, giving up just one walk! Each Giant made $1,142; each of the losing Athletics received $382.

Matty's achievement made him a superstar. He was already extremely popular with his teammates, who knew they could always count on him. He was not only a great thrower but also a great pitcher who kept a detailed mental record of his pitches and also the strengths and weaknesses of his opponents. Mathewson's sharp mind was legendary among his colleagues. He was to play chess and checkers simultaneously against several opponents and was unbeatable at card games. McGraw once fined Matty $500 for playing poker with his teammates because McGraw worried that Matty's talent for winning might cause dissension.

Hopes were high for a third pennant in 1906, but Mathewson missed the start of the season after contracting diphtheria. The team suffered several debilitating injuries, most notably league-leading hitter Mike Donlin's broken leg, and the pitching staff collapsed. Matty managed to win 22 games but pitched only 266 innings. But the Giants probably would not have won under any circumstances because the Chicago Cubs won a record 116 games, losing just 36. At the end of the season, Henry Mathewson joined his famous brother and pitched two games for the Giants. His brief career ended after one more appearance in 1907.

The Giants retooled in 1907 with a lot of rookies and came in fourth. Leading hitter Mike Donlin left the team, dissatisfied with management's failure to give him a $600 raise in return for agreeing to a no-drinking clause in his contract. In 1908, McGraw plotted redemption, starting with spring training in Marlin, Texas, where the players could concentrate on baseball away from distractions. Matty was at the top of his game. Besides the fadeaway, he threw a moving fastball, a slowball (for a change of pace), a drop curve, a spitball, and a "dry spitter" that died when it got to home plate. Moreover, he was so respected, his biographies relate, that umpires would ask him for advice if they missed a play. The Giants made two expensive minor league acquisitions at this time. They bought pitcher Rube Marquard for a record price of $11,000 from Indianapolis (American Association [AA]) and catcher John "Chief" Meyers for $6,000 from St. Paul (AA).

The 1908 race for the NL pennant was a three-team competition among the Giants, Cubs, and Pirates. Matty carried the pitching staff, appearing in fifty-six games and finishing two-thirds of his starts. One of the most unforgettable games in baseball history occurred on September 23, when the Giants and the Cubs played at the Polo Grounds. The Cubs had beaten the New Yorkers in a doubleheader on the previous day, placing the two teams in a virtual tie. An estimated thirty thousand fans attended the game that pitted Matty against Jack Pfiester. The game was tied, 1–1 when, in the bottom of the ninth after one out, the Giants' Mike Devlin singled. A force-out and a single by first baseman Fred Merkle, starting his first game of the season, followed. Next up to bat was Al Bridwell, who singled up the middle for the apparent game-winning hit. Merkle headed for second and turned in jubilation toward the clubhouse, never bothering to touch second, which was often done then. Second baseman Johnny Evers chased the ball, which by then probably had been tossed into the stands. After retrieving a ball, Evers attracted the umpire's attention, who called out Merkle for failing to touch second. The umpires then suspended the game as a tie to prevent a riot. The close pennant race ended with the Giants winning their last three games to tie the Cubs for the league lead. The NL ordered that the suspended game be replayed at the Polo Grounds to select the champion.

About thirty thousand fans attended the big game, and thousands watched from nearby Coogan's Bluff. The Giants took the lead, but Matty could not hold it, losing 4–2 and giving the Cubs the league pennant. Matty was superb all season long with a record of 37–11 in 390.2 innings and an ERA of 1.43 with 12 shutouts. He finished 34 of 44 starts, struck out 259 batters, and walked 42, less than one per game.

The Giants faltered over the next two seasons as several of their veterans retired. Matty was still superb, winning 25 games while pitching 275 innings yielding merely 36 walks; his ERA was 1.14, still the fifth lowest in major-league history. Then in 1910 he went 27–9 (the most wins in the majors that season) and pitched 318 innings. The Giants played their first postseason exhibition series that year against the Highlanders, following a tradition already well established in other cities with two major-league teams. The six games attracted over 100,000 fans, earning each victorious Giant $1,110 for a week's work at a time when the average major leaguer earned about $3,000 for a full season.

Major-league franchises were becoming very profitable. The value of a franchise, worth $50,000–$100,000 in the early 1900s, increased by 1,000 percent in a decade. The Giants were among the most profitable teams in the major leagues because of the high quality of their team and its large potential audience in metropolitan New York. Freedman had sold the team to Brush in 1902 for about four times what he paid for it seven years earlier. Brush also did very well with the team, which earned about $100,000 a year from 1906 to 1910. In 1919, Brush's heirs sold the franchise for $1 million to Charles Stoneham, a Tammany curb-market broker. In the following year the Giants earned $296,803, an NL record.

One of the most important developments in the baseball business in this era was the replacement of the dangerous wooden ballparks that often burned down. The profitability of major-league baseball and declining construction costs made it possible to build fireproof ballparks out of concrete and steel. These new structures provided safe, comfortable, attractive facilities to better compete with other commercialized entertainments. The construction of fireproof parks began in 1909 with the building of Philadelphia's $500,000, 20,000-seat Shibe Park. Soon after, Pittsburgh's tripledecked Forbes Field was built, and one year later, Chicago's Comiskey Park. By 1916, nearly all the major-league parks had been fireproofed and had an average capacity of about twenty-five thousand seats. These privately constructed civic monuments were at the urban periphery in middle-class or underdeveloped areas where relatively cheap sites were purchased or leased on a longterm basis. They were known as "grounds," "fields," or "parks," rural metaphors that reinforced the national pastime's pastoral image.

The Giants built their fireproof park in 1911 following a fire that destroyed the old wooden Polo Grounds. They briefly played at the Highlander's Hilltop Park and then moved into the new, classically designed Polo Grounds, which eventually had a seating capacity of fifty-five thousand. The new Polo Grounds, like other contemporary fields, had unique dimensions that reflected the size of the lot. Right field was only 258 feet from home plate; left field, 277 feet; and center field 500 feet.

In 1911, the Giants were NL champions and McGraw's ideal team. They bunted, hit-and-ran, took the extra base, and stole 347 bases, a major-league record. Matty, who was earning $10,000 a year, had another great season, going 26–13 with an ERA under 2 in 307 innings. In the World Series the Giants played an outstanding Philadelphia Athletics squad, renowned for its "$100,000 infield" and led by Frank "Home Run" Baker, who won four straight AL home-run championships (1911–1914) without hitting over 12 home runs in any single year (an amazingly low number by 1990s' standards). Matty won the first game in New York 2–1, but back in Philadelphia the Athletics—the "A's"—won on a Baker home run. Matty pitched the following day, but Baker hit another homer in the ninth to tie the score, and the Athletics won in extra innings. It rained six straight days, giving Matty a lot of rest for the next game, but he lost 4–2. The Giants won the fifth game but lost the World Series in six games. A record 180,000 fans attended the games, earning the Athletics each about $3,400 and the Giants, $2,346.

During this Series, newspaper columns appeared that were signed by ballplayers, although they were actually ghostwritten. Journalists responded by organizing the Baseball Writers Association to protect their interests. American League president Ban Johnson, a former sportswriter, was a leading critic of the ghostwritten stories, which were often very critical of organized baseball yet frequently unseen by the players who had the bylines. Mathewson had a syndicated column that was written for him by John N. Wheeler, a *New York Herald* journalist and founder of the North American Newspaper Alliance. In 1913 the *Chicago Daily News* surveyed readers about Matty's column. They responded that the essays were interesting, that Mathewson was smart enough to have written them had he chosen to, and that the paper should keep printing the articles. Wheeler also ghostwrote Mathewson's instructional volume *Pitching in a Pinch* (1911), which discussed players' superstitions, strategy, jinxes, luck, and umpires. Mathewson offered positive judgments about his peers and described several of his era's greatest games. Wheeler and Mathewson subsequently collaborated on a series of boys' books with alliterative titles— *Pitcher Pollack, Catcher Craig, First Base Faulkner,* and *Second Base Sloan.* These books featured ballplayers as role models for youngsters.

The Giants toured Cuba after the 1911 season, playing exhibitions against top local teams that included many players of color. African-American athletes had been barred from organized baseball in the United States since 1898, and only the Walker brothers in

1884 had ever played in the majors. Americans were already familiar with the high quality of Cuban baseball because of Cuban players on African-American teams, the outcome of four major-league tours of the island after 1908 and the presence in 1911 of light-skinned Cubans in the majors. The greatest Cuban ballplayer was pitcher José Mendez, the "Black Mathewson," whose skin color prevented McGraw from bringing him back to New York to play for the Giants.

The Giants repeated as NL champions in 1912, going 103–48. They continued to play McGraw's aggressive style with 319 stolen bases. Matty won twenty-three games but was surpassed by teammate Rube Marquard's twenty-six wins. In the World Series the Giants faced the Boston Red Sox, who were playing their first year in Fenway Park. The Sox had a superior outfield led by Tris Speaker and a talented young pitcher in twenty-three-year-old Smokey Joe Wood, whose record was 34–5. The Giants lost three of the first four games but rallied to tie with the Red Sox.

Mathewson pitched the deciding seventh game, which was tied 1–1 and went into extra innings, the first Series final ever to go to extra innings. Wood relieved for Boston in the tenth inning and allowed the Giants to take the lead. Clyde Engle led off the Boston frame by hitting a short fly that was muffed by center fielder Fred Snodgrass in one of the most famous misplays in baseball history. Engle reached second. Harry Hooper then hit a shot on the first pitch to deep right center, seemingly a sure double, but Snodgrass made a stunning catch and held Engle at second. The next batter walked, and then Speaker singled, tying up the game, and took second on the throw in. Following an intentional walk, Larry Gardner hit a sacrifice fly to win the game and the Series.

Despite the stunning defeat, Mathewson's heroic image continued to grow. After the season, his admiring fans gave him an automobile. Matty had already appeared on the vaudeville stage in 1910, doing comedy sketches for seventeen weeks at the Hammerstein Theater for $1,000 a week. Two years later he starred in the film *Breaking into the Big Leagues* and cowrote a baseball comedy about a scheming female club owner, *The Girl and the Pennant,* that ran for twenty performances. Author Lester Chadwick began a juvenile series, Baseball Joe, that was patterned on Mathewson and eventually sold millions of copies. Even Matty's teammates considered him a hero. Catcher John "Chief" Meyers recalled, "How we loved to play for him. We'd break our necks for the guy. If you made an error behind him or anything of that sort, he'd never get mad or sulk."[1] Mathewson's peers offered him the presidency of the Fraternity of Baseball Players of America, a union established in 1912 that sought higher wages, better working conditions, and protection for players against capricious decisions by the National Commission. Mathewson begged off, but he did serve as a vice president.

In 1913 the Giants won their third straight pennant with a record of 101–51. Matty, who was making $12,000 a year, led the way with 24 victories in 306 innings. His control was impeccable, walking only 21 batters during the season, and he set a record of 68 straight innings without a walk. The Athletics faced the Giants again in the World Series. They captured the first game, but Matty outdueled Eddie Plank in the second, winning 3–0 in ten innings, and drove in the winning run. But the Athletics won the next three games, including the final; Plank topped Matty 3–1 to take the championship. This was Mathewson's last Series appearance. He had played in five Series championships; and his total World Series record was 5–5, with 10 complete games in 11 starts, 4 shutouts, and an ERA of 1.15.

In 1914 the outlaw Federal League, bankrolled by several rich men such as oilman Harry Sinclair, declared itself a major league. It sought the services of many star players, such as Ty Cobb, Walter Johnson, and Mathewson, who was offered $20,000 after the 1915 season to switch teams. Although none of the top stars joined the "Feds," they and lesser players used the leverage of a rival league to negotiate lucrative new contracts. Cobb, for instance, signed a new contract with the Detroit Tigers in 1915 that raised his salary from $12,000 to $20,000. The Federal League merged with the other major leagues after the 1915 season, depriving players of any option after 1915 but to sign with their old teams at unfavorable terms.

Matty's last great season came in 1914 when he won twenty-four games, five by shutouts. The Giants started the 1914 season well but faltered in the second half, losing the league pennant to the Boston Braves. The Giants fell to last place in 1915 and Christy's record sagged to eight wins and fourteen losses. Matty was now no better than the third or fourth starter. In mid-July 1916, struggling with a 3–4 record and an ERA approaching 3, he was traded along with two other players to Cincinnati for shortstop-manager Buck Herzog. Mathewson became the Reds' new manager. The Reds finished in seventh place, 60–93 (25–45 under Matty) but improved to fourth the following year.

The United States declared war on Germany just before the start of the 1917 season, but it had little impact on major-league baseball that year. In New York, where Sunday baseball was still not allowed, the Giants staged a game on Sunday, August 19, against the Reds, ostensibly to raise money for Army relief but primarily to test the local blue laws that banned professional baseball on the Sabbath. Matty had never played on Sundays for reasons of personal conscience. But he considered his participation that

Sunday as a statement promoting social democracy. He now recognized the merits of enabling working-class men to attend a ball game on their only day off. Managers McGraw and Mathewson were arrested for violating the Sunday penal codes. Magistrate Francis X. McQuade dismissed the complaint and praised the managers for their support of Sunday baseball. Two years later the state legislature legalized Sunday ball, deciding that returning soldiers who had fought for freedom in Europe should not have their own liberty curtailed by strict blue laws.

In 1918 the federal government called for a scaling back of the baseball season and issued a "work or fight" order requiring all eligible men to participate in essential war-related work or be drafted. Eventually, 255 major leaguers served in the military, but many players, including Babe Ruth and Joe Jackson, took jobs in shipyards or steel mills, primarily as ballplayers on company teams, to fulfill their service obligations.

Besides the potential loss of ballplayers, Reds' manager Mathewson had another big problem, the integrity of his first baseman, Hal Chase. Chase was considered the best fielding first baseman of the day and was NL batting champion in 1916. However, there had long been rumors that he gambled on games and had not always played his best. Mathewson became convinced that Chase was too skillful to get to the base as late as he often did for throws or to make as many errors as he did, for example, frequently throwing off line to pitchers covering first base. In August 1918, Mathewson heard that Chase had offered a bribe to a Giants pitcher and suspended him for his lax play. Formal charges were brought after the season, but despite damaging testimony, NL president John A. Heydler acquitted Chase to protect baseball's good name. Chase joined McGraw's Giants in 1919, and he continued trying to fix games. In August, McGraw took him out of the lineup and later dropped him from the roster. The Chase affair foreshadowed the dark clouds gathering over baseball. After the World Series that year, played between the Cincinnati Reds and the Chicago White Sox, eight White Sox players were accused of fixing the Series. The scandal became known as the Black Sox scandal. In 1920, Chase was indicted by the Cook County grand jury that was investigating the scandal, but he was never tried.

Mathewson left the Reds in August 1918 to accept a commission as a captain in the chemical warfare service, training recruits in the hazards of poison gas. While serving in France, Matty was exposed to mustard gas, which seriously damaged his health. When he returned to the states, McGraw hired him as his assistant manager.

Matty covered the 1919 World Series for the *New York Evening World*. He sat at the games with Hugh Fullerton, the preeminent baseball writer of the day, who suspected a fix was under way. They carefully watched the action and drew numerous red circles on their scorecards when they spotted a dubious play. The Black Sox scandal was an important symbolic event at a time when many old-stock Americans were worried about the future of their country and disillusioned. After World War I the Senate had failed to approve the peace treaty ending "the war to end all wars." Growing fears at home of radicalism led to the Red scare. Racial antagonisms led to the Chicago race riot. Economic discontent resulted in major railroad and steel strikes, a general strike in Seattle, and a police strike in Boston. The country seemed to be coming apart. If baseball, the institution that epitomized American traditional values, was corrupt, what hope was there for the future? The acquittal of the Black Sox players (jurors carried the players out of the courtroom on their shoulders) seemed to restore national self-confidence and paved the way for the "golden age of sports."

In 1920, Mathewson's doctors diagnosed his illness as tuberculosis, a potentially fatal disease, and sent him to Saranac Lake in upstate New York to seek a cure. The Giants staged a benefit for him on September 30, 1921, with an old-timer's game preceding the regularly scheduled contest. The $50,000 raised for Matty's medical expenses set a record for sporting-event benefits and reflected the public's esteem for him. In 1923, Mathewson's health apparently was improving, and Judge Emil Fuchs, owner of the Boston Braves, made him the president of the team. But his condition continued to worsen, and he was merely a figurehead president. He died from tuberculosis pneumonia at Saranac on October 7, 1925, at the age of forty-five.

Mathewson was eulogized as no American athlete before him. W. O. McGeehan of the *New York Herald Tribune* called him "the best loved and most popular of all American athletes. . . . If baseball will hold to the ideals of this gentleman, sportsman and soldier, our national game will keep the younger generation clean and courageous and the future of the nation is secure."[2] *Commonweal*, the liberal Catholic magazine, similarly lauded him: "Certainly no other pitcher ever loomed so majestically in young minds, quite overshadowing George Washington and his cherry tree or even that transcendent model of boyhood, Frank Merriwell. . . . Such men have a very real value above and beyond the achievements of brawn and sporting skill. They realize and typify in a fashion the ideal of sport—clean power in the hands of a clean and vigorous personality."[3]

Frank Merriwell, the athletic hero of contemporary juvenile literature, was a fictional role model for American boys, but Christy Mathewson set a real-life example. In his athletic career and personal life he was the ideal role model for his admiring young fans, teaching them the importance of hard work, fair play, citizenship, and respect for others.

Matty's greatness is also reflected in the numbers: a lifetime record of 373–188, third place in major-league history for wins and shutouts, his completion of 435 out of 552 games, and his role in leading his team to five pennants. He was honored in 1939 as one of the first five men elected to the Baseball Hall of Fame. But more than that, he was an American hero who embodied, both on and off the field, all the finest qualities that the game represented, and he provided an ideal role model for American youth.

Notes

1. Lawrence Ritter, ed., *The Glory of Their Times* (New York: Macmillan, 1996), 167.

2. Ray Robinson, *Matty, an American Hero: Christy Mathewson of the New York Giants* (New York: Oxford University Press, 1993), 217.

3. "Editorial," *Commonweal* 2 (October 21, 1925), 579.

Suggested Readings

Ray Robinson, *Matty, an American Hero: Christy Mathewson of the New York Giants* (New York: Oxford University Press, 1993), is the only biography of Mathewson. Charles C. Alexander, *John McGraw* (New York: Viking, 1988), is a biography of Mathewson's manager and close friend. Lawrence Ritter, ed., *The Glory of Their Times* (New York: Macmillan, 1966), includes interviews with ballplayers who were Mathewson's contemporaries. Fred Lieb, *Baseball As I Have Known It* (New York: Coward, McCann and Geoghehan, 1977), is a valuable memoir by a major baseball journalist. Steven A. Riess, *Touching Base: Professional Baseball and American Culture in the Progressive Era* (Westport, CT: Greenwood Press, 1980), examines the relationship between professional baseball and American society during the period 1900–1920, emphasizing New York City baseball. David Q. Voigt, *American Baseball*, vol. 2, *From the Commissioners to Continental Expansion* (Norman: University of Oklahoma Press, 1970), provides an overview of major-league baseball history from 1900 to 1960; Harold Seymour, *Baseball*, vol. 2, *The Golden Years* (New York: Oxford University Press, 1971), is the best analysis of the major leagues from 1900 to 1930. Benjamin G. Rader, *American Sports: From the Age of Folk Games to the Age of Televised Sports,* 3d ed. (Englewood Cliffs, NJ: Prentice-Hall, 1996), is the standard text on sports history. For a fascinating fictional analysis of Mathewson, see Eric Rolfe Greenberg, *The Celebrant: A Novel* (Lincoln: University of Nebraska Press, 1993).

10

James Michael Curley and the Politics of Ethnic Resentment

James J. Connolly

James Michael Curley was one of the most colorful politicians in American history. His long run on the stage of Boston politics is largely attributable to his ability to turn his Irish heritage to electoral advantage. Since their arrival in the mid-nineteenth century the Boston Irish had been regarded as second-class citizens by working-class Protestants and upper-class Brahmins, who excluded them from the city's power structure. By 1900 the Irish had gained a toehold in the economy and government, but Curley did not let his constituents forget the slights of the past. In fact, he embellished them, aiming his barbed wit at upper-class Yankees, whom he labeled as prejudiced and discriminatory.

The revision of Boston's charter in 1909 changed the cadence of politics in Boston by downgrading the role of political parties and elevating the importance of the media and publicity. James Connolly, a political historian, traces how Curley adapted to the new era by manipulating ethnic images and exploiting the media. Connolly's story of Curley's ascent in Boston touches on two fundamentals of urban politics in the Progressive Era: the campaign to restrict the influence of party politics and the persistent relevance of cultural groups in electoral politicking. Connolly argues that reforms forced urban politicians to rely more heavily on the media to win elections and that this new style accentuated ethnic consciousness, at least in Boston. Reformers had changed some rules of politics, but they did not eliminate traditional cultural identities or the antagonisms among them.

James J. Connolly is assistant professor of history at Ball State University in Muncie, Indiana. He is the author of *The Triumph of Ethnic Progressivism: Urban Political Culture in Boston, 1900–1925* (1998) as well as several articles and essays on ethnicity and politics in the early-twentieth-century United States.

During the fall of 1904, James Michael Curley sat in a downtown Boston jail cell. His promising political career hung in the balance. Two years earlier, government officials had caught him, then a member of Boston's Common Council, taking a civil service examination for a constituent. Two men, James Hughes and Bartholomew Fahey, had sought jobs as letter carriers, positions that required successful completion of a written test. Having failed the exam already, they approached Curley and asked for help. He offered to take the test in their place, and on the appointed day proceeded with a colleague to the Federal Building in downtown Boston. The two impostors signed in as Hughes and Fahey and took the test. The deception failed; the two men were even seen copying each other's answers. Within a year the imposters were tried and convicted of attempting to defraud the U.S. government. After a long appeal, they were each sentenced to two months in jail.

The conviction might have ruined Curley's political career. Many Bostonians were outraged. Leaders of the local Democratic party organization were embarrassed and withdrew all support for him. But instead of trying to sweep the incident under the rug and quitting public life, Curley embraced it. Curley ran for reelection while the appeal was pending, brazenly declaring that he "did it for a friend" who needed a good job to support his wife and children. After all, civil service tests, he and others argued, were simply roadblocks erected by wealthy Yankees to keep poor immigrants from getting good jobs with the government. The pitch worked and Curley was reelected. The following year, he won a seat on the board of aldermen while serving his prison term, finishing fifth among the thirteen successful candidates in a citywide race. His success was at least partly attributable to the publicity he earned from the civil service case and the outrageous novelty of a political campaign conducted from a jail cell.

This experience taught Curley an important lesson. He could win support by cultivating ethnic resentment. In Boston, a city where Irish immigrants and their descendants made up more than half the population and where other immigrant groups were arriving rapidly, the arousal of a collective sense of ethnic grievance through mass publicity was an effective political strategy. Curley based his political career on this approach. But he did more than simply exploit existing grievances; he was able to rewrite the city's history in a way that redefined what it meant to be Irish in Boston.

Curley's approach was successful because of changes in American politics sparked by progressive reform. Progressivism, a loose term encompassing a broad and varied array of reform activity, reflected a growing concern about the consequences of rapid industrialization, urbanization, and immigration. An important part of this reform surge centered on politics. Dissatisfied with the corruption and inefficiency that plagued party politics in this era, reformers campaigned to restructure American public life. They sought to eliminate the party machines that used government jobs and services as rewards for political support and replace them with professionally run bureaucracies devoted to serving the public interest. (Civil service examinations were part of this effort.) These reforms were particularly successful in Boston, where a revision of the city charter undermined the power of party organizations.

Such reforms had unintended consequences as well. The decline of parties meant the decline of neighborhood political institutions. Without these grassroots groups, politics became more media-driven as candidates and officeholders sought new ways to reach prospective voters. Instead of relying on ward-level party organizations to turn out voters, politicians used advertising and publicity to communicate directly with the public. Those candidates who could attract voters' attention most effectively stood the best chance of winning.

In Boston no politician did this better than Curley. Demonstrating an ability to shape popular perceptions that would make television-age politicians envious, he convinced the Irish Americans in Boston that they were the victims of an ongoing campaign of discrimination at the hands of the city's Yankee elite, despite the fact that they were a numerical majority and controlled the city's politics. This mind-set encouraged their collective action in local affairs, if only to battle a common enemy. Even more important for Curley, he was able to project an image of himself as the spokesman and champion of the Boston Irish, the man who would lead the battle to overthrow their "Yankee overlords." Largely as a result of his efforts, ethnic resentment in Boston intensified sharply during the early twentieth century even though Boston's immigrants—and particularly its Irish majority—now dominated the city's public life as never before.

James Michael Curley's early life offered few indications that he would become the most powerful politician in twentieth-century Boston. He was born in 1874, the son of poor Irish immigrants, at a time when no Irishman had ever served as mayor of the city and only a handful had been elected to office. Curley's family lived in Roxbury, a crowded, working-class neighborhood south of downtown Boston. His father, a laborer, died when Curley was ten; his mother scrubbed floors to keep the family afloat. Leaving school after his father's death, Curley took a succession of jobs as a newsboy, a delivery boy, a drugstore clerk, a machine operator in a piano factory, and a traveling salesman.

This firsthand struggle with poverty, which would help shape Curley's politics, was typical of the nineteenth-century Irish experience in Boston. The city was an inhospitable place for the impoverished Irish peasantry that began pouring into the city during the 1840s and continued coming at a steady clip through the rest of the nineteenth century. Almost all of these newcomers were Catholic in a city established by Puritans and with a long history of anti-Catholic violence and discrimination. Moreover, the economic elite that emerged in Boston over the first half of the nineteenth century had close commercial and cultural ties to England, Ireland's most hated enemy. The Boston Irish thus were not only poor, they found themselves in a uniquely hostile city, one where the phrase "no Irish need apply" was a common part of job advertisements.

Politics emerged as one of the few avenues of advancement open to these Irish immigrants. Whereas banking, medicine, and the upper reaches of the legal profession remained Yankee preserves through the late nineteenth century, the Irish, by virtue of their growing numbers and their almost uniform loyalty to the Democratic party, made headway in politics. In 1884 Hugh O'Brien became the first Irish mayor of Boston and by the 1890s, Irish surnames dominated the rosters of the city's Common Council and board of aldermen.

With few other options, Curley naturally gravitated to the political arena at an early age. It was a field for which he was well suited. Gregarious, sharp-witted, and endowed with a superb voice (which he had cultivated at the Staley School of the Spoken Word), he was recruited as a teenager to speak on streetcorners for local politicians. He first ran for a seat on the Common Council, representing Roxbury's Ward 17 in 1897 at the age of twenty-two. He lost that bid, as well as a second attempt the following year, because he did not have the support of either of the two rival Democratic clubs in his district. He finally earned the endorsement of one group and won, beginning a stretch of eighteen straight years in elective office.

As the beginning of Curley's career suggests, organizational support was paramount to political success. Local nominations were made by the Democratic party caucus (in Roxbury, as in the other Irish sections of Boston, the Democratic nominee was a sure winner in the general election). The caucus also selected slates of delegates to party conventions, where nominees for citywide and statewide offices were chosen. Caucuses were run by the ward committee, and the members of that committee often adjusted the rules to favor the candidate of their choice. Thus, control of the ward committee and the local caucuses provided significant advantages, and competition for this control was fierce. In 1890s Roxbury, two main factions fought for control of the Ward 17 committee, a situation typical of most of Boston's Irish districts at the time.

Curley was too ambitious to be a mere cog in someone else's machine. In 1901 he broke with the dominant faction in the ward and launched his own organization, the Tammany Club. The name was provocative. Tammany Hall was the Irish-run Democratic political machine in New York City. Over the last half of the nineteenth century it had earned a well-deserved reputation for corruption. But it was also a symbol of Irish power, and it was this connotation that Curley evoked. Both the name and the club were a success. It quickly became the leading faction in the ward, and Curley came to be viewed as the political "boss" in the district. Although he faced several sharp challenges, Curley and his organization dominated Roxbury's political life for the next decade.

From this base, Curley's political fortunes rose. Capitalizing on his growing popularity and a reputation for generosity highlighted by the civil-service-exam case, Curley won seats in the Massachusetts house of representatives, the board of aldermen, and the U.S. House of Representatives over the next ten years. Finally, in January 1914, he was elected to a four-year term as mayor of Boston, the first of four successful bids for that office over the next forty years. He would also serve a term as governor of Massachusetts in the 1930s and another term in the U.S. House of Representatives during the 1940s.

By the time Curley reached the mayor's office, politics in Boston—as in most cities during this era—had changed sharply. As early as the 1880s, reformers had campaigned to revamp the city's political structure. They argued that too much power rested in the hands of local party officials, who determined which men held office and, even more important, how city money was spent. Between 1885 and 1909, Boston implemented a series of reforms that began shifting power out of the hands of neighborhood politicians and into the hands of the mayor and appointed experts who presumably would run the city and spend its money more honestly and efficiently. Pro-reform forces also convinced the state legislature to start tinkering with the election process in the hope of weakening the power of political parties, which in Boston's case especially meant the Irish-dominated Democratic party.

The culmination of these efforts came in 1909 when the state legislature rewrote the entire city charter. Under the new arrangements the power of the purse moved from the city council (which had represented neighborhood interests) to the mayor, who was supposed to spend city money to benefit the whole community. The legislature also approved drastic alterations in Boston's electoral system. It eliminated the existing process, in which each party nominated candidates for all offices, including the seventy-five local representatives on the Common Council and the twelve district-based aldermen. After charter reform, the city council shrank to one chamber with just nine members. These officials, as well as the mayor, would be elected on an at-large basis. Political parties could not officially participate in municipal elections; prospective candidates earned nominations by gathering signatures on a petition.

These institutional changes transformed Boston politics. Neighborhood-based party organizations seemed to disappear almost overnight. Without a major role to play in choosing local representatives, they lost much of their clout and much of their prominence in the city's public life. "There isn't much demand for places on the ward committee as there formerly was," one observer noted at the time; "the ward committee, as an instrument for political power, is becoming a vain and empty thing."[1]

Boston office-seekers now faced a new challenge. Since they had to run for at-large offices, they needed to be able to win voter support in every section of the city. In the past, the network of Democratic ward organizations had accomplished that task, each supplying the necessary votes from its district. In their absence, politicians needed to connect with and win over voters directly. The best way to do that was to use advertising and publicity.

Fortunately for those aspiring to municipal office, the urban press was evolving in ways that complemented the political changes of the era. Newspapers during the nineteenth century had tended to operate in one of two ways: they were either partisan or independent. Partisan papers openly sided with one or the other of the two major parties; independent papers remained neutral on partisan issues and sometimes aloof from popular concerns altogether. By the turn of the century, a new style had emerged that combined political independence with sensational reporting, entertainment, and new visual tactics. This new "yellow journalism" influenced the approach of all but the most hidebound of city dailies. It attracted a wide urban readership that included working-class immigrants, making the urban press an increasingly effective medium for public figures seeking a popular audience. But for politicians to prosper in this context, they would have to be able to create the kind of stir that attracted sensation-minded editors.

No politician in Boston—perhaps none anywhere—took better advantage of these changes than James Michael Curley. His career was marked by outrageous statements and frequent controversies, many of which were calculated to win public attention. Even after he had served his term in prison for the civil-servic-exam case, he repeatedly revived the issue to burnish his image as the friend of the downtrodden and to attract press coverage. For instance, when challenged about his criminal record by a member of the audience (probably a Curley plant) during a 1910 campaign speech, Curley quickly explained that he took the exam "for a man who had a wife and five children starving for want of food and who had not earned a dollar in many months." According to the local newspaper, "he then forgave his disturber amidst great enthusiasm."[2] Interruptions of this sort, followed by a swift rejoinder from Curley, were a staple of his public speeches. These staged clashes also revived the issue, earning him fresh publicity each time it came up.

Curley also exhibited a more sophisticated ability to shape press coverage than most of his peers. One example is an incident during his first campaign for mayor in late 1913. Word reached Curley of a Roxbury woman, Mrs. William Doane, whose husband had died just before Christmas, leaving her penniless. He gave her the money to pay for the funeral and to buy the clothes she needed, the kind of gesture that earned Curley his reputation for generosity. But he did not present the money directly to Mrs. Doane. Instead he handed it to a newspaper reporter, who in turn delivered it to her and reported the favor in his newspaper, further widening Curley's image of benevolence. Other politicians made sure their favors earned popular notice, but few demonstrated Curley's flair and consistency.

As mayor, Curley grew even more skillful at managing press coverage. Boston in Curley's day had as many as ten daily papers, some delivered in the morning, others in the evening. Many people read one of each. Curley's principal opponents were generally businesspeople rather than professional politicians and had work schedules that forced them to pursue politics at night. These "evening politicians" prepared their public statements late in the day for consumption in the next morning's papers. Curley was a full-time politician and acutely aware of the need to mold public opinion. He made sure he responded to morning-edition attacks in time for the afternoon paper. Boston's newspaper readers often had his counterattack in hand even before they had encountered his opponents' charges. Meanwhile, Curley's salvos went unanswered until the next day, giving them time to settle in the public mind. With such tactics, he adroitly shaped popular perceptions on the key questions of municipal affairs.

Reaching a mass audience was one thing, but winning citizens' support was another. To do so, Curley needed to give the public a reason to vote for him. He did so by presenting Boston's public life as a pitched battle between the city's Yankee elite, often described as Brahmins, and its Irish community and by making himself the leader of the Irish in that contest. In his telling, this small group of wealthy, cranky Yankees was conspiring to deny the Irish the power they deserved as a majority in the city. These Yankee efforts to put down the Irish were part of a larger historical pattern and required Boston's Irish to unite and rise up against their oppressors. The best way to overcome the oppressor was, of course, to vote for Curley.

Curley's version of Boston's social and political history was not merely a fabrication. Numerous vicious attacks on Irish-Catholic immigrants had occurred during the nineteenth century. In 1834, a mob attacked a Catholic convent just outside the city and burnt it to the ground. During the 1850s, the strongly anti-immigrant American (or "Know Nothing") party flourished in and around Boston, spurred on by the flood of immigration that followed the potato famine in Ireland. Even as late as the 1880s and 1890s, opponents of Irish power had successfully worked to defeat the city's first Irish mayor and remove all of the Catholic members from the Boston school committee. Curley often cited these and other aspects of Boston's conflict-ridden ethnic history to buttress his depiction of present-day ethnic relations in the city.

Nevertheless, Curley provided a distorted view of both the present and the past. Although the Brahmin presence in local public life remained significant, it paled in comparison to Irish activity. Boston's largest immigrant group dominated city politics, overrunning whatever prejudice stood in its way. Irish-American politicians made up most of the city council, both before and after the city charter change, and more often than not, the mayor was also of Irish descent. Granted, Irish economic power lagged behind its political authority, but the collective fortunes of the Irish in Boston were not in quite as dire shape as Curley suggested. Moreover, he focused his animosity on a supposed clique of resentful, wealthy Brahmins who were using their economic and social power to deprive the Irish of power. Yet many of the members of this group had been staunch defenders of Irish civil rights during earlier ethnic controversies. The most powerful source of anti-Irish activism in nineteenth-century Boston had not been the city's elite but working-class Protestants, those who had competed directly with Irish Catholics for social and economic advantage. The Irish prevailed in this competition, as they did in local politics, and Curley might easily have presented himself as the representative of a triumphant group poised to inherit the reins of civic power in one of the nation's oldest and most important cities.

But the politics of ethnic resentment worked better as a tool for mobilizing and uniting his supporters, and Curley used it to great effect. Group identities are rooted in history and memory, as Curley was keenly aware, so he focused much of his rhetorical energy on Boston's past. This strategy allowed him to paint twentieth-century Brahmins as the latest in a long line of elitist oppressors that stretched back to old England as well as to early New England. This depiction of an ongoing conspiracy created a common enemy that required unified opposition. It also implied that the Boston Irish were a victimized group, a self-understanding that would persist well beyond the opening decades of the century. That one man could have so great an impact on the identity of a specific social group is testimony to the importance of the political changes of that era and to his talent for manipulating public discourse.

Sometimes Curley's revision of New England history took a humorous turn. Miles Standish, he once declared, was an Irish mercenary hired by the Pilgrims "to do their fighting for them." In Curley's account, Samuel Adams and his raiding party had prepared to dump tea in Boston harbor by consuming ale at an Irishman's saloon. And according to him, the real beginning of the American Revolution did not occur in Lexington and Concord but in New Hampshire several months before, when an Irishman led a raid on a British munitions supply. Though tongue-in-cheek, these rhetorical jabs mattered. They undermined popular respect for the city's Yankee past and helped explain why the Irish triumph over a hostile Yankee Boston was celebrated.[3]

Curley's fullest and most denigrating depiction of Boston's Anglo-elite came in 1916, midway through his first term as mayor. He offered it in response to a 1916 speech by Brahmin reformer John F. Moors that lamented the growing political dominance of the Irish and the corresponding decline of Yankees in civic affairs. Describing the original Irish immigrants as "mostly peasants" whose descendants now ruled the city, Moors complained that "not a rich man's son under forty years of age today is taking an important part in the political life of this city."[4]

Moors's remarks gave Curley the perfect opportunity to unleash one of his patented diatribes against the city's Anglo-elite, who were conspiring to defy the Irish quest for power and legitimacy. Drawing on one of the main currents of social thought during the Progressive Era, he framed his indictment in evolutionary terms. Moors was "a pathetic figure of a perishing people who seek by dollars and denunciations to evade the inexorable and inevitable law of the survival of the fittest"; a member of "a strange and stupid race, the Anglo-Saxon beaten in a fair, stand-up fight, he seeks by political chicanery and hypocrisy to gain the ends he lost in battle, and this temperamental peculiarity he calls fair play."[5]

Not only were Boston's Brahmins hypocritical, they were anti-democratic. Curley mocked Moors for lamenting Irish political dominance in a predominantly Irish city: "How absurdly American this was, the majority daring to rule the minority; but that is one of the peculiarities of the American system so different from the Anglo Saxon system of the man doffing his hat and pulling his forelock to his masters and betters."

Once again, there was historical precedent for this kind of elitist hypocrisy, according to Curley. The colonial era was not filled with heroic figures despite the accounts of history books; it was a time "when the traders in rum, salt cod and slaves were engaged with the New England Historical Genealogical Society in fabricating family histories." From his perspective, the rise of the immigrant

Irish was Boston's redemption, a democratic tide that washed away the city's hierarchical, hypocritical past. Paraphrasing Boston's William Cardinal O'Connell, Curley proclaimed: "The Puritan is passed; the Anglo Saxon is a joke; a newer and better America is here."

Curley was not finished yet. Moors had made his remarks to the Women's Department of the National Civic Federation, a fact Curley used to depict Boston's Yankee leaders as effeminate and thus ineffective men. Moors and his Brahmin supporters became "clubs of female faddists, old gentlemen with disordered livers, or pessimists croaking over imaginary good old days and ignoring the sunlit present." Boston needed "men and mothers of men," Curley proclaimed, "not gabbing spinsters and dog-raising matrons in federation assembled." By contrast, Irish rule in Boston promised the leadership of a "virile, intelligent, God-fearing, patriotic people." This image of a snobbish, effeminate group of Yankees wringing their hands over growing Irish power became a central piece of Boston folklore in the twentieth century.

Curley emerged from this historical context as the leader of the Irish effort to overthrow Yankee rule. He was, as he later explained in his autobiography, "the tribal chieftain who led the invading Irish" in their battle against "State Street carpet-baggers and Boston Bourbons." The "Brahmins" were "the Back Bay and Beacon Hill Hatfields who, around the turn of the century, became embroiled in a picturesque struggle with the Irish McCoys." Boston's Brahmins, the book went on to explain triumphantly, "were and are . . . the top, homogenized members of the Yankee overlords who, after repelling the British twice, during the Revolution and the War of 1812, were conquered by a horde of invading Irish." Curley, of course, was at the head of that invasion.[6]

During his first term as mayor, Curley worked assiduously to craft his image in this context, as the voice and symbol of an ascendant Irish Boston. Perhaps his most audacious act was the construction of an elaborate home for himself and his family in the fashionable Jamaica Plain section of Boston. Curley orchestrated an ethnic controversy around it, probably to distract public attention from the fact that he had persuaded contractors to build the house for free in exchange for lucrative city contracts. He planted a phony letter in the *Boston Post*, the leading paper among the city's Irish working class, supposedly from an indignant Yankee neighbor complaining about the shamrocks Curley had carved into the shutters of his new home. The pretense allowed Curley to engage in some amusing Yankee bashing. At a Roxbury rally he declared that "the shamrocks are here to stay" and that the neighbor could "close his shutters" or "wear a blindfold" if he didn't want to see them. He added that he had begun construction of the house on St. Patrick's Day "and didn't do it by accident either." Although the manufacturing of this incident was exposed a few days later, it allowed Curley to portray himself as the embodiment of an Irish Boston proudly fighting the slurs and deprecations of haughty Yankees.[7]

There was more than rhetoric to Curley's claim that he represented Irish Boston. He reinforced his claim to this role by delivering services and benefits to his constituents. As often as possible he did so directly, arranging jobs, and personally providing services to individual supporters. But he had neither the time nor the resources to cater to the entire city or even its large Irish population. To win collective support, he spent large sums of city money in a fashion that benefited Boston's working-class, ethnic majority.

Here too, Curley benefited from the political changes of the Progressive Era. Prior to charter reform in Boston, city spending was initiated by neighborhood representatives serving on the city council, who naturally made sure that substantial amounts were directed to their districts. In the hopes of curtailing the logrolling this system encouraged, the architects of the 1909 city charter not only eliminated district representation, they also placed the responsibility for determining the city budget in the mayor's hands. The city council's role was simply to approve or reject the budget submitted by the mayor.

When Curley assumed office, he used this power to direct city spending in ways that would benefit ethnic Boston, especially its Irish districts. Charlestown, South Boston, Roxbury, Dorchester, and other Irish neighborhoods received numerous improvements under Curley's leadership. Meanwhile, predominantly Yankee sections and the downtown business district earned far less attention and support. These spending priorities concretely demonstrated his allegiance to the city's Irish community. Curley also advocated policies and projects that served the interest of the city's ethnic working class, including the construction of a city hospital, increased benefits for city laborers, and social welfare programs to assist the poor.

Complaints about Curley's policies and the money they cost only fueled the resentment he cultivated. When some of the city's businesspeople successfully pressured the city council to veto Curley's budgets, which they thought were extravagant and wasteful, he was able to represent these efforts as yet another example of the anti-Irish machinations of Brahmin Boston. This tactic also insulated him from increasingly frequent charges of corruption and inefficiency, which came to be seen as merely the latest episodes in the long-running efforts of Yankee Boston to undermine Irish power.

The primary critic of Curley and his mayoral policies was the Good Government Association (GGA), a municipal reform group launched by local business leaders in 1903. Although it had endorsed Irish candidates in the past, it came to be seen as anti-Irish when it criticized Curley, a reputation it found difficult to counter because its executive committee, which determined its policies, did not include any Irish Americans. By 1915, the GGA had had enough of Curley, who, it charged, was padding the city payrolls with his supporters, spending beyond the means of the city, and illegally favoring some city contractors over others. The GGA endorsed city council candidates pledged to oppose him. For a time it succeeded: the GGA endorsees on the council vetoed his spending proposals, and the association persuaded the state legislature to deny him the power to borrow additional money.

Initially Curley sent subtle signals that such opposition was inspired by ethnic prejudice. When the GGA led efforts to deny Curley the power to gain a $500,000 loan for street repairs, he responded by threatening to cut off power to the Back Bay, a wealthy Yankee section of the city. The implication, of course, was that the GGA represented the interests of that part of Boston but not the interests of its ethnic districts. In another instance, Curley charged that the GGA represented "wealth, refinement, and corruption," code words that his supporters by now clearly recognized as a reference to Brahmin Boston.[8]

As the clash between Curley and the GGA escalated, his rhetoric grew more direct. When Curley ran for reelection in late 1917, the GGA mobilized against him, endorsing a wealthy Yankee candidate, Andrew Peters, instead. Charging Curley with wasteful and dishonest spending that not only damaged the city but took resources away from the American effort in World War I, the association presented Curley as a massively corrupt political boss. Curley responded by characterizing the GGA campaign as an attack on the city's Irish. A Curley ad in *The Hibernian*, a local Irish-American weekly, described the contest as "a fight between the Irish and anti-Irish forces" and urged "every red-blooded son of the race" to back Curley. "The Peters Issue Is—Down with the Irish," it read; "The Good Government Issue Is—Down with the Irish." "A vote for Peters," the ad concluded, "is a vote for the anti-Catholic, anti-Irish combination."[9] He also compared his opposition to the American Protective Association, an anti-Catholic, anti-immigrant group that campaigned against Irish power in late-nineteenth-century Boston. GGA opposition to Curley thus became the latest manifestation of the Brahmin campaign to block the Irish ascent to power. Even two decades into the twentieth century, when the Irish had clearly established themselves as the numerical and political majority of the city, Curley argued that they remained threatened by Yankee prejudice and discrimination.

These claims proved politically effective over the long run, ensuring Curley a solid block of Irish votes in every local contest. Although Curley lost the 1917 mayoral election when two other Irish candidates cut into his vote, he recaptured the mayor's office in 1921. In that election, he carried a substantial majority of the Irish vote even though the GGA nominated an Irish politician to oppose him. In ensuing years, he could count on strong support in the Irish quarters of the city, particularly in working-class Irish districts, where his depiction of Boston's character proved a persuasive explanation of the hardships they experienced in an economically stagnant city. Curley's exploitation of ethnic resentments also made him popular in Boston's substantial Italian and Jewish communities, but never to the degree evident in Irish Boston.

Perhaps the best measure of the support Curley earned was his own career. He used the loyalty of blue-collar Irish Boston to win two more terms as mayor, another in Congress, and even a term as governor of Massachusetts during the Great Depression. (He also served another term in jail, this time for mail fraud.) Although his power had slipped somewhat by the middle of the twentieth century, he remained a potent figure in Boston public life right up to his death in 1958.

Yet the electoral consequences of Curley's appeal were less significant than the power it had in defining the Irish place in Boston. He convinced most members of the city's largest ethnic group that they were victims of ethnic oppression, a perspective that would endure well beyond the Progressive Era. Even as late as the 1940s, after several decades of Irish rule, this siege mentality persisted. When the African-American population in Boston began to grow during World War II, one city councilman still insisted that the Irish were the true "minority race" in Boston, a perspective that pervaded the city's response to civil rights efforts during the second half of the twentieth century.[10] Such comments succinctly expressed the perception of the Boston Irish that Curley had fostered: They were the one and only oppressed group in Boston. No others need apply.

By most accounts, this mentality and the identity that flowed from it had their roots in Irish social experiences in nineteenth-century Boston. They were also the product of the emergence of a modern, media-driven political culture and, in particular, of the efforts of one man—testimony to the power of individual leaders to shape social relations and communal identities in the public life of twentieth-century America.

The origins of this mentality also show that ethnic identities are not primordial. They are not simply fixed attributes based on blood ties stretching back many centuries. Rather they are fluid, shifting social phenomena whose meaning and boundaries change in response to political and social circumstances. The identity of the twentieth-century Boston Irish was not entirely new, but what it meant to be Irish in Boston was significantly different in 1920 than in 1880. More important, the sense of victimization that defined the Boston Irish was not inevitable. A story of progress and political success might also have provided a plausible context through which the Irish could have understood their place in Boston. But political changes, and the manner in which James Michael Curley capitalized on them, made the more resentful perspective dominant.

Here lies the central irony of Curley's political success. Political changes that at first glance appeared to undermine the local, tribal nature of American society had the opposite effect, at least in Boston. The emergence of a mass-media-based politics and the centralization of municipal authority made it possible for an ethnic demagogue such as Curley to triumph. As a result, ethnic conflict intensified instead of lessening, as most modernization scenarios would predict. In an era when group allegiances seem to matter more than ever, the story of Curley and the Boston Irish shows the importance of considering the connections between the development of a modern political order and the persistent power of ethnic identities.

Notes

1. *Charlestown Enterprise,* September 9, 1911.

2. *South Boston Gazette,* September 24, 1910.

3. Jack Beatty, *The Rascal King: The Life and Times of James Michael Curley, 1874–1958* (Reading, MA: Addison-Wesley, 1992), 168.

4. Ibid., 169.

5. For the quotations presented in this and the following three paragraphs, see the *Boston Journal* clipping (n.d.) in James Michael Curley Scrapbooks, vol. A-1, Boston Public Library.

6. James Michael Curley, *I'd Do It Again: A Record of All My Uproarious Years* (Englewood Cliffs, NJ: Prentice-Hall, 1957), 1–2.

7. *Boston Post,* December 14, 1915; clipping from the Records of the Good Government Association, Candidate Files, James Michael Curley File, box C.2, file 2, Massachusetts Historical Society, Boston.

8. *Boston Advertiser,* May 18, 1915; clipping from the Records of the Good Government Association, Scrapbooks, vol. 14, Massachusetts Historical Society, Boston.

9. *The Hibernian,* December 13, 1917; clipping from the Martin Lomasney Scrapbooks, vol. 26, Massachusetts Historical Society, Boston.

10. John F. Stack Jr., *International Conflict in an American City: Boston's Irish, Italians, and Jews, 1935–1944* (Westport, CT.: Greenwood Press, 1979), 140.

Suggested Readings

Jack Beatty, *The Rascal King: The Life and Times of James Michael Curley, 1874–1958* (Reading, MA: Addison Wesley, 1992), reviews Curley's life and career. Curley told his own story in James Michael Curley, *I'd Do It Again: A Record of All My Uproarious Years* (Englewood Cliffs, NJ: Prentice-Hall, 1957). The place of the Irish in Boston politics is recounted in Thomas O'Connor, *The Boston Irish: A Political History* (Boston: Northeastern University Press, 1995).

James J. Connolly, *The Triumph of Ethnic Progressivism: Urban Political Culture in Boston, 1900–1925* (Cambridge, MA: Harvard University Press, 1998), examines politics in the Hub at the turn of the century. Insightful analyses of Progressive Era politics are offered by John D. Buenker, *Urban Liberalism and Progressive Reform* (New York: W. W. Norton, 1973); Richard L. McCormick, *From Realignment to Reform: Political Change in New York State, 1893–1910* (Ithaca, NY: Cornell University Press, 1981); Michael E. McGerr, *The Decline of Popular Politics: The American North, 1865–1928* (New York: Oxford University Press, 1986); and Thomas R. Pegram, *Partisans and Progressives: Private Interest and Public Policy in Illinois, 1870–1922* (Chicago: University of Illinois Press, 1992).

11

Hiram Johnson and the Dilemmas of California Progressivism

Philip VanderMeer

Politics can be a rough sport, especially if your father is a well-positioned adversary. This is the situation that Hiram Johnson faced when he challenged the status quo in California, where his father was a member of the old-guard wing of the Republican party. Philip Vander-Meer, a political historian, reviews the life of this complex politician whose career illuminates the contradictions of the "progressive move-ment." To Johnson, progressivism meant the eradication of political cor-ruption, boss rule, and the influence of the Southern Pacific Railroad in politics.

Johnson was an adept politician who learned how to attract voters, who elevated him to the governorship in 1910. Under his tutelage, law-makers adopted a battery of reform measures in 1911 and in 1913. Johnson's program and his lobbying among lawmakers to pass the leg-islation represented the new level of gubernatorial leadership that was characteristic of the Progressive Era. His independent style also reflect-ed the rise of autonomous election campaigns in which candidates relied more on their own organizations than on a political party. Later in his career, when he had entered the U.S. Senate, Johnson retreated from his insurgency and accepted support from old-guard Republicans. By this time he had softened his earlier critique of wealth and became consumed with blocking U.S. military intervention abroad. Professor VanderMeer sees the twists and turns in Johnson's career as emblem-atic of progressivism generally.

Philip VanderMeer is associate professor of history at Arizona State University, where he teaches late-nineteenth- and early-twentieth-century American history. He is the author of *Hoosier Politicians: Politi-cal Culture and Officeholding in Indiana, 1896–1920* (1985) and coeditor of *Belief and Behavior: Essays in the New Religious History* (1991). His articles include "Congressional Decision-Making and World War I: A Case Study of Illinois Congressional Opponents," in *Congressional Studies* 8 (1981) and "Congress and Other Legislatures" in *The Encyclopedia of the American Legislative System* (1994).

Hiram Johnson dominated California politics for over a genera-tion. He was a clever political strategist and an outstanding orator, and his actions and policies inspired both ardent devotion and intense dislike. As governor (1911–1917) he led the progressive forces in an increasingly important state. In 1917 he moved to the U.S. Senate, where he served until his death in 1945, making his tenure in the upper house one of the longest on record. He began his career as an ardent progressive and finished in the company of conservative isolationists. He was also the first of many California contenders for the presidency. Besides its unique aspects, Johnson's early career also resembles those of other progressive politicians. His sudden election as governor of a major state, the success and prominence of his program, the power of his oratory, his combative spirit and driving ambition, mirror traits of men such as Woodrow Wilson, Theodore Roosevelt, and Robert LaFollette. Thus, although most of Johnson's senatorial career goes beyond the Progressive Era and, hence, the time frame of this essay, examining his activities during the early twentieth century illuminates both the immediate influences on his life and career—the reputation and behavior of his father, the conflict between integrity and ambition, and the dynamics of California politics—and the broader challenges of defining progressive policies, coalition building and third-party politics, and the difficulties of maintaining reform movements.

Hiram was the second son of a volatile, irascible, and domineering father whose style, shady reputation, political prominence and affiliations, and position on political issues significantly shaped the early stages of Hiram's life and career. Grove Johnson was born in 1841 in Syracuse, New York, where he became a lawyer and school board member. Indicted in 1863 for falsifying endorsements on two promissory notes, he fled to the West and in 1865 moved to Sacramento. Although he quickly repaid the Syracuse debts, he continued to behave unscrupulously: in 1867 he falsified voter registration lists, and in his 1871 bid for state senate, which he lost, he was charged with producing counterfeit ballots that used disappearing and invisible inks. In an era of party loyalty, Grove was also criticized for switching to the Democratic party in 1871 and back to the GOP in 1877. Yet his ability was recognized by both parties; as a Democrat he served on the state party committee and was twice nominated for the state senate; as a Republican he was elected to the state legislature in 1877 and 1879, and during the 1880s he regularly served on the platform committee of Republican state conventions. During the latter decade he did not seek elective office. Instead, he focused on developing his legal practice, which he did successfully, for he was shrewd, highly articulate, and had an excellent memory. He was also aggressive, quick tempered, and sarcastic, and he could be amazingly vituperative.

Hiram was born in 1866 in Sacramento, and his education in Sacramento schools and at home was focused on the memorization of literary passages and oratory, which he practiced as class valedictorian. After graduating from high school in 1882, Hiram worked in his father's law office, learning shorthand reporting until he began attending the University of California in 1884. His promising academic career was cut short and his life changed, however, when he married his pregnant girlfriend in 1887. Moving next door to her parents in a house built by her father, Hiram worked as a stenographer and studied law with his father. Admitted to the bar in 1888, he joined his father and brother, Albert, in a law firm that was successful but doomed to dissolution.

Grove's domineering and inflammatory personality provided the general conditions for this family breakup, but his political beliefs and his revived pursuit of elective office, beginning with an unsuccessful bid for Congress in 1892, were the specific causes. In 1893, Albert left the firm and abandoned his father's politics. In 1894, Grove ran again, and in his successful campaign he criticized the Southern Pacific Railroad. The SP, as it was called, owned millions of acres, was the largest single employer in the state and connected with innumerable other economic interests, and was a very powerful and pernicious political force within California. Politically active from its origins as part of the first transcontinental railroad, in 1893 the SP began operating through the Southern Pacific Railroad Political Bureau to dominate the Republican party and, through bribery and coercion, to obtain further economic opportunities from the legislature and throughout the state.

Grove's criticism of the SP was legitimate but misleading, for he had been and would soon again be closely allied with the politically powerful railroad. Having chastised his predecessor for supporting a generous refinancing of SP's debt, Grove defended an even more generous measure in 1895. Defeated for reelection in 1896 and denounced by William Randolph Hearst's San Francisco *Examiner,* Grove responded with a vicious personal attack on Hearst that reveals his style and perspective: "We knew him to be a debauch, a dude in dress, an Anglomaniac in language and manners, but we thought he was honest. We knew him to be licentious in his tastes, regal in his dissipations, unfit to associate with pure women or decent men, but we thought 'Our Willie' was honest." A "blackmailer" and "tatooed with sin," he was "ungrateful to his friends, unkind to his employees, [and] unfaithful to his business associates."[1]

Hiram campaigned for his father in 1892 and 1894, but differences appeared by 1896, when he still supported Grove but did not campaign for him. After the election he, too, left his father's law firm and politics. This breakup began nearly fifteen years of intense political and personal conflict between the two—what various historians have described as "bitter enmity" or "loathing." Grove became one of the most influential old-guard Republican leaders, serving in the California State Assembly from 1898 to 1904 and from 1906 to 1910, chairing major committees, and acting as one of the main political agents and defenders of the SP. Hiram increasingly opposed bossism, the old guard, and the SP—all closely identified with his father—and at crucial moments in his political and professional career he was confronted by his father's activities or reputation. Most important, in contrast with his father's shady reputation, Hiram earnestly pursued the reality and image of integrity.

In 1899, Hiram and Albert campaigned for George Clark, a reform mayoral candidate in Sacramento. After the defeated incumbent refused to leave his office on a technicality and Hiram appealed successfully to the California State Supreme Court, Clark appointed him city attorney. In 1901, Clark ran as an independent, provoking a direct political conflict between Hiram and Albert, who managed Clark's campaign, and Grove, who supported the machine. Hiram spoke frequently and passionately against "boss rule"; Grove announced that "the head of the Johnson family is still out for the Republican ticket. Children make mistakes; the old man never does!"[2] The reformers won handily, but the following year, when they competed for the Republican state convention, the organization marshaled its resources. Hiram angrily denounced involvement by the SP, but Grove and the regulars were easily victorious.

Hiram and Albert then moved to San Francisco, where their law firm was immediately successful. As a skilled researcher, Albert initially helped, but he was losing a battle with alcoholism and died in 1906. Hiram was invigorated by the opportunities in San Francisco and soon became one of its most prominent attorneys. In court he spoke quickly and used few notes, relying on his memory and his ability to extemporize. Like other successful lawyers of the era, he relied more on emotional appeals than on detailed analysis of the law. Like his father, Johnson could scathingly denounce persons he opposed. He sometimes shouted at witnesses, challenged persons or accepted challenges to fight, and on two occasions even struck an opposing attorney in court. His theatrical and emotional style, added to his mastery of detail, won him numerous verdicts and popular attention.

Johnson's prominence increased when the San Francisco district attorney, William Langdon, hired him as a special prosecutor for several cases in 1906, most significantly the San Francisco corruption trials. For the previous half-century, San Francisco politics had been tumultuous and infused with the charges and reality of corruption. The "Blind Boss" of the 1880s, Christopher Buckley, was ousted by reform Democrats and was eventually followed by the leader of Democratic reform, Mayor James Phelan. After several effective terms, a bitter strike in 1901 seriously damaged Phelan's reputation and weakened the party's relationship with labor. In the resulting political chaos, Abraham Ruef moved adeptly to transform San Francisco politics and create major opportunities for himself as a behind-the-scenes boss. He orchestrated the creation of a new, municipal party, the Union Labor party, and selected as its mayoral candidate Eugene Schmitz, who was the leader of the musicians' union and concertmaster of a local orchestra. Ruef, Schmitz, and members of the San Francisco City Council Board of Supervisors then solicited and accepted bribes on an outrageous scale.[3]

Public outcry led to the hiring of a special prosecutor, Francis J. Heney, who had successfully prosecuted grafters in Oregon. Johnson was hired as an assistant, helping with the grand jury, preparing cases, and delivering the opening and closing statements in the Schmitz trial. Schmitz was convicted, but Johnson resigned in October 1907 because of friction with Heney. A year later, after Heney was seriously wounded in an assassination attempt, Johnson rejoined the effort and secured the conviction of Ruef. In this case, as in the Schmitz trial, observers remarked on the savage nature of his summation.

Despite these convictions, the graft prosecutions lost public support, partly because labor unions and the Union Labor party felt unfairly assaulted and also because business owners lost interest when prosecutors began focusing on bribe payers. The prosecutions effectively ended in 1909 when Heney, who had recovered from his wound, lost the race for district attorney. For Johnson, the graft trials brought fame and demonstrated the dangers of corporate power; for California they further fueled the rise of the progressive movement.

Progressivism in California, as elsewhere in the nation, involved diverse sources, support, and issues. Such diversity has sometimes led historians to question whether the term has any central meaning or if it should be abandoned. But participants during this period, certainly in California, used it regularly to describe others and as a means of self-identification. Thus, in a specifically political context it is helpful and even necessary. Talking about progressives can also be confusing because the label has been applied simultaneously to an array of political actors: public officials, political action groups, leaders, and voters. The problem is compounded by examining the movement over time, for ideas about policies and the relationships between individuals and factions changed.

Despite these difficulties, it is clear that initially there was an identifiable group of California progressives and that Hiram Johnson was the central figure—as governor and senator, as a leader of the Lincoln-Roosevelt League, and as a spokesman for progressive issues and values. Like his progressive supporters and colleagues, Johnson supported various causes, but he started with a core belief in an active and selfless public that was threatened by political corruption and, more generally, by the growing economic and political power of corporations. Like many progressives, Johnson perceived himself in a struggle between the people and concentrated wealth, between good and evil. Like many other progressives, such as Theodore Roosevelt and Robert LaFollette, Johnson talked frequently and explicitly about fighting, mixing the character trait of determination with the physical activity of boxing; he described himself as a fighter and posed with his fists clenched. Mere politicians might seek compromise, but Johnson and progressives fought for truth.

Progressivism in California, as in many other states, grew out of earlier, urban protest movements. The graft prosecutions in San Francisco followed a reform movement of the 1890s, which had taken organized form in the Committee of One Hundred and had produced a new city charter. In Los Angeles, reform efforts also began in the 1890s with the Direct Legislation League, the League for Better Government, and the Committee of Safety, which uncovered a network of graft and corruption. In 1902 reform groups coalesced into the Municipal League of Los Angeles and obtained a new city charter in 1903. Reformers expanded their efforts to control government more directly in 1906 by organizing the Non-Partisan Committee of One Hundred; in the municipal elections of that year they won most city offices.

The initial core of the state's progressive movement was the Lincoln-Roosevelt League. Building on the municipal reform movements, it was first organized by Edward Dickson, an editor at the Los Angeles *Express,* and Chester Rowell, editor of the Fresno *Republican,* who were upset by the manipulation and corruption at the 1907 session of the state legislature (symbolized by the presence of Boss Ruef on the floor of the legislature). A meeting in August 1907 brought together thirty-eight men who called their organization the League of Lincoln-Roosevelt Republican Clubs. George Mowry, the first scholar of California progressivism, described this group as being urban, old-stock Americans, middle and upper-middle class, primarily lawyers and journalists, antimonopolists and critical of both corporations and unions, individualists who feared class conflict and class consciousness. However, as both Mowry and subsequent historians noted, the initial group included a range of interests, and this diversity increased with the success of the movement.

And the movement was quickly successful. Starting with victories in several 1907 local elections, in 1908 it elected a surprising number of delegates to the Republican state convention, and numerous state legislators. When the new legislature met, the Lincoln-Roosevelt League lobbied successfully for stronger railroad regula-·tion. In addition, Johnson, who was vice president of the league, was the spokesman for a direct primary bill. This role brought him into direct conflict with his father, who chaired the Judiciary Committee of the lower house and denounced primaries as "wicked innovations." Although Hiram's bill was defeated, the legislature did enact a primary for all state offices, a measure that would have major consequences for state politics and for Johnson.

The Lincoln-Roosevelt League approached the new primary in 1910 with a keen recognition that beating the SP and the old guard would take careful planning and great activity. They chose a full slate of candidates but focused especially on picking someone to run for governor, a wise decision, since previous governors had actively thwarted reform efforts. After considering several possibilities, especially Francis Heney, in February they settled on Hiram Johnson and overcame his initial resistance. Johnson was an excellent choice because of his reputation and public visibility, his strengths as a public speaker, and, as became increasingly apparent, his abilities as a perceptive political strategist. More than anyone else, Johnson realized that the primary system made it essential to cultivate the new nominating power—the voters—so he started early and worked at it harder. Initially, Johnson campaigned with other Lincoln-Roosevelt League candidates, but he grew frustrated with the league's poor organization and felt that the other candidates (including his running mate) were boring speakers. As a result, he set up his own personal organization and toured the state in a red Locomobile. For each stop, his staff arranged advance publicity and identified the prominent persons; in smaller towns he attracted a crowd with his car and a cowbell. Campaigning almost nonstop from March until August, Johnson delivered over six hundred speeches and some days spoke up to 15 times. He was well suited for such a campaign, for he was an excellent stump speaker. Dramatic, passionate, and full of moral fervor but also entertaining, he studiously and effectively gauged the temper and mood of his audiences.

From the first, Johnson presented himself unequivocally as a progressive Republican. Privately he complained that President Taft spoke only of dollars and not people, and publicly he claimed affinity with Theodore Roosevelt and Robert LaFollette. Whether consciously or not, he also imitated Roosevelt's speaking style, gestures, and language ("bully"). More specifically, he announced, "I am going to make this fight in an endeavor to return the government of California to the people and take it away from the political bureau of the Southern Pacific Company."[4] Johnson persisted with this specific approach throughout the campaign. Although sometimes he also mentioned electoral reforms, the focus of his message remained narrow and consistent: elect Hiram Johnson and oust the SP from control of California government. This strategy had certain advantages. It allowed him to criticize the power and wealth of an unpopular corporation while identifying himself with the people and a defense of democracy. This approach was both emotionally satisfying and popular. It was also a straightforward message that represented his intentions on becoming governor and that was helpful after he was elected.

Of course, reality was more complex than Johnson or other progressives suggested. The SP was wealthy and wielded considerable political power: it bribed legislators and municipal officials, and it resisted efforts to reduce its rates. However, it had less influence than Johnson and others contended, shown partly by the 1909 legislation that strengthened rate regulation. Second, opponents of the SP included other, powerful economic interests—shipping and manufacturing firms, large ranchers and farmers, and newspapers. Johnson's campaign, particularly in traveling to rural areas of the state, clearly recognized this fact and sought the support of these interests.

Johnson's approach also brought him into conflict with his father, still a prominent supporter of the railroad. Grove even threatened to campaign directly against his son, which would have been painful and awkward, since Hiram always refused to criticize his father publicly. Amazingly, the Los Angeles *Times* argued that Hiram was falsely critical of the SP and that he was still controlled by his father. Nothing could have infuriated Johnson more than attacks on his integrity, on the central plank of his platform, and on his relationship with his father. Hiram responded with a vicious denunciation of the publisher, Harrison Gray Otis, that was reminiscent of his father's early attack on Hearst: "He sits in senile dementia, with gangrened heart and rotting brain, grimacing at every reform, chattering impotently at all things that are decent, frothing, fuming, violently gibbering, going down to his grave in snarling infamy. . . . He is the one thing that all Californians look at, when, in looking at Southern California, they see anything that is disgraceful, depraved, corrupt, crooked and putrescent."[5]

The Lincoln-Roosevelt League's candidates, including Johnson, succeeded in the August primary, winning most nominations for statewide office, several for Congress, and many for the state legislature; in September they also won control of the Republican party. In the general-election campaign, Johnson resumed his grueling schedule, delivering hundreds of speeches throughout the state. This campaign was more difficult because his Democratic opponent, Theodore Bell, had legitimate reform credentials, having run in

1906 as a railroad critic and continuing his criticism in 1910. But Johnson did not hesitate, condemning Bell's studied moderation as weak, opportunistic, and insufficient to deal with the problem.

When the votes were counted, Johnson had beaten Bell by a convincing margin, the other Lincoln-Roosevelt League candidates were also successful, and, apparently, progressives controlled the state. In terms of drama, consequences, and perceptions at the time, this was one of California's most crucial and decisive elections. But in 1910 the results were not necessarily a reliable indicator of the future; nor for various reasons should they have been comforting to Johnson as the progressives' leader. First, Johnson had won only a plurality of the vote (45.9 percent), not a majority—partly because minor-party candidates had won nearly 15 percent. However, these candidates did as well for other state offices, whereas Republicans had won majorities in these races. Second, party affiliation best explains an individual's votes, and Johnson's strength correlates moderately well with votes for President Taft in 1908 and for other Republicans in 1910—but only moderately well. Other Republicans held Taft's 1908 voters, but Johnson's vote was lower by 15 percent in the Sacramento Valley, 10–20 percent in the Bay Area, and 10 percent in the southern counties. Finally, since other Republican winners had previously been elected to state office, it might appear that new progressives generally had less support. However, two strong progressives running in districts that covered large parts of the state received essentially the same support as Republicans who won statewide races.[6] This outcome was encouraging for progressives but less so for Johnson. He had won and on a clear platform, but his future electoral success would depend on his actions as governor. He could now feel relieved about his father, who had failed to win reelection to the legislature and, after Johnson won, resigned from the brief remainder of his legislative term. Hiram Johnson was, thus, finally freed from this embarrassment and frustration.

Immediately after the election, Johnson deepened his identification with national progressives, traveling east to visit LaFollette and Roosevelt, proclaiming himself a progressive and an "insurgent." In his inaugural address, Johnson presented as his guiding principle a belief in "the absolute sovereignty of the people" and argued that "nearly every government problem that involves the health, the happiness, or the prosperity of the state has arisen because some private interest has intervened or has sought for its own gain to exploit either the resources or the politics of the state." Thus, the theme of his address and his "first duty" was seeking "to make the public service of the state responsive solely to the people." Focusing primarily on the structure of government rather than its policies, he advocated a variety of direct-democracy measures (initiative, referendum, recall, and direct primary) and railroad regulation, as well as nonpartisan and civil service reforms. Following a pattern recently begun by other reform governors, Johnson set a tone of democratic simplicity and had no inaugural ball or parade.[7]

During his six years as governor, Johnson participated in creating much significant legislation. Assessing his role or that of any executive is difficult because the political process is often obscure and because the context for such activity—the assumptions regarding the proper role of executive and legislature as well as the nature of the political forces involved—can vary so significantly. Johnson did little to create or draft new legislative initiatives; yet within the context of his time and movement, as an executive he was clearly one of the most significant and active progressive leaders. As governor, Johnson sent special messages to the legislature to define some legislation and called special legislative sessions to obtain speedy passage. He helped select the chairs of legislative committees. More important, he actively and successfully lobbied legislators on behalf of progressive legislation and even threatened to campaign against those who opposed key measures. Finally, he campaigned vigorously to develop public support for progressive proposals.

Johnson's own legislative initiatives largely concerned matters of administration and budget, the areas traditionally accepted as a governor's responsibility. That Johnson did not draft and present other legislation certainly reflects his personality, political interests, and skills. He was not an intellectual or a political philosopher; he was, instead, a skillful and perceptive political fighter who sought to advance the goals of his movement. Moreover, progressives did not lack for policy initiatives. Thus, to evaluate Johnson as governor requires assessing his role as executive and in the legislative process, plus the diversity and change within the progressive movement.

Johnson's first concern (and that of most progressives) was railroad legislation, and he worked with the legislature to significantly strengthen railroad regulation, giving the railroad commission power to set rates, to investigate complaints about rates, and to assess the value of railroad property. A related measure, passed later in the same session, authorized the commission to regulate utilities—gas, water, electricity, telephone, and telegraph.

Second, Johnson worked to obtain passage of various measures that advanced direct democracy and reduced the influence of political party organization: the initiative, referendum, and recall, plus the direct election of senators; direct primaries for legislators; and nonpartisan elections for judges and school boards. On another political matter, women's suffrage, Johnson was silent; whether this silence was motivated by personal or political reasons is unclear, but he did not obstruct the measure and was subsequently a strong supporter. Johnson cooperated with the legislature in creating a conservation commission, providing free textbooks, establishing teachers' pensions, and reforming school curricula. Finally, Johnson won adoption for his own proposal to create the California Board of Control, which would audit state institutions and prepare a comprehensive state budget.

Two final categories of government policy appealed to different parts of the California progressive movement, the kind of diversity historians have considered fatal to a meaningful use of the term "progressive." At least during the early years of Johnson's governorship, however, these policies represented different but not divergent parts of a coalition. Progressives from the southern part of the state were more interested in legislation controlling moral behavior, matters that Johnson said little about. The legislature abolished racetrack gambling and slot machines and legalized local option voting on liquor. Legislators from the northern part of the state, especially from the Bay Area, sometimes opposed such proposals but certainly were much more supportive of various labor laws, which some southern Californians opposed. As a candidate, Johnson had said little regarding labor, and progressives had generally emphasized other issues. As governor, however, Johnson worked diligently to obtain the passage of numerous important labor laws: a workers' compensation system, regulation of child labor, requirements for payment of wages, and an eight-hour law for women workers. Johnson also balanced the interests of the pro-labor north with the (generally) anti-union south by opposing both a compulsory arbitration bill and a measure to reduce the use of court injunctions in labor disputes. In all, labor won a remarkable thirty-nine of the forty-nine measures it sought, and it responded by supporting Johnson at the polls thereafter.

The extraordinary activity and productivity of the 1911 legislature won it and Johnson national acclaim. In 1913 and especially in 1915, Johnson offered far fewer legislative recommendations, and on balance the legislature enacted less significant measures, some largely expanding or revising existing programs. These measures included the establishment of commissions for industrial accidents, for industrial welfare, and for immigration and housing. Legislation strengthened the workers' compensation system, set a minimum wage for women, and created a state water board. The political system was further changed by electing county and township officers on a nonpartisan basis, creating a merit and civil service system, and allowing candidates to cross-file in the primary, that is, to run simultaneously for the nomination in more than one party. Johnson asked primarily for a slight tax increase in corporation taxes to balance the state budget (which was passed) and for a central administrative body (which was not created). Another piece of morality legislation, an antiprostitution "red light abatement" law, was passed, again without Johnson's participation. The most memorable law passed in 1913 effectively prohibited any Japanese from owning land in California. The Wilson administration argued against it, but Johnson contended that this law merely prohibited aliens from owning land, as did laws in eight other states, and that it was U.S. law that prohibited Japanese from becoming citizens. In truth, the law was blatantly and cruelly discriminatory, but in signing it Johnson was accepting a measure that the overwhelming majority of legislators and California voters favored.

Johnson's governorship occurred in a period of enormous political turmoil that posed momentous political challenges. Although politics always involves choices—between ideology and pragmatism or even between integrity and victory—this era involved especially difficult decisions. One can understand Johnson and his behavior only by closely examining the various opportunities and dilemmas he faced. By late autumn 1911, Johnson was in an enviable position. Having presided over a dramatically successful legislature and known as a friend of Roosevelt's, he was suddenly a nationally prominent player in "insurgent" efforts to replace President Taft. An important supporter of Theodore Roosevelt at the 1912 national convention, he was outraged by Taft's theft of the GOP nomination, and he led Roosevelt delegates out of the convention. He was a major leader in the new Progressive party, serving as temporary chair to organize its convention, and as Roosevelt's vice presidential running mate he mounted a frenetic, nationwide campaign. It was, he believed, a struggle "in behalf of humanity," but he and other California progressives faced a terrible problem: having worked so long and so hard to control the GOP and thus the state, they did not wish to relinquish this control to the old "forces of greed."

Therefore, unlike progressives in most other states, the California insurgents did not formally break with the Republican party. In fact, Roosevelt was the Republican nominee on the California ballot.[8] Following their defeat, California progressives and Johnson faced difficult choices. Divisions within the progressive coalition led Johnson to request less legislation in 1913, for he perceived that "communities will stand just so much reform legislation at one time" and even felt "our legislation has brought us to the very verge of disaster."[9] Although the future of the national Progressive party seemed increasingly doubtful, Johnson's commitment to reform and his reaction to criticism from conservative Republicans about the loyalty—and essentially the integrity—of progressives remaining within the GOP finally convinced him to create the California Progressive party in December 1913.

Not all progressives agreed with this action, for reasons of sentiment and practicality. What made this decision not completely impractical was the unique opportunity progressives had created with the 1913 cross-filing law: it enabled them to run in both Progressive and Republican primaries and, in effect, to exclude conservative Republican opposition from the ballot. Nevertheless, in 1914 progressives engaged in serious internecine battles. Ideological strains and personal conflicts, Johnson's ambivalence about serving in the Senate or running again for governor, his fears of electoral failure, and his jealousy of potential rivals and his critical view of Heney led to acrimony. Although Johnson and most other progressive candidates won, Heney lost the U.S. Senate race, and he and his supporters were greatly embittered.

In 1916 the conflict between ideology and practicality became even more complicated as progressives attempted to rejoin the GOP without conceding their principles. Failing to obtain an acceptably blended slate of delegates to the Republican national convention, Johnson and other progressives attended their own party's national meeting, but Roosevelt betrayed their hopes of forcing some concessions. Furious with the former reformer now turned warrior but not completely alienated by the Republican nomination of Charles Evans Hughes, Johnson returned to California to ponder a very difficult decision. The demise of his party meant returning to a Republican party again controlled by conservatives. To prevent this outcome he could run for the Senate, but he would have to win the Republican primary, in which 300,000 progressives were ineligible to participate, against the united opposition of conservatives and without support from the Hughes camp. Ultimately, he decided to lead a crusade to retake the party. Conservatives also saw the contest in this light and even used Hughes in their efforts.

Johnson won the primary and general elections, and progressives retook the legislature and party as well, but Hughes's candidacy in California was damaged, and with this loss went the presidency. Although Johnson endorsed and spoke for Hughes, he was suspicious of him—angry at being ignored but not wanting to be vindictive. However, as he wrote to Chester Rowell in August, he had no doubts about his priorities or what was at stake: "In 1910 we kicked the Southern Pacific out of the government of California. In 1916, through Mr. Hughes, the inherited Southern Pacific millions are again [seeking] to control the State." He concluded that he could afford to lose the Senate race but asked, rhetorically, "Can I afford, can I supinely permit that which I've so consistently fought, the destruction of which has been my consuming thought politically, again to command my State?" Rather than let the old guard rule, he would accept defeat for Hughes or for himself.[10]

A final political battle involved Johnson's resistance to the succession of Lieutenant Governor William Stephens as governor until March 1917. Johnson clearly felt ambivalent about moving to Washington and was jealous of any successor, but he also had specific complaints. First, he was angry that southern California interests had forced him in July 1916 to appoint Stephens as lieutenant governor after the death of John Eshleman, whom Johnson very much respected. He disliked Stephens as being too interested in prohibition and not enough in workers. Finally, as he later explained, he considered Stephens too shallow, weak, and indecisive to advance the progressive cause.

Those feelings grew, yet Johnson did not participate in the 1918 gubernatorial contest—in part because the only challenger entered the race too late. But Johnson's inaction also reflected some keen understanding of progressives and reform. First, since Stephens had retained Johnson's appointees and continued his policies, opposition would seem simply a matter of pique, not principle. Second, nearly all the progressives held office, and they had endorsed Stephens. And as Johnson noted to a friend, these were "the sort of men" who, "after they have thus declared themselves, will not for any person change."[11] Following the primary, Johnson blamed himself and others for failing originally to select someone better than Stephens, but he also reflected philosophically on the movement, claiming that "our present position is that which comes to all reform movements. We fight gloriously. We finally win. Power comes to us, with all that power means; and then, with the weakness of human nature, loving that power, we forget that for which we fought in our love of it and our desire to retain it. It is the usual breakdown of the moral fiber of men who attain ease, and influence, and distinction, and position. The process has ever been the same."[12]

When Johnson came to Washington in March 1917, the Senate's attention was on war. Johnson supported American participation, but from the beginning he attempted to define a domestic progressive agenda on war issues, a "radical, progressive war program to which we could adhere and which might ultimately be of benefit to the movement so fastly [sic] waning and disintegrating."[13] Deeply concerned about civil liberties, he strongly opposed censorship provisions of the espionage and sedition laws. He accepted the draft as a military necessity but argued that wealth should also be conscripted. He thus wished to raise more revenue through taxes and less from bonds and to increase taxes on businesses and the wealthy. He shied away, however, from the leading advocate of such taxes, Senator LaFollette, mainly because LaFollette's antiwar views had made him quite unpopular, but also because Johnson himself disliked some of his colleague's opinions. Johnson willingly accepted government control of the communication systems and the railroads, but in 1918 he was outraged by a level of compensation to railroad companies that he considered gross overpayment. In general, Johnson emphasized the irresponsibility, selfishness, and failures of the wealthy. By early 1918 he talked fearfully of labor's reaction to inequitable policies, but by late summer he had concluded that union labor had been bought off by hours and wage concessions, which meant that "the great middle class of people" were left to "foot the bills and pay the price."[14]

But foreign policy was most important in this era, and it provided a turning point for Johnson's opportunities and his perspective on politics, policy, and his role. His anger at the subordination of domestic issues and at the power of businesses and banks fueled his concerns about America's relationship with the rest of the world. A believer in American exceptionalism and unilateral action, and skeptical of all other nations, he adamantly resisted any expansion of U.S. commitments abroad. He denounced having U.S. troops fight in Russia or guaranteeing the borders of other countries as an invitation to "world wide imperialism" and being directed by "the International Banker."[15] Wilson's view of America's role in the world fully mobilized him. Johnson had initially opposed the president on partisan grounds; he had become increasingly upset by the administration's war policies, which he felt were coercive, dictatorial, and favored business; but he became an implacable opponent of the president because of Wilson's peace plans, especially the League of Nations. Though Johnson periodically despaired of defeating the league, and against strong criticism from various friends and allies who saw its progressive aspects, he became one of the leading "irreconcilable" senators opposing the league, even trailing Wilson around the country to speak against him.

Johnson's campaign against the league intersected with his other campaign, begun in May 1919 and announced in December, for the Republican presidential nomination. He originally intended to emphasize domestic issues, but as the league debate intensified, Johnson increasingly focused on that issue. This focus brought him important backing, but it also cost him the support of many of his former progressive colleagues. He won six primaries, but as Roosevelt's experience in 1912 had shown, a handful of primary victories could not, for most Republican delegates, counterbalance party irregularity or questionable policies. But more devastating than his ultimate loss was Johnson's experience in trying to win California delegates. Anxious, hurt, and angered by the defection of former allies to a new California progressive leader, Herbert Hoover, he was horrified to learn that his own slate of delegates included many of his former enemies. "In all my political life I have never felt as I felt when I read that list. I have had just one asset, and that was, my unyielding independence. I have reached such position as I have had with the people of California because of their belief in my sincerity and my obstinacy for the right, and because they think I would never compromise with dishonesty or dishonest men." Johnson felt that the delegation's composition eliminated any slim hope of winning, but even more it "marks the beginning of a new policy on my part of compromise, intrigue, and perhaps surrender. I realize that I could justify myself . . . but I think I have ever been intellectually honest, and I will not either lie to myself or console myself with any such specious reasoning. The severest blow to my political career has now fallen upon me."[16]

In fact, Johnson continued this campaign, and his career extended another twenty-five years. Still, this campaign does mark a crucial divide in his activities and self-perception. In contrast to the positive and creative efforts of his California years, as a senator Johnson increasingly indulged what he called his "natural" bent toward individualism, criticism, and opposition. After a period of lethargy in the early 1920s, his interest in progressive concerns revived, and for a decade he supported some domestic reform measures. But by the mid-1930s his opposition to budget deficits, labor militancy, and FDR put him firmly on the conservative side. In the 1920s he also began paying great attention to patronage and "pork" for California, including Hoover Dam and higher tariff duties for agricultural products. Johnson had always been a political realist, but he had also tied his efforts to clear progressive goals. Weakening those goals, playing traditional politics, and accepting reelection support in 1922 from conservatives and former enemies reflect more than a tactical shift and the kinds of compromises he would not have made before 1920. He even tried again for the presidency in 1924, but his campaign was so bland that he provided no meaningful alternative even to Calvin Coolidge.

His greatest activity as a senator involved periodic crusades against American participation in international affairs. Abandoning anti-imperialism in favor of economic nationalism and isolationism in the early 1920s, he was virtually alone until the mid-1930s, when his bitter obstructionism to virtually any American efforts to influence the course of world events was joined by a few other senators. In poor health by 1940, Johnson suffered a stroke in 1943 and from then until his death on August 7, 1945, was little involved in Senate affairs. His last public position was to oppose American participation in the United Nations. He thus ended his career as a caricature of the man he had been thirty years previously, a man who had blended public good and personal advancement and who carefully balanced personal integrity and ambition.

Notes

1. *Congressional Record,* 54th Cong., 2d sess. January 8, 1897, 593.

2. Sacramento *Union-Record,* October 17, 1901, as quoted in Michael A. Weatherson and Hal W. Bochin, *Hiram Johnson: Political Revivalist* (Lanham, MD: University Press of America, 1995), 11.

3. Here, again, the actions of Hiram's father cast a shadow across his son: Grove introduced a bill into the legislature that would have substantially aided Ruef, and it was rumored that he was considering assisting in Ruef's legal defense. Walton Bean, *Boss Ruef's San Francisco: The Story of the Union Labor Party, Big Business, and the Graft Prosecution* (Berkeley: University of California Press, 1952), 181.

4. As quoted in H. Brent Melendy and Benjamin F. Gilbert, *The Governors of California* (Georgetown, CA: Talisman Press, 1965), 308.

5. Los Angeles *Times,* April 6, 1910.

6. The vote for Lieutenant Governor Albert Wallace, from Los Angeles, was nearly identical to Johnson's. The other progressives were John Eshleman, railroad commissioner from the southern Third District; and U.S. Representative William Kent, whose district included counties in the Sacramento Valley to the Pacific coast. As a result of Johnson's loss of support, his strength was not in the south, as most historians have said, but in counties along the Nevada border and on the central coast.

7. Inaugural address of Governor Hiram W. Johnson, in Franklin Hichborn, *Story of the Session of the California Legislature of 1911* (San Francisco: James H. Barry, 1911), i–ii. On inaugural styles see the example of Thomas Marshall of Indiana in Philip VanderMeer, *The Hoosier Politician: Officeholding and Political Culture in Indiana, 1896–1920* (Urbana: University of Illinois Press, 1985), 22.

8. Taft's write-in status helps explain his poor showing in the state.

9. Johnson to Meyer Lissner, December 12, 1912, Johnson Papers, Bancroft Library, University of California, Berkeley, as quoted in Weatherson and Bochin, *Johnson,* 69.

10. Hiram Johnson to Chester Rowell, [n.d., August 20?] 1916, Rowell Papers, Bancroft Library, University of California, Berkeley, as quoted in Spencer C. Olin, *California's Prodigal Sons: Hiram Johnson and the Progressives, 1911–1917* (Berkeley: University of California Press, 1968), 165.

11. Johnson to Eustace Cullinan, August 10, 1918, reprinted in Robert E. Burke, ed., *The Diary Letters of Hiram Johnson* (7 vols), vol. 2, *April 1918– December 1918* (New York: Garland, 1983).

12. Johnson to Hiram Johnson Jr., August 30, 1918, reprinted in Burke, *Diary of Johnson,* vol. 2.

13. Johnson to sons, April 23, 1917, reprinted in Burke, *Diary of Johnson,* vol. 1, *April 1917–March 1918.*

14. Johnson to Amy Johnson, August 10, 1918, reprinted in Burke, *Diary of Johnson.* vol. 1.

15. Johnson to Archibald Johnson, December 25, 1918 reprinted in Burke, *Diary of Johnson,* vol. 2.

16. Johnson to sons, March 18, 1920, reprinted in Burke, *Diary of Johnson,* vol. 3, *1919–1921.*

Suggested Readings

Richard Coke Lower's *A Bloc of One: The Political Career of Hiram W. Johnson* (Stanford, CA: Stanford University Press, 1993) is an excellent, detailed study that provides many insights and a balanced perspective on Johnson. Also useful is Michael Weatherson and Hal Bochin, *Hiram Johnson: Political Revivalist* (Lanham, MD: University Press of America, 1995), which focuses especially on Johnson as an orator. George E. Mowry's classic study *The California Progressives* (Berkeley: University of California Press, 1951) is still valuable on progressivism. Spencer C. Olin, *California's Prodigal Sons: Hiram Johnson and the Progressives, 1911– 1917* (Berkeley: University of California Press, 1968), provides a more positive view of Johnson and a more detailed view of his administration, whereas Kevin Starr, *Inventing the Dream: California through the Progressive Era* (New York: Oxford University Press, 1985), is very critical of the movement and often scathing in his treatment of Johnson. Michael Paul Rogin and John L. Shover analyze the basis of progressive voting support in *Political Change in California: Critical Elections and Social Movements, 1890–1966* (Westport, CT: Greenwood Press, 1970).

For San Francisco politics and society see Walton Bean, *Boss Ruef's San Francisco: The Story of the Union Labor, Party, Big Business, and the Graft Prosecution* (Berkeley: University of California Press, 1952); and William Issel and Robert W. Cherny, *San Francisco, 1865–1932: Politics, Power, and Urban Development* (Berkeley: University of California Press, 1986).

Johnson's war activities and policies are covered in Robert David Johnson, *The Peace Progressives and American Foreign Relations* (Cambridge, MA: Harvard University Press, 1995); Ralph Stone, *The Irreconcilables: The Fight against the League of Nations* (New York: W. W. Norton, 1970); and David M. Kennedy, *Over Here: The First World War and American Society* (New York: Oxford University Press, 1980).

12

William S. Sims
Naval Insurgent and Coalition Warrior

Kenneth J. Hagan

Fighting is one of the smallest aspects of military operations.
—W.S.S., 1917

Although the United States has possessed two coastlines since 1848, the Atlantic Ocean dominated maritime strategy for most of the nation's history. Before Japan evolved as a Pacific power, American naval leaders looked eastward at Great Britain as the most likely adversary. William S. Sims, a career naval officer who rose to the rank of four-star admiral during World War I, challenged this conventional wisdom. Sims was a born iconoclast who delighted in firing salvos at orthodox assumptions. Kenneth Hagan, an expert in naval history, highlights the admiral's controversial career and his contribution to America's success in World War I.

Commissioned in 1882, Sims witnessed fundamental changes in military technology during his four decades in uniform. Developments in gunnery and speed, he believed, outmoded Captain Alfred Thayer Mahan's premise that battleships should form the center of U.S. naval strategy. When the German military buildup caused alarm among officials in the United States, Sims encouraged cooperation with Britain. In 1917 he was assigned as the American naval liaison in London, where he developed the system of convoying ships as a defense against German submarines. When the United States officially entered the conflict, Sims assumed command of American naval operations in the European theater. In retirement, Sims continued to rail against battleships, foreseeing the day when air power would reduce the great ships to tactical dinosaurs. Sims's outspoken criticism of naval tradition reflects the growing pains in the American military as technology and diplomacy propelled the nation toward a wider global involvement.

Kenneth J. Hagan is professor emeritus of the U.S. Naval Academy and a member of the adjunct faculties of the Naval War College and the Naval Postgraduate School. A specialist in the history of naval policy, he is the author of *This People's Navy: The Making of American Sea Power* (1991), several other works about the American navy, and coauthor of *American Foreign Relations: A History* (1995).

William Sowdon Sims was born of a Canadian mother and American father on October 15, 1858, in the village of Port Hope, on Lake Ontario, midway between Toronto and Kingston, Canada. This geographic happenstance caused the future naval officer to be mistaken for a Canadian and to be accused of excessively pro-British sympathies despite the fact that he rose to become a four-star admiral in the U.S. Navy, the highest rank existing in the American armed services prior to World War II. Sims's graphic retort was, "Had I been born in a stable would I have been a horse?"[1]

In June 1876, Sims entered the U.S. Naval Academy as a resident of the state of Pennsylvania, where he had lived for four years. After graduating with a lackluster academic record in 1880, he served two years as a "passed midshipman" aboard the obsolescent wooden steam frigate *Tennessee*. Commissioned in 1882, Ensign Sims was launched on what augured to be an unremarkable career in a navy marked by material decay, an overabundance of officers, and a polyglot cadre of enlisted men gathered from the wharves of the world's seaports. He could not know that in his first decade of commissioned service he would witness the transformation of the American navy from an antediluvian appendage of a continental and fundamentally agrarian trading nation into the cutting edge of a major industrial and imperial world power.

At the end of the Civil War the U.S. Navy had ranked high among the world's naval powers in number of ships, but the military and naval retrenchment that characterizes most postwar periods in American history soon decimated the force. In 1873 a crisis erupted over the Spanish execution of crewmen seized on board the *Virginius,* a merchant vessel of U.S. registry operating in Cuban waters. The American navy experienced profound embarrassment in assembling a ragtag fleet that staggered with great difficulty and no appreciable speed toward Spanish Cuba, where the outcome of a naval engagement was problematical. Diplomacy saved the day for the U.S. Navy, but the imbroglio generated a decade of intense lobbying by naval officers and their political supporters for modernization of the service. Antimilitary sentiment gradually waned, and by the early 1880s Congress was willing to fund a renaissance of the navy.

The "new navy" of the 1880s and afterward differed from the old in several fundamental ways. Wooden hulls gave way to ones of iron and then steel; sails yielded to steam-driven propulsion systems; small muzzle-loading smoothbore cannon were replaced by much larger breech-loading rifled guns that eventually reached a bore diameter of sixteen inches; electricity was introduced to train and elevate the new guns. To employ the revolutionary new ships, a fresh strategy was devised at the U.S. Naval War College in Newport, Rhode Island.

Established by Secretary of the Navy William E. Chandler in 1884 in response to the lobbying of Rear Admiral Stephen B. Luce, the War College attracted a faculty of highly intelligent uniformed reformers, the most famous of whom was Captain Alfred Thayer Mahan. The lectures Mahan gave in the college's first years were published in 1890 as *The Influence of Sea Power upon History, 1660–1783.* This classic study of the Anglo-French struggle for dominance of the oceans in the age of sail paved the way for American adoption of a strategy of battle-fleet engagements aimed at destroying the enemy's fleets in the age of steam. The objective was to break the opponent's will to fight and win command of the seas. The new Mahan dogma would govern the U.S. Navy for the next century.

The technological and intellectual metamorphosis sweeping the U.S. Navy in the 1880s and 1890s provided the largely self-taught Sims with the perfect stimulus for honing his intellect and for expressing critical viewpoints on ship design and naval gunnery. As the intelligence officer on board the six-year-old cruiser *Charleston* on the China Station in 1895, Sims expertly detailed for the Navy Department the characteristics of the Japanese and Chinese warships that fought the protracted Battle of the Yalu River during the Sino-Japanese War. As U.S. naval attaché in Paris from 1896 until late in 1900 he meticulously cataloged the alarming superiority of the gunfire systems atop the steel warships of Britain, France, and even Russia. During the Spanish-American War he constructed a spy network in the Iberian Peninsula whose function was to keep Washington informed of the strengths, weaknesses, and disposition of the Spanish home fleet.

Some of Sims's reports reached the desk of the compulsively energetic assistant secretary of the navy, Theodore Roosevelt. A keen student of American naval history, a patron of the Naval War College, an admirer of Mahan, and a fierce exponent of naval expansion, Roosevelt took time "to add my personal appreciation" and admiration for "the energy, zeal, and intelligence" of Sims's assessments of European warships and naval building programs. The assistant secretary gushed: "I am very much pleased; you have done *well;* your report and enclosures were as interesting as anything I have recently read."[2]

On May 6, 1898, Roosevelt abruptly left the Navy Department to become a "lieutenant colonel of a regiment of mounted riflemen," that is, second-in-command of the Rough Riders. His mythic charge up San Juan Hill in the Spanish-American War catapulted him from that unlikely billet to the vice presidency of the United States in the election of November 1900. In the same month, Sims boarded the recently completed thirteen-inch-gun battleship *Kentucky,* bound for the Far East. The auspicious relationship between politician and naval officer seemed over, but within a year the assassination of President William McKinley carried Roosevelt to the White House, where he soon received a personal letter regarding naval policy from Lieutenant William Sims.

The China Station to which Sims returned at the beginning of 1901 was radically altered from what it had been during his tour aboard the cruiser *Charleston* in 1895–96. At that time the United States firmly controlled only one Pacific possession west of San Francisco, the remote island of Midway, and the American Asiatic Squadron had relied on British naval stations on the China coast to fuel and repair its steel warships. Now, as a result of the 1898 war with Spain, American territorial possessions stretched across the Pacific from Hawaii to the Philippines, where establishment of a major U.S. naval base eliminated the unsettling dependence on the Royal Navy.

Sims thus arrived in 1901 as an imperialist, a member of the "white race" whose superiority, he thought, should manifest itself in warship design.[3] He came aboard the USS *Kentucky,* one of the navy's newest battleships, a class of ship not available to Commodore George Dewey when he annihilated the Spanish fleet in Manila Bay on May 1, 1898. And whereas Dewey had been asked to leave Hong Kong by a British governor fearful of not appearing neutral, Sims and his shipmates on the *Kentucky* were welcomed aboard British men-of-war in Hong Kong and at English naval officers' clubs in Chinese cities. As Sims recalled, "We got to know the officers very well." From these new friends the American learned a great deal about gunnery in the Royal Navy. He became a particular admirer of Captain Percy Scott, the innovator of "continuous-aim firing," a technique that radically increased the accuracy of ships' guns by keeping the target constantly in the gunners' sights.

During his two years on the China Station, Sims bombarded the Navy Department with highly technical analyses extolling Scott's methods and discrediting the inadequate armor protection and faulty interior structure of the turrets of the U.S. Navy's latest ships. Frustrated by what he viewed as the Navy Department's stifling of his reports, he audaciously took his case directly to President Roosevelt. On November 16, 1901, Sims wrote a personal letter to the president, alleging "the extreme danger of the present very inefficient condition of the Navy, considered as a fighting force." The irrepressible lieutenant unfavorably contrasted the rapidity and accuracy of American naval guns with that exhibited by "our possible enemies, including the Japanese." Years later he publicly conceded that by writing to the president he had been guilty of "the rankest possible kind of insubordination."[4]

Roosevelt was not a man to take offense at the circumvention of normal bureaucratic channels, although he did chide Sims for being an alarmist: "I think you [are] unduly pessimistic, as you certainly were at the outset of the Spanish-American War, when, as you may remember, you took a very gloomy view of our vessels even as compared with those of Spain."[5] But he ordered navywide distribution of the critical evaluations Sims had recently submitted and invited him to write again. The radical critic had found a patron at the highest level, a point not lost on the officer in charge of naval personnel, Rear Admiral Henry C. Taylor. Himself a naval reformer and one of only two or three very senior officers who approved of Sims's campaign, Taylor ordered the maverick back to the United States for a tour as the inspector of target practice.

From October 1902 until the end of the second administration of President Theodore Roosevelt, Sims savored his position as the navy's authorized, free-wheeling critic. He continued to correspond with Percy Scott, now his counterpart as the British inspector of target practice. In an early visit to London he met with Admiral John Fisher, the First Sea Lord, and Admiral John Jellicoe, the director of naval ordnance. Both were gunnery enthusiasts. Sims and Jellicoe would meet again, on a more nearly equal footing, in World War I. In the meantime, Sims was witnessing at close hand the historic Anglo-American diplomatic rapprochement of the early twentieth century.

At Fisher's insistence, the British North America and West Indies Squadron was dissolved and its ships recalled to England, leaving the U.S. Navy as the unquestioned master of the Caribbean and Gulf of Mexico. The Royal Navy's withdrawal from age-old cruising grounds facilitated enforcement of President Roosevelt's "corollary" to the Monroe Doctrine, the pledge of December 1904 that henceforth the United States would police the area. At the same time, London also agreed to unilateral American construction and fortification of the Panama Canal, which became a secure conduit for emergency transfers of the U.S. Navy's battle fleet from its home waters in the Atlantic to danger zones in the Pacific. Japan's stunning military and naval victories in the Russo-Japanese War of 1904–05 dramatized the vulnerability of America's new insular possessions in the Pacific and demonstrated the strategic necessity for interoceanic mobility of a fleet that was growing at an average rate of one battleship per year.

While Sims was goading the U.S. Navy to improve its gunnery, Fisher was secretly creating a qualitatively new battleship, the *Dreadnought*. Completed in December 1906, this fast, heavy, and thickly armored "all-big-gun ship" mounted a main battery of ten twelve-inch guns. Sims and most other experts immediately recognized that the vastly extended range of the *Dreadnought*'s large guns rendered all existing battleships vulnerable and hence obsolete. The U.S. Navy had to respond in kind, but construction of an American equivalent was nearly checked when Alfred T. Mahan published an article in the June 1906 issue of the U.S. Naval Institute's *Proceedings,* arguing that speed and great guns were not essential in a modern battleship.[6] What counted to him was the age-old Nelsonian willingness of a commander to close with the enemy and slug it out with an array of guns of various calibers aimed at selected parts of the enemy's ships.

Mahan's pen carried so much weight with Congress that his article might have paralyzed American development of a *Dreadnought* had not Sims joined the debate. In response to a request from President Roosevelt, who favored the all-big-gun ship, Sims composed and published a refutation of Mahan's data and logic. Further, he visited England in December 1906 and, through his friendships with Fisher and Jellicoe, arranged a clandestine tour of the highly secret leviathan. Sims's description of the *Dreadnought* was used by President Roosevelt to help ram through Congress an authorization for the battleships *Delaware* and *North Dakota,* popularly regarded as America's first dreadnoughts. In the public debate over the all-big-gun ship, Lieutenant Commander Sims had bested the most venerated naval writer ever produced by the United States.

Appointed to the additional duty of naval aide to President Roosevelt in November 1907, Sims moved toward center stage, poised to stimulate the construction of a fleet centered on American derivatives of the *Dreadnought*. His immersion in the bitter intraservice debates over such arcane technological matters as optimal thickness and placement of belts of armor plate earned a unique reward from the old Progressive he served. In the last days of his presidency, Theodore Roosevelt ordered Sims to take charge of a battleship, an honor universally reserved for senior naval captains who had previously distinguished themselves as commanding officers of smaller warships.

Sims had never held command at sea, and his naval rank of commander placed him one level below that of a captain. Even his admirers were shocked. A future chief of naval operations, Captain William S. Benson, wrote to congratulate him and to complain that for the sake of naval tradition and the morale of the officer corps the president should first have promoted Sims and then given him command of a battleship. This sensible observation aside, the command of a major combatant vessel presented the naval insurgent with a rare opportunity to continue at sea his crusade for further modernization of fleet technology and procedures, an absolute necessity if the navy was to keep pace with the runaway expansion of American overseas power.

The global reach of the United States was evidenced by the around-the-world cruise of the "Great White Fleet," lasting from December 1907 to February 22, 1909. With barely a week left in office, President Roosevelt boarded the luxurious presidential steam yacht *Mayflower* in Hampton Roads, Virginia, to preside at the glorious homecoming of the sixteen battleships of the Atlantic Fleet. Beside him stood his ebullient naval aide, who seven days later would take command of the returning *Minnesota*. Built at a cost of $7.5 million and commissioned in 1907, the *Minnesota* was one of the finest pre-dreadnoughts in the U.S. Navy. Mounting four twelve-inch guns and a host of mixed batteries, it could achieve a speed of eighteen knots. Under Sims the *Minnesota* served as the flagship of a battleship division of the Atlantic Fleet.

Commander Sims characteristically turned the ship to his own purposes. He revived his shipboard practice of besieging the Navy Department with brutally frank criticism of its warships and weapons, but he also began to hone a unique style of leadership. He showed great solicitude for the well-being of his junior officers and, more significant, for the enlisted crewmen of the *Minnesota*. He deplored the draconian punishments often inflicted by commanding officers on enlisted men guilty of misconduct, most particularly extended periods of restriction to the ship. Although he decried the effect of "white slavery" on the prostitutes in harbors, he reasoned that protracted denial of sexual gratification—"the most compelling of all passions"—would drive enlisted sailors to outright desertion from the ship and the navy.[7] For these men he practiced and preached a high standard of morality. He urged them not to become drunk but if intoxicated to return to the ship for their own safety, and he imposed punishments that were in his mind humane. Monetary fines were his favorite measure. The result was a "happy ship," that is, a proficient crew imbued with high morale and genuine affection for this benign father figure who was the navy's most rebellious son in his own dealings with icons of higher authority.

Perhaps the most insubordinate act of Sims's entire career took place while he was commanding officer of the *Minnesota*. In late 1910, as part of a goodwill mission undertaken by the Atlantic Fleet, his ship was ordered to visit England and France. Germany, then in the midst of a major naval race with England, was not included on the itinerary. To compound the insulting exclusion, the crews of the *Minnesota* and other ships in the division participated in a week of festivities culminating in two banquets hosted by the Lord Mayor of London at the historic Guildhall. On December 2, the Lord Mayor's welcome included what Sims described as a confident assertion that the United States would come to the British Empire's aid if it were ever seriously threatened by a foreign enemy. Intoxicated by the oratory and ceremony, Sims the next day replied in kind: "If the time ever comes when the integrity of the British Empire is seriously menaced by an external enemy, it is my opinion that you may count upon every man, every dollar, every drop of blood, of your kindred across the sea."[8]

This gross indiscretion soon became a matter of serious political concern for President William Howard Taft, who was no less a proponent of battleship construction than his predecessor. Thanks to backing from the secretary of the navy and other friends in the cabinet, Sims suffered only a public reprimand in the form of a "general order" forbidding naval officers to make undiplomatic speeches in the future. He easily could have been relieved of command and forced into retirement, in which case the naval history of World War I would have been quite different. Instead, he was promoted to captain and whisked off to study at the Naval War College.

When he emerged from Newport to take command of a flotilla of destroyers in July 1913 he discovered an absence of doctrine to guide tactics in battle. As if he were the proctor in a seminar, he began to gather officers from all the ships and conduct mock battles on the deck of his flagship's wardroom. This "war college afloat," as Sims referred to it, gradually formulated sound procedures for systematic and coordinated night torpedo attacks by destroyers on the fleet's battleships.

For Sims, both personally and professionally, the importance of his command of the flotilla cannot be overemphasized. By working collegially in a conference system with his officers to develop and perfect tactics, he was consciously or unconsciously emulating the technique followed so successfully by Horatio Nelson and his "band of brothers" prior to the battles of the Nile (1798) and Trafalgar (1805). The bestowal of exceptional trust and confidence from on high engendered a deep sense of loyalty among Sims's subordinates, several of whom gladly rejoined him in London when he supervised the U.S. naval forces in the eastern Atlantic during World War I. Furthermore, for a mind conditioned to thinking of heavily armored ships and big guns, the seagoing experience with thin-hulled small warships opened vast new possibilities about how to fight a naval war.

On October 25, 1915, Captain Sims was detached from the flotilla and ordered to command of the spanking new battleship *Nevada,* a supership displacing nine thousand tons more than the standard-setting *Dreadnought.* The experience of command was itself uneventful, but it coincided with a monumental event in the naval history of World War I. On the afternoon of May 31 and in the dark early hours of June 1, 1916, the only major battle-fleet action of World War I took place in the North Sea, south of Norway and west of the upper portion of the Danish peninsula known as Jutland.

With desperate aggressiveness, the German High Seas Fleet attempted a breakout to disrupt the Royal Navy's strangling command of the approaches to European ports. In a complex running battle with the British Grand Fleet lasting about twelve hours, the Germans were met, contained, and forced back to their base in northern Germany. To everyone's dismay, the Jutland engagement left the naval routine where it had been since August 1914: the Royal Navy patrolled on blockade offshore, and the German battle fleet lay tucked safely in Continental harbors.

Washington learned of the Battle of Jutland on June 3. The impact was felt sharply in Congress, which quickly authorized the largest American naval expansion in history. Intended to create "a navy second to none," the 1916 naval act emphasized construction of battleships and battle cruisers. Their purpose was to prepare for two-ocean naval warfare against coalitions involving combinations of Japan, Germany, and Great Britain. Like the battle that provoked its swift enactment, the measure had precious little to do with the victory at sea in World War I.

During the hearings leading up to the 1916 act, at which he had testified, Sims remained preoccupied with commanding the *Nevada*. But suddenly and quite unexpectedly he became the beneficiary of one of the administrative reforms he had championed: rationalization of the promotion system. Early in 1916, Secretary of the Navy Josephus Daniels, an ardent reformer of naval traditions, persuaded Congress to abolish the hoary practice of advancing captains to the rank of rear admiral solely on the basis of their longevity. He replaced it with a system of promotion based on merit as evaluated by a board of the navy's most senior officers. The first admirals' "selection board" picked Captain Sims for promotion to flag rank in August. He suddenly was too senior to command a single ship, however grand it might be. On January 1, 1917, Rear Admiral Sims was packed off once again to Newport, Rhode Island, this time as president of the Naval War College. His tour lasted less than three months.

By January 1917 the United States had spent almost two and one-half years attempting to maintain a policy of qualified neutrality toward the two warring blocs in the stalemated war in Europe: the Triple Alliance dominated by Germany and the Austro-Hungarian Empire on the one hand and the Triple Entente of Great Britain, France, and Russia, on the other. A highly lucrative transatlantic trade in foodstuffs and war matériel gradually had grown up between the thriving agricultural and industrial giant of North America and Britain and France. Commercial and financial relations with Germany simultaneously withered because the Royal Navy had effectively closed hostile ports on the Continent. The

German navy struck out against this lack of economic neutrality in the only way it could: with submarine attacks against Allied and neutral shipping.

President Woodrow Wilson stubbornly insisted that Americans had the right to travel into German-declared submarine war zones on belligerent-owned liners as well as on American ones. He also advanced an outdated proposition derived from commerce raiding in the age of sail: the predator must issue a warning of imminent attack for the sake of the passengers and crew aboard the targeted vessel. He refused to concede that the U-boat represented a revolution in commerce raiding. It could not warn its victims in advance for fear of being rammed or shot out of the water by an armed merchantman. Germany protested stridently but largely acceded to Wilson's unrealistic demands throughout 1915 and 1916 in order to avoid U.S. entrance into the war on the side of the Anglo-French allies.

In January 1917, overly confident German naval officers persuaded the government of Kaiser Wilhelm II that unlimited U-boat attacks on the heavily loaded transatlantic cargo ships flooding Britain with war munitions and food from the United States could drive England out of the war within six months. According to this calculation, the United States would enter the war, but mobilization of its armed forces would take so long that America's military and naval participation could not alter the outcome. On January 31, Berlin announced that starting the next day German submarines would attack without warning and sink all vessels, enemy and neutral, found in or near British waters. President Wilson was incensed. He ordered the severance of diplomatic relations with Germany and waited anxiously for the toll of sunken ships to mount.

Germany's declaration of unrestricted submarine warfare was the most momentous single event in the professional life of William S. Sims. He had barely assumed his position as president of the Naval War College when he received a telephone call from Washington, ordering him to report at once to the Navy Department. There he learned that in a cable dated March 23 the American ambassador in London, Walter Hines Page, had requested the immediate dispatch of "an Admiral of our own Navy who will bring our Navy's plans and inquiries." Page explained the benefits that would accrue to the United States: "The coming of such an officer of high rank would be regarded as a compliment and he would have all doors opened to him."[9] President Wilson, who had decided for war, informed Secretary of the Navy Daniels, "The main thing is no doubt to get into immediate communication with the Admiralty on the other side (through confidential channels until the Congress has acted) and work out the scheme of cooperation."[10]

Sims was the man of the hour, chosen despite—or because of—his well-known pro-British sympathies, first publicly vented in London's Guildhall in 1910. By March 31 he was under way on the fast passenger liner *New York*, traveling incognito in civilian clothes with his aide, Commander John V. Babcock. He brought no war plans, only verbal orders. The exact nature of his instructions later became a matter of dispute among himself, Secretary of the Navy Daniels, and William S. Benson, the chief of naval operations. The refusal of official Washington to commit itself in writing to a decidedly unneutral act prior to the president's request for a congressional declaration of war is quite understandable. It proved highly advantageous to Sims when he met in London on April 10 with an old comrade, Admiral John Jellicoe.

Congress had declared war on April 6, so Sims's reunion with Jellicoe constituted a meeting of allied commanders rather than a shadowy consultation between belligerent and neutral senior officers. It was a sobering experience for Sims, who had arrived in England confident that the British had the war at sea well in hand. On the contrary, Jellicoe somberly informed him, German submarines were ravaging British and neutral shipping at such a rate that the Allied powers unquestionably would lose the war for want of food and matériel, possibly as early as August, certainly by October. Sims later remembered that he had asked Jellicoe, "Is there no solution for the problem?" The First Sea Lord had replied, "Absolutely none that we can see now."[11] As Sims realized, "The thing must be stopped."[12]

It was a perfect opportunity for the young admiral from across the Atlantic, who came unencumbered by restrictive orders and who was blessed with a lifelong habit of creative thinking. Within four days of arriving in London, Sims fired off a cable to the Navy Department outlining Britain's desperate plight and prescribing the remedy. The U.S. Navy should immediately dispatch a "maximum number of destroyers . . . accompanied by small anti-submarine craft" and the government should provide an unlimited volume of merchant tonnage.[13] Then, in cooperation with innovative junior British naval officers and with the support of Prime Minister David Lloyd George, Sims encouraged a strategic about-face in the admiralty. On April 30, the sea lords agreed to experiment with the convoying of merchant vessels by destroyers "as the general plan of campaign."[14] This concession would lead to Allied naval victory in World War I, but only after Sims convinced his own government that convoys held the key to the defeat of the U-boats.

For at least four months, American naval strategy in World War I was the subject of an acrimonious transatlantic debate. From London, Sims and Ambassador Page beseeched Washington to send every seaworthy destroyer to escort convoys of merchant vessels through U-boat-infested waters off the English coast. President Wilson and Secretary of the Navy Daniels agreed that the submarine constituted the chief threat to the Allied cause, but they seriously doubted that the peril facing Great Britain was quite so extreme as portrayed by Page and Sims, both of whom wore haloes radiating Anglophilia. British laggardness in prosecuting the war against the submarine irritated Wilson, and for a time he thought that direct attacks against bases on the Continent and massive mine-laying would prove more destructive to the U-boats than convoys escorted by destroyers.

Wilson, Daniels, and the doubters within the Navy Department were not unreasonable men. Many old salts in and out of uniform questioned whether merchant vessels on the high seas could remain "on station" in tight formations flanked by protective warships. Differences in ships' speeds, uneven conning skills of helmsmen and dark nights could easily dissolve formations, leaving stray merchantmen to be picked off by submarines. What finally won over the president and secretary of the navy was the accumulating documentation of the gradual but inexorable reduction in the monthly rate of U-boat sinkings of merchant ships as the convoy system was expanded by the admiralty and the U.S. Navy's man in London.

At the height of the war, Sims oversaw 370 ships of all classes, 5,000 officers, and 70,000 enlisted men distributed among 45 bases in the British Isles and on the Continent. He divided most of his days and nights among his London residence in the Carlton Hotel, the admiralty, and his own headquarters at the American embassy in Grosvenor Square. As a commander of operating ships the admiral enjoyed the perquisite of a flagship. His flagship, the *Melville,* was a destroyer tender named after a naval engineer and it remained moored throughout the war at the Royal Navy base in Queenstown, Ireland.

Sims was drawn to Queenstown because it was home for the American destroyers that escorted the merchant cargo vessels on the last leg of their journey from New York or Hampton Roads to their destinations in southern England. Many of their skippers had served under Sims when he commanded the destroyer flotilla from 1913 to 1915. He also was intrigued by the British commander at Queenstown, Admiral Sir Lewis Bayly, whom the eminent naval historian Sir Julian Corbett considered "the father of destroyer tactics and organization."[15] Nicknamed "Old Frozen Face" by irreverent American sailors, Bayly exercised command over the U.S. destroyers when they were at sea on convoy duty. Their arrival at Queenstown, he later said, had made "all the difference" to the success of the convoys.[16] Together, Bayly and Sims proved that in an Anglo-American naval war against a continental European power's unleashed submarines, the convoying to safety of cargo vessels loaded with war matériel held the best hope for maritime victory.

The figures speak for themselves. When Sims first arrived in London, Admiral Jellicoe predicted that in April 1917 the U-boats would sink 900,000 tons of merchant transports. By December 1917 the Allies were losing 350,000 tons per month. In October 1918, the month before the war ended, the U-boats could sink no more than 112,427 tons. This massive reduction in loss with the corollary monthly increase in tonnage of matériel being shipped from the United States was accomplished between May 1917 and November 1918 by fifteen hundred convoys of eighteen thousand ships. The U.S. Navy provided about 27 percent of the escorting destroyers in British waters, the Royal Navy 70 percent. Simultaneously, the United States initiated a separate category of shipments: troops and their equipment that were routed to Brest, France, on a more southerly track around the British Isles. Sims and the admiralty protected the convoys of this war-winning force of two million American soldiers with the loss of only a single troop transport.

The American admiral repeatedly cited the Anglo-American disparity in combatant vessels to justify the subordination of his destroyers to the British operational commander. His was a perfectly defensible stance, but at the same time he undercut himself with official Washington by appearing unnecessarily sycophantic in his relations with the admiralty in London. In early 1918 the British offered him honorary membership on the Board of Admiralty, an unprecedented distinction that would have made him privy to the innermost deliberations of the Royal Navy's central headquarters. Secretary of the Navy Daniels forbade acceptance, saying later, "I regarded it as rather a love of glitter and foreign recognition and honor than anything else."[17] The Navy Department refrained from taking any further action inimical to its London commander for the rest of the war, and in December 1918 it even promoted him to the rank of full—that is, four-star—admiral. It was a bittersweet, ephemeral reward for Sims. Once he left the London command he had to revert to two-star rank, the highest permanent grade in the U.S. Navy at the time.

The postwar American navy had little room in its inner sanctum for a senior officer who was blatantly enthusiastic about close cooperation with the Royal Navy. Secretary Daniels and Chief of Naval Operations Benson coldly excluded Sims from the peace negotiations of January–May 1919, and they went to Paris personally to shape U.S. naval policy toward the principal American ally of the recent war. In a memorandum of March 13, 1919, Benson threw down the anti-British gauntlet: "In the past Great Britain built with the exclusive idea of keeping a safe superiority over the German fleet. In the future her sole naval rival will be the United States, and every ship built or acquired by Great Britain can have in mind only the American fleet."[18]

Appalled at the resurrection of an Anglophobic naval policy, Sims sailed for home. At his request, he returned to the presidency of the Naval War College, a bully pulpit for the navy's aging critic. On the bottom of his orders, he wryly noted "how pleased all hands are to give me the College. It relieves them from the embarrassment of [not] knowing what to do with me."[19]

Another monumental international race in warship construction loomed, but the war had left Great Britain economically prostrate, and the end of hostilities had rekindled traditional antimilitary sentiment in Congress. Finding it fiscally impossible to indulge in a costly battleship-building program, the leaders of the two countries sought redress in a diplomatic solution. At the Washington Conference on the Limitation of Armaments, held in 1921–22, an agreement to limit the gross tonnage of battleships and heavy cruisers was reached by the United States, Great Britain, Japan, France, and Italy. Much disparaged by American naval officers as a political capitulation, the arrangement gave the United States battleship parity with Britain for the first time in history.

In the era of treaty limitations, Rear Admiral Sims played his habitual role as the most outspoken uniformed critic of American naval orthodoxy. He began his postwar crusade on December 17, 1919, with a letter to Secretary Daniels protesting inequities in the secretary's system of awarding medals for meritorious service. He was very quickly and willingly led into a protracted Senate committee hearing on the Navy Department's conduct of the war at sea. From March through May 1920, he attempted to persuade the American public that the Wilson administration was culpable for failing prudently to man and equip the navy for a European war during the two-year period of neutrality preceding U.S. belligerency. Sims also charged that the refusal of Secretary Daniels and the Washington naval bureaucracy to commence extensive transatlantic convoys had protracted the war for six months. His first case faltered on varying perceptions and definitions of neutrality, and his second assault was too patently self-serving to win widespread respect. The brazen attack on the top civilian leadership undermined Sims's credibility as a high-minded if flamboyant skeptic and destroyed his hope for massive administrative reform of the Navy Department.

William S. Sims retired from active duty on October, 14, 1922, at the mandatory age of sixty-four. He continued to reside in Newport, Rhode Island, until his death fourteen years later. Vigorous to the end, he gave speeches and wrote articles urging the disestablishment of the U.S. Naval Academy for failing properly to train young men in the essentials of leadership. He recognized at a very early date that the aircraft carrier would be the mainstay of the battle fleet of the future. "Therefore," he wrote in March 1922, "the battleship is dead."[20] These were the ultimate heresies. In the navy of the 1920s and 1930s the battleship was the weapons system around which all others revolved. Likewise, the Naval Academy was and remains the institutional or emotional heart of the U.S. Navy, far more so than any fleet or shore establishment.

With a morbid and ironic twist of fate, Sims's prediction about the battleship's demise was borne out on December 7, 1941, when aircraft from carriers of the Imperial Japanese Navy severely damaged the American battle fleet moored at Pearl Harbor, Hawaii. One of the battleships sunk on that dreadful Sunday morning was the old *Nevada,* of which Sims had been the first commanding officer.

The tragedy forced the U.S. Navy to depend almost exclusively on carrier-launched aircraft to fight the monumental and tide-turning World War II battles in the Pacific—Coral Sea, Midway, the Philippine Sea. In the entire four-year panorama of the Japanese-American war there would be but one solitary battle-fleet engagement conforming to the ideal that Mahan had ordained for the twentieth-century American navy. It was fought at Surigao Strait in the Philippine Islands in October, 1944. Like the Battle of Jutland in the previous war, its strategic impact was marginal. At the same time, unrestricted American submarine attacks on Japanese shipping proved once again that an island nation could not hope for maritime victory if it did not convoy its tankers, cargo vessels, and troopships.

In the Atlantic, the British and Americans—unstintingly reinforced by the Royal Canadian Navy—once again instituted a well-coordinated system of transoceanic convoys. Countless naval escorts protected the vital shipments of matériel flowing from North America to England and the Soviet Union, and a highly sophisticated campaign of antisubmarine warfare steadily depleted the numbers of U-boats sent to sea by Nazi Germany. The Anglo-American naval coalition first forged by Admiral Sims in 1917 was revived and solidified into another historic victory at sea. Today, on the eve of the twenty-first century, it is the bedrock of American foreign policy and naval strategy.

To use a nautical term, the transatlantic partnership is "180 degrees out" from what Passed Midshipman Sims knew on board on the *Tennessee,* when the Royal Navy loomed as the world's most lethal threat to American national security. That William Sowden Sims helped in ways small and large to end a century of mutual hostility between the two major English-speaking powers is certainly the most significant and lasting transformation brought about by a man who always sought change while wearing a uniform that symbolizes permanence, conservatism, and tradition. He was the perennial outsider in the ultimate insider's organization. As he himself said of the navy at the height of his power and prestige: "I have never liked it. I would rather have been in a productive occupation. There has never been a time when I have not been uncomfortable in a uniform."[21] Paradox defined the man.

Notes

1. William S. Sims quoted in Elting E. Morison, *Admiral Sims and the Modern American Navy* (Boston: Houghton Mifflin, 1942), 7.

2. Theodore Roosevelt, quoted in ibid., 49.

3. For Sims on the superiority of "white men" as naval architects, see U.S. Congress, *Hearings before the Select Committee of Inquiry into Operations of the United States Air Services, House of Representatives,* 68th Cong., pt. 4, 1925, 2977–78.

4. Sims to Theodore Roosevelt, November 16, 1901, quoted in Morison, *Sims,* 102–104; Sims in 1916 before the House Committee on Naval Affairs, quoted in Morison, *Sims,* 328.

5. Theodore Roosevelt to Sims, December 12, 1901, quoted in Morison, *Sims,* 104-105.

6. Alfred T. Mahan, "Reflections, Historic and Other, Suggested by the Battle of the Japan Sea," U.S. Naval Institute *Proceedings* (June 1906): Sims responded with "The Inherent Tactical Qualities of All-Big Gun, One-Caliber Battleships of High Speed, Large Displacement and Gunpower," *Proceedings,* December, 1906, 1337–66.

7. Sims quoted in Morison, *Sims,* 332.

8. Ibid., 281.

9. Walter Hines Page quoted in Josephus Daniels, *Our Navy at War* (New York: Doran, 1922), 36.

10. Woodrow Wilson to Josephus Daniels, March 24, 1917, quoted in Mary Klachko and David F. Trask, *Admiral William Shepherd Benson: First Chief of Naval Operations* (Annapolis, MD: Naval Institute Press, 1987), 57.

11. John Jellicoe, quoted in William S. Sims, *The Victory at Sea* (London: John Murray, 1920), 7.

12. Ibid., 10.

13. Cable, Sims to U.S. Navy Department, April 14, 1917, in Sims, *The Victory at Sea,* 319.

14. John V. Babcock, quoted in Morison, *Sims,* 351.

15. Julian Corbett, quoted in ibid., 378.

16. Lewis Bayly, quoted in Arthur J. Marder, *From the Dreadnought to Scapa Flow,* vol. 4, *1917: Year of Crisis* (London: Oxford University Press, 1969), 275.

17. Josephus Daniels in 1920 congressional hearings, quoted in Morison, *Sims,* 391.

18. William S. Benson and Captain Frank H. Schofield, memorandum dated March 13, 1919, quoted in Kenneth J. Hagan, *This People's Navy: The Making of American Sea Power* (New York: Free Press, 1991), 262.

19. Sims, quoted in Morison, *Sims,* 467.

20. Sims to W. F. Fullam, March 1922, in ibid., 506.

21. Ibid., 430.

Suggested Readings

Two surveys of American naval history provide different and yet complementary perspectives on the background and context of the Sims era: George W. Baer, *One Hundred Years of Sea Power: The U.S. Navy, 1890–1990* (Stanford, CA: Stanford University Press, 1994); and Kenneth J. Hagan, *This People's Navy: The Making of American Sea Power* (New York: Free Press, 1991). Despite the modest title, the most comprehensive analysis of the U.S. Navy in the years of Sims's greatest activity is the two-volume work by William R. Braisted, *The United States Navy in the Pacific, 1897–1909* and *1909–1922* (Austin: University of Texas Press, 1958, 1971). The relations between the top civilians and officers in the Navy Department are ably discussed in two books by a leading naval historian, Nathan Miller: *Theodore Roosevelt: A Life* (New York: William Morrow, 1994); and *FDR: An Intimate History* (Lanham, MD: Madison Books, 1991).

For Sims's entire career, nothing can touch the elegantly written biography by Elting E. Morison, *Admiral Sims and the Modern American Navy* (Boston: Houghton Mifflin, 1942). The life of Sims's towering 1906 protagonist is critically recounted in Robert Seager II, *Alfred Thayer Mahan* (Annapolis, MD: Naval Institute Press, 1977), and Mahan's writings are imaginatively reexamined in Jon Tetsuro Sumida, *Inventing Grand Strategy and Teaching Command: The Classic Works of Alfred Thayer Mahan Reconsidered* (Baltimore, MD: Johns Hopkins University Press, 1997). "Jacky" Fisher, the Royal Navy, and the *Dreadnought* are creatively rendered in Jan Morris, *Fisher's Face: Or, Getting to Know the Admiral* (New York: Random House, 1995).

The Great War at sea is thoroughly explained in Paul G. Halpern, *A Naval History of World War I* (Annapolis, MD: Naval Institute Press, 1994). Sims's months in London are vivified in David F. Trask, *Captains and Cabinets: Anglo-American Naval Relations, 1917–1918* (Columbia: University of Missouri Press, 1972). Admiral Benson's side of the war story is the subject of Mary Klachko and David F. Trask, *Admiral William Shepherd Benson: First Chief of Naval Operations* (Annapolis, MD: Naval Institute Press, 1987).

13

Edith Wharton and the Spirit of Noblesse Oblige

Alan Price

Edith Wharton was born to a well-to-do family in New York City during the Civil War and died in France during the Spanish civil war. Although she enjoyed the privileged life, her passion was writing, which she pursued by authoring forty-seven books. She counted Theodore Roosevelt, the Vanderbilts, and the Rockefellers among her acquaintances, but her closest friends were members of the literary community. Many of these intellectuals had relocated in Paris, where social mores were more flexible than in America. Edith Wharton joined these expatriates in 1909 and was residing in Paris when World War I broke out in 1914. Alan Price, a professor of English and a Wharton biographer, examines this chapter of her life.

The war diverted Edith Wharton's attention from writing and refocused it on the refugees that streamed into Paris. Resolving to ease their predicament, she began by soliciting charitable funds and organizing a sewing room, but her relief work evolved into programs that housed, fed, educated, and provided medical care for hundreds of refugees. Dreading the possibility that German *Kultur* might spread across Europe, Wharton privately criticized American reluctance to join the Allies. After the United States had entered the war, Wharton was distressed by the American Red Cross, which swept aside small, private relief efforts in favor of a centralized operation. Her embitterment at this affront was one of many that made World War I a dividing line, in Price's opinion, between the "age of innocence" and a new world "without taste, a world without an aristocracy or intellect."

Alan Price is professor of English at Pennsylvania State University at Hazleton. He is the author of *The End of the Age of Innocence: Edith Wharton and the First World War* (1996), and several articles on Wharton and other American writers.

T he American novelist Edith Wharton would seem to be an unlikely candidate for the title of social worker during the Progressive Era in American history. Yet as we shall see, Wharton saved the lives of thousands of Belgian and French civilian refugees during the opening months of World War I, well before the United States entered the conflict in April 1917. When the war began in August 1914, she feared that if Germany won, it would mean "the crash of civilization." Through the following months she organized several relief organizations and charities, many of which bore her name. She was rewarded for her heroic efforts with the highest decorations France and Belgium could bestow.

Who was Edith Wharton? And why would this wealthy American writer living in France choose to become involved so deeply in war relief work? Wharton was the author of forty-seven books: she wrote novels, short stories, travel books, texts on house and garden design, and essays. The story of her life can be best traced, however, in the context of the various places she chose to live during her long and productive life.

She was born Edith Newbold Jones in New York City in 1862 and died in France in 1937. She was a daughter of an upper-middle-class family of English and Dutch ancestry. As was the case with the family of Henry and William James, Edith Wharton's parents offset a post-Civil War decline in their family income (derived largely from rental properties in New York City) by moving to Europe for a few years. Although it may seem paradoxical to us, upper-middle-class families of the 1860s and 1870s found that it was actually cheaper to live in Europe than in the United States, where the effect of the depression of the 1870s eroded rental incomes. The young Edith Jones spent the late 1860s and the early 1870s living in hotels and rented apartments in Spain, France, Italy, and Germany.

In 1885, Edith Jones married Teddy Wharton. He unfortunately had none of his wife's literary interests, and though both tried, the marriage was not a happy one. They were divorced in 1913 after Teddy's mental problems led to a complete breakdown of the marriage. While they were married, through the 1880s and the 1890s, they lived in New York during the winter and in Newport, Rhode Island, during the summer. They took frequent trips to Europe as well. They built a home together in Lenox, Massachusetts, where both spent the happiest years of their marriage. But after 1907, when Edith Wharton began renting apartments in Paris, France became her home for longer and longer periods.

Wharton inherited some money, but she made the major portion of her income from her pen. Her novels sold very well, and they were frequently turned into plays and movies during her lifetime. Even with her interest in the past, it should be noted that she was no Luddite. She loved what the automobile had done for travel, and she embraced the telephone. From 1905 on she owned a series of automobiles, one of the first women to do so. Her friend the novelist Henry James would claim with characteristic literary exaggeration that Wharton would sweep down on his quiet village like "an angel of devastation," pluck him up, and carry him off on motor trips through England and France.

Like Henry James, Wharton felt more comfortable in Europe than she did in her native United States. For many American writers, especially women, the act of becoming an expatriate was liberating. Wharton was introduced to French literary circles in 1909 by the French novelist Paul Bourget. Paris was especially congenial to American writers, especially those like Gertrude Stein and Djuna Barnes who were seeking cultural and sexual freedom. Wharton could move easily in either French or American circles in Paris, since more than ten thousand Americans lived there—enough to support their own newspaper, the *Paris Herald*.

Wharton's earliest novel was set in Italy, but James told her to "do New York" as the subject of her fiction. His advice was valuable; her two best-known novels, *The House of Mirth* (1905) and *The Age of Innocence* (1920), for which she won the Pulitzer Prize in 1921, are both set in New York. Edith Wharton was, after all, the author of *Ethan Frome* (1911), that most chilling of American New England tales.

Wharton was very much a product of the tradition of noblesse oblige, the principle that those with wealth or those who have been born into a higher economic and social class have also inherited an obligation to help those who are less fortunate. As a young woman she received some training in volunteer organization by serving on local boards of the Society for the Prevention of Cruelty to Animals in New York City and later in Lenox, Massachusetts. Also in Lenox she was active on the local library board. However, it was not until the beginning of World War I that her genius for organizing and administering charities became apparent.

Wharton was essentially a social and philosophical conservative in the root sense of "one who conserves or maintains." Wharton believed in a general sense of fitness in life. She was not an obvious snob about family lineage or aristocratic titles, but she was a snob about breeding and learning. She preferred an oligarchy of taste and erudition, a meritocracy of learning. She favored a society that would protect, if not favor, the connoisseur. In politics, Wharton was what may be called a traditionalist and a conservative. She was not a fan of a total democracy. She recognized that with the rise of new wealth after the Civil War, the traditional balance between old inherited money and inherited social obligations was upset. As an alert novelist she recognized that the major shift in social class and income distribution then under way would be a rich field for writers of fiction. In a 1905 letter to Dr. Morgan Dix, rector of Trinity Church in New York, she observed: "Social conditions as they are just now in our new world, where the sudden possession of money has come without inherited obligations, or any traditional sense of solidarity between the classes, is a vast and absorbing field for the novelists."[1]

Like many others of her social class and background, Wharton usually stayed well away from the arena of politics, both as a subject for her fiction and as a place for personal friendships. It is true, however, that she was a friend of Theodore Roosevelt. They may have met as young people in the lively New York City social scene. Through the early 1880s, Roosevelt and his wife attended Mrs. John Jacob Astor's elaborate holiday balls, for example, where the young Edith Jones and her brothers were frequently guests. Wharton was four years younger than Roosevelt and shared with him a history of respiratory problems brought on by anxiety.

Their first recorded meeting was in August 1902, when she spent two hours chatting with the president at a christening in Newport, Rhode Island. She saw him again the following month when a carriage accident near Pittsfield, Massachusetts, threatened to cancel his planned public appearance. Despite injuries to his face and to one knee, Roosevelt insisted on going ahead with his speech. Wharton told a friend that his "few quiet and very fitting words . . . to the crowd gathered" belied his image as a "bronco-buster."[2]

In 1905 she had lunch at the White House with Roosevelt. They discussed Wharton's recent novel *The Valley of Decision*, and the president was of the opinion that her protagonist should have been of a higher moral order. Throughout their friendship they shared a love of books and literature, and Wharton was impressed by Roosevelt's political ideals. She defended her friendship, for example, to Harvard University President Charles Eliot Norton, who thought of Roosevelt as "the good cowboy become President." When Roosevelt was on his way home from Africa in 1910, he stopped in Paris and insisted on visiting his old friend Edith Wharton.

Because Roosevelt was denied the nomination from his Republican party in 1912, he ran as an independent in his own Bull Moose party and lost to Woodrow Wilson. This loss predisposed Wharton to dislike Wilson, who had defeated the person Wharton thought most ably represented her political ideals—Theodore Roosevelt. When the war began, she urged Roosevelt to come to Europe to report on the destruction firsthand, claiming that only he could convince the American people to join the war effort. He contributed a rousing, fiery introduction to her elaborate gift book *The Book of the Homeless* (1916), designed to raise money for her charities.

It is perhaps understandable that in a friendship based on respect for each other's writing, Wharton's final tribute to the man she saw as her political ideal should come in the form of literature. Roosevelt appears in a thinly disguised form as the governor of New York in Wharton's novel *The Age of Innocence*. He tells the hero,

Newland Archer, that Archer is exactly the kind of man the country needs in political office. When Roosevelt died in January 1919, she wrote a poem, "Within the Tide," published in the *Saturday Evening Post*.

Edith Wharton's life was bracketed by wars. She was born during a bitterly cold January week in 1862, when the line of military camps stretched from northern Virginia through Kentucky to Cairo, Illinois. She died in 1937, the year that General Francisco Franco and his insurgents waged war against the Spanish Republican Army, which was supported by the International Brigade with its scattering of American writers. Her friend Teddy Roosevelt fashioned his public reputation during his military exploits in the Spanish-American War. Wharton's own literary career was interrupted, almost bisected, by World War I.

She was one of a number of American writers, primarily women, who became involved in war charities during the opening months of the conflict in Belgium and France, well before the United States abandoned its official policy of neutrality. Wharton was among the twenty-five thousand American women who volunteered for war-related work in Europe, Serbia, China, and Russia.[3] During the four years and three months of the war, she witnessed a transformation wherein economic and political power shifted from a Europe bled white by the war (more than ten million dead) to the United States, which emerged relatively unscathed (115,000 dead).[4]

In 1914, the year World War I started, Wharton's plans were to begin a new novel during a leisurely summer at a rented estate in England. Those plans were, of course, destroyed when the German army invaded Belgium and soon crossed into northern France. For the next year, Wharton threw her energies into organizing and raising money for several large civilian war charities.

Wharton's relief efforts began simply enough with a sewing room. The need was obvious. Several thousand working women in Paris had been thrown out of their jobs by the military mobilization in early August 1914. With the mobilization of the army, French male civilians in the hundreds of thousands put on their military uniforms, checked their assignment papers, and reported to designated railroad stations, from where they would be shipped to the front.

Meanwhile, in Paris hundreds of shops, cafes, and small businesses immediately closed, leaving previously employed female workers without a means of support. If these women were from the distant provinces of France—as was the case with thousands of them—and had come to the capital city to earn enough to support themselves and send a few francs back home, they were suddenly out of luck.

Wharton soon found herself engaged in a problem that at other times might have offered material for her as a novelist. The French labor ministry was upset with the French Red Cross for encouraging wealthy French women to take up wartime sewing. As Wharton wrote to a friend in America, "The silly idiot women who have turned their drawing-rooms into hospitals (at great expense), & are now making shirts for the wounded, are robbing the poor stranded [sewing workers] of their only means of living."[5]

We think of Paris as the capital of fashion, so an example from the fashion industry may give us some idea of the financial crisis. Contemporary newspaper reports noted that dresses normally costing $150 to $200 dollars were selling at wartime prices of less than $40 dollars, if one could get to Paris to buy them. In the last two weeks of August, usually the busiest season for shipping dresses to America, orders declined by 75 percent. Three-quarters of the dress shops on the normally busy rue de la Paix were closed. The street itself, one observer said, presented "a long, gray expanse—broken only at intervals—of forbidding iron shutters."[6] The famous dressmaker Paul Worth turned his idled workrooms into a hospital. The president of the French Fashion Association announced on August 19, 1914, that since the closing of the Paris *salons de couture,* where the majority of them had been employed, more than 300,000 women were out of work.[7] Estimates of unemployment in Paris during fall 1914 ran as high as 44 percent, and the displacement was particularly hard on female workers.[8]

At the request of the head of one of the branches of the French Red Cross, Wharton quickly organized a workroom for women, many unmarried and from the provinces, who had been thrown out of their jobs by the mobilization. The most immediate need was to find something for them to do that would allow them to earn a livelihood. Wharton's first workroom served out-of-work seamstresses and secretaries from her own Seventh and the neighboring Sixth District in Paris. Beginning with several pieces of calico cloth, as well as a budget of $1,000 raised from her friends, she established a workroom able to support twenty unemployed women. Each worker was given one franc a day (the equivalent of twenty cents) plus a midday meal consisting of soup, a meat stew with vegetables, and fruit.

Later Wharton's workroom offered employment to as many as ninety French women at a time. Wharton oversaw the work and secured orders from American friends. Some of the seamstresses had worked for the famous fashion houses. Wharton's sewing room soon established a reputation for producing fine lingerie, as well as bandages for the hospitals and knitted socks and gloves for the men in the trenches. After a few weeks at Wharton's workroom, the women were encouraged to leave and do their sewing at home, allowing spaces for a long line of applicants looking for work.

By October and November, Paris was flooded with refugees from Belgium and the invaded provinces of northern France. The French government could barely keep up with its own homeless, so the poor Belgians were forced to find shelter in railroad stations, in large sporting arenas, and on the streets. Again the need was obvious. With French, Belgian, and American friends, Wharton established the American Hostels for Refugees, a charity that provided housing, food, employment, medical services, and education—even Montessori classes for children of nursery-school age. During its first month of operations the American Hostels (and here the word "hostels" simply means a temporary home) lodged and clothed 878 refugees, found work for 153, and served 16,287 free meals. Within a year the organization was caring for five times that number of refugees.

The American Hostels for Refugees soon opened more houses, each with an inexpensive restaurant, reading rooms, a small medical clinic, and a sewing workroom. With her social connections, Wharton was able to see that the American ambassador in Paris visited whenever she opened a new facility.

Wharton's philosophy of social assistance was that the refugees should become self-sufficient as soon as possible rather than remain dependent on the charity of others. She explained, "The aim of our committee is always to enable the refugees to form a home for themselves rather than remain in the Hostels."[9] To support these rapidly growing charities, she raised money through her friends in France and England. In the United States her sister-in-law formed Edith Wharton Charity committees in Boston, New York City, Montclair, New Jersey, and Washington, DC. Soon there were charity fairs featuring tables of fine lingerie sewn in Wharton's workroom in Paris. During the summer, Wharton's loyal sister-in-law arranged house-party entertainments at the fashionable resorts of Newport, Rhode Island, and Bar Harbor, Maine, all to support Wharton's charities.

All of this organizing and fund-raising for refugee organizations left Wharton little time for writing. When her publisher asked her about a promised novel, Wharton told him that the demands of the war had destroyed any possibility of concentrated work on it. She wrote, "For the present there is too much to do for the unfortunate creatures all about one to think of literature."[10]

Things in New York that first winter of the war, according to her publisher Charles Scribner, were going along about as usual. The editors of the *Literary Digest* surveyed 367 American writers and editors; they announced in their November issue that 105 favored the Allies (England and France), that only 20 were for the Central powers (Germany and Austria), but that the vast majority, 242, favored neutrality.[11]

Edith Wharton's own highly critical attitude toward the official American policy of neutrality during the opening years of the war needed to be closely guarded. Although she was raising money publicly in the United States to support her French and Belgian charities, it would not do to criticize too openly America's neutral position in the conflict. In her private Christmas letter to a friend, however, Wharton downplayed her own contributions but soon warmed to the theme of America's absence:

> There is no merit in digging 12 hours a day at the nearest "social" job this huge disorganization may have put in one's way. It's the only means of keeping a little oxygen in one's lungs—and I can imagine how you must feel the great weight of that deserted place. The only consoling thought is that the beastly horror had to be gone through, for some mysterious cosmic reason of ripening and rotting, and the heads on whom that rotten German civilization are falling are bound to get cracked—and that, this being so, the crash has come at a moment that seems to find the other nations morally ready. I wish I could include the U.S.—but it sticks in my innards that the great peace-treaty-Hague-convention protagonist shouldn't rise in its millions to protest against the violation of the treaties she has always been clamouring for. We are smug just now, aren't we?[12]

To her niece she wrote that, of course, Americans ought to give generously to civilian charities in France "to atone for the cowardice of their government." And in a moment of anger she anticipated her friend Henry James's action of renouncing his American citizenship: "The whole thing makes me so sick with shame that if I had time— & it mattered—I'd run round to the Préfecture de Police & get myself naturalized, almost anything rather than continue to be an American."[13]

In 1915, Wharton made visits to several locations on the French front, where she distributed medical supplies for the French Red Cross while collecting impressions for a series of evocative war essays that appeared first in *Scribner's Magazine* and were later collected in her book *Fighting France* (1915). By summer she had begun another literary project, *The Book of the Homeless* (1916), an elaborately illustrated anthology with contributions from the leading writers, artists, and composers of the period. Wharton's war work was becoming widely known, and her reputation in Paris as well as the United States allowed her to collect contributions from Joseph Conrad, Thomas Hardy, Henry James, Igor Stravinsky, W. B. Yeats, Claude Monet, and many others.

Her charities also continued to grow during 1915. The Belgian government was so impressed by Wharton's work with adult refugees that it asked if she could care for a small group of orphaned and abandoned children from Flanders. She said yes. With less than twenty-four hours' notice, she received sixty young girls. She had barely settled them when she received two hundred more! Soon the Children of Flanders Rescue Committee was caring for more than six hundred children and another two hundred aged and infirm Flemish refugees. Realizing that the children would return to Belgium after the war and would need to have native skills with which to make a living, Wharton set up lace-making, gardening, and carpentry classes.

The work with the charities frequently left her exhausted. She began to take periodic rest trips in 1915 to get back to her writing. A cycle of exhaustion and recovery was soon established. She would perform administrative and fund-raising tasks for the war charities in Paris until she reached a point where illness and fatigue would force her doctor to send her away, usually to the south of France, for several weeks. The rest cures, however, rarely accomplished the goal. Often she had barely gotten her first wind when the deaths of close friends or the needs of the charities would shatter her peace and drive her back to Paris more tired than when she had left.

By 1916, Wharton was beginning to receive official recognition for her war work (the French government awarded her the Legion of Honor in 1916), but public honors were quickly overshadowed by private griefs (the deaths of her dear friends Henry James and Egerton Winthrop). She was slowly able to get back to her first love—writing fiction. During summer and autumn she wrote the novella *Summer,* which with its passion she called her "hot Ethan."

Also in 1916 she could see that all of her humanitarian efforts would waste away in the scourge of tuberculosis unless something were done immediately, and on a large scale, to limit the sweep of that disease. She had already established a number of convalescent homes to care for the ill among her own refugees, but the disease was rampant among the soldiers coming out of the damp, rat-infested trenches. She joined several other prominent Americans in France, where she served as a vice president for the Tuberculeux de la Guerre, a large charity with official French government sanction. She set up demonstration sanatoriums using the American method of fresh-air cures for French soldiers and civilians suffering from the disease. Wharton convinced the French to allow citizens and returning soldiers with the disease to convalesce near the sea or in the mountains, somewhere away from the dank air and enclosed hospital spaces of the city.

In 1917, America entered the war and Wharton began her struggle with a charity octopus—the American Red Cross. Her salvation might have come with the arrival of the American Red Cross in summer 1917, but it did not. She never publicly revealed her disagreements with the organization. However, her unpublished letters, an especially rich source for understanding the politics of American relief aid during World War I, reveal her growing frustration. Moreover, they make clear that Wharton's disillusionment with the American Red Cross after 1917 was representative of what other American women in France felt. Scores of private relief agencies organized and administered by American women during the first three years of the war were unceremoniously swallowed up in a vast centralizing wave. Fourteen months after America entered the war and only three weeks before the armistice, Wharton told her sister-in-law, "The feeling against the Red Cross is not only as strong as it was but far stronger within the last two or three months . . . and apparently their purpose is to strangle all the independent war charities."[14]

After the United States entered the war, Wharton withdrew increasingly from the management of the charities. She was still officially recognized; she had meetings with General John Pershing and Woodrow Wilson's representative, Colonel Edward M. House, when they came to Paris in June 1917. But she moved to the Pavillon Colombe, a small estate in the village of St. Brice-sous-Forêt some twenty miles from Paris, and into a private imaginative space with her brief war novel *The Marne* (1918). Her fiction written during the war and that which uses the war as a subject investigates themes of family struggles and the social politics of civilian war charities.

Though Wharton's humanitarian war work was widely recognized (the French Legion of Honor and the Belgian Queen Elizabeth's Medal), her writing from the war years has been largely dismissed by literary historians as an embarrassing passage during which she fell prey to propaganda. Even her most ardent admirers are left with uncomfortable questions: How did a sophisticated social satirist turn so quickly into a partisan war propagandist? What led Wharton, with her rich sense of irony, to turn her pen to sentimental fiction and propaganda essays?

To understand Wharton's decision, we need to remember that the phenomenon of American authors turning from fiction to propaganda to sway a neutral American reading public and to aid war charities was not uncommon in 1914–1917. Dorothy Canfield Fisher, Mary Roberts Rinehart, Gertrude Atherton, Alice B. Toklas, and Gertrude Stein participated in and wrote about relief activities in Belgium and France. Even that most detached of social observers,

Henry James, wrote propaganda pamphlets and public letters to American newspapers urging support for the Norton-Harjes ambulance units in France and for the Belgian refugees in London.

For James and Wharton the proposed imposition of German *Kultur* (the term used by German intellectuals to justify the war) was an unconscionable violation of cultural boundaries. As expatriates and as writers of exquisite sensitivities, James and Wharton used their isolation from their native culture to heighten perception and contrast. For them the idea of Germany imposing a master culture on France or England or Italy was not just a political and military invasion, it was an assault on the cultural gradations that made their art possible.

Edith Wharton, it is true, wrote with uncharacteristic passion and obvious political commitment during the early portion of the war. She learned during the course of the war, however, to modulate her pitch and to hit and hold "the tremolo note" when its effects served her ends. This shift in rhetorical tone is instructive. When the war began, her dominant tone had been satire with a strong secondary suit in irony. She and Henry James were swept uncritically into a total condemnation of Germany, and in German *Kultur* they foresaw "the crash of civilization." They quickly concluded that they could not remain silent in the face of official American neutrality.

With her keen sense of noblesse oblige, Wharton makes an especially illustrative case of the tension that many American writers felt between the disinterested code of their craft, on the one hand, and their sympathy for the Allies and the refugees, on the other. Wharton's unpublished correspondence with her editors from the war years reveals a writer whose literary identity was being tested as she became involved with, and began to write about, subjects covered by a popular fiction she had rejected.

Part of Wharton's reaction to the cataclysm of the war was social and aesthetic. For Wharton, the war was an obvious assault on the order of life, on decorum. Wharton entered one type of world when she left the United States for France, but she witnessed the emergence of another type of world after the war. Even though England and France won the war, the world Wharton had valued was largely lost. It was obliterated by the mass world, a world without taste, a world without an aristocracy of intellect. Finally, the convergence of historical forces that transformed Wharton from an ironic social satirist into a partisan war reporter represents one of the few periods in her life when she was not in control of what happened. The war was not just a shock; it was a catastrophe that threatened one's ability to make a world. For a novelist who made fictional worlds and for a woman who created aesthetic spaces (her houses and their gardens), the loss of control was potentially devastating. World War I ushered in the true end of the age of innocence.

To return to our original questions: Why did the American novelist Edith Wharton become a social activist during World War I? What did she know about raising hundreds of thousands of dollars for refugees? What training had she had to administer several large war charities caring for thousands of people? What did the author of *Ethan Frome* and *The Age of Innocence* know about charity work? In answering these quite appropriate questions, we need to consider the convergence of several circumstances and skills in Wharton's life.

First, she was well connected with the upper social classes in both France and in the United States. She could call on ambassadors and wealthy philanthropists because she knew them. When General Pershing reached Paris in June 1917, for example, one of the first people to whom he sent formal greetings was Edith Wharton. When the Belgian ambassador needed to house orphaned children from Flanders, he called Madame Wharton. When the French department of health began to fight the scourge of tuberculosis in 1916, it modeled its new hospitals on those Wharton had already established to care for her refugee children. And whether the name was Astor or Vanderbilt or Rockefeller, Edith Wharton could write to each of them directly or have a friend write a personal note.

The second thing to remember about Edith Wharton is that she had had experience since childhood in administering a staff. Today we may grumble at the thought of this society lady ordering her servants around, but we can appreciate what it meant to hire, fire, direct, and pension a staff that rarely numbered less than ten. For starters, there were her secretary, her personal maid, her butler, her chauffeur, her cook. And that is just the small personal staff that always traveled with her. In addition she always had maids to maintain her large houses, a staff in the kitchen, and—because she loved flowers—a small army of gardeners. By 1914, Wharton was divorced, and control of this corps of servants fell entirely to her.

Finally, an artist understands the necessity of organization. Consider that by the time of the war Wharton had already written more than half of her forty-seven books. In her artistic life and in her personal life, she had organizational and executive talents in abundance. She was nearly fifty when the war began. She had connections with the great and she had great talents. The war was a terrible, but strangely appropriate, opportunity to display both. Could she have run a corporation? Could she have led an army? Emphatically "yes." But those opportunities were not open to her. As a woman she was allowed to care for the welfare of civilian refugees—and that she did magnificently.

Notes

1. Edith Wharton, letter to Dr. Morgan Dix, December 5, 1905, reprinted in R. W. B. Lewis and Nancy Lewis, eds., *The Letters of Edith Wharton* (New York: Charles Scribner's Sons, 1988), 99.

2. R. W. B. Lewis, *Edith Wharton: A Biography* (New York: Harper & Row, 1975), 113.

3. This number is an estimate offered by Dorothy Schneider and Carl J. Schneider, *Into the Breach: American Women Overseas in World War I* (New York: Viking Press, 1991), 11, and app. A, 287–89.

4. Schneider and Schneider, *Into the Breach,* 2. Other sources break down the deaths this way: 1 million French, 722,000 British, 2 million Germans, 600,000 Italians, 1.8 million Russians. In percentages of those who served who were killed, France "led" the way with 17 percent, followed by Germany, 16 percent; Britain, 12 percent; Russia, 12 percent; and the United States, 3 percent. J. M. Winter, *The Experience of World War I* (New York: Oxford University Press, 1989), 202, 206.

The most recent statistic comes from John Steele Gordon: "At 11:00 A.M. on November 11, 1918, as the guns fell silent after fifty-one months and 8,538,315 military deaths," "What We Lost in the Great War," *American Heritage* 43 (July-August 1992): 89.

5. Wharton to Bernard Berenson, August 22, 1914, in Lewis and Lewis, *Letters of Edith Wharton,* 334.

6. Charles Inman Barnard, *Paris War Days* (Boston: Little, Brown, 1914), 40.

7. "Orders for Dresses Would Help French Working Women," *New York Herald,* August 20, 1914, 3.

8. Winter, *World War I,* 170.

9. Wharton to the *New York Herald,* February 25, 1915.

10. Wharton to Charles Scribner, December 29, 1914, Scribner Archives, Department of Rare Books and Special Collections, Princeton University, Princeton, New Jersey.

11. Patricia R. Plante, "Edith Wharton and the Invading Goths." *MidContinent American Studies Journal* 5 (Fall 1964): 20. Charles A. Fenton has described World War I as "a literary fracture" between Wharton's generation, as exemplified by the members of the National Institute of Arts and Letters in 1914 and the generation that followed: Hemingway, Dos Passos, Fitzgerald, Faulkner. See Fenton, "A Literary Fracture of World War I," *American Quarterly* 12 (1960): 119–32.

12. Wharton to Gaillard Lapsley, December 23, 1914, Wharton Papers, Collection of American Literature, Beinecke Rare Book and Manuscript Library, Yale University, New Haven, Connecticut.

13. Wharton to Beatrix Farrand, c. December 1914, quoted in Eleanor Dwight, *Edith Wharton: An Extraordinary Life* (New York: Harry N. Abrams, 1994), 287.

14. Wharton to Mary Cadwalader Jones, October 19, 1918, Wharton Papers, Collection of American Literature, Beinecke Rare Book and Manuscript Library, Yale University, New Haven, Connecticut.

Suggested Readings

Shari Benstock, *No Gifts from Chance: A Biography of Edith Wharton* (New York: Charles Scribner's Sons, 1994), a recent full-scale biography, offers a sensitive feminist reading of Wharton's life. Eleanor Dwight, *Edith Wharton: An Extraordinary Life* (New York: Harry N. Abrams, 1994), gives the reader a wonderful sense of place, which was so important to Wharton; this biography contains more than 330 photographs and illustrations. R. W. B. Lewis, *Edith Wharton: A Life* (New York: Harper and Row, 1975), won both the Pulitzer and Bancroft Prizes and remains both a highly readable and detailed biography. Alan Price, *The End of the Age of Innocence: Edith Wharton and the First World War* (New York: St. Martin's Press, 1996), examines Wharton's astonishing activity during World War I.

Edith Wharton, *The Age of Innocence* (New York: D. Appleton, 1920), is the author's best-known novel and the first one she completed after the war. The story follows the life of a New Yorker who on his engagement day discovers a fascinating "other woman." *A Backward Glance* (New York: D. Appleton, 1934) is Wharton's autobiography and tells us a great deal about her friendship with Henry James and others and includes a chapter on the war. Wharton's *Fighting France: From Dunkerque to Belfort* (New York: Charles Scribner's Sons, 1915), a collection of magazine articles from the French front, offers some of the best reportage of the war. R. W. B. Lewis and Nancy Lewis, eds., *The Letters of Edith Wharton* (New York: Charles Scribner's Sons, 1988) shows Wharton's intelligence and wit and put a personal face on this daunting writer. *A Son at the Front* (New York: Charles Scribner's Sons, 1923; reprint ed., De Kalb, Northern Illinois University Press, 1995) is Wharton's best war novel; she never got the story to the front, but she dissected the behind-the-lines scene of the war relief organizations in Paris.

Suggestions for Further Reading

Good starting places to explore the Gilded Age and Progressive Era are Nell Irvin Painter, *Standing at Armageddon: The United States, 1877–1919* (New York: W. W. Norton, 1987); and John W. Chambers, *The Tyranny of Change: America in the Progressive Era, 1890–1920* (New York: St. Martin's Press, 1992). The latter volume contains an extensive bibliography. Ray Ginger, *Age of Excess: The United States from 1877 to 1914* (New York: Macmillan, 1965), provides a colorful statement of the period written from a critical point of view. Samuel Hays, *The Response to Industrialism, 1877–1920* (Chicago: University of Chicago Press, 1957), and Robert Wiebe, *The Search for Order* (New York: Hill and Wang, 1967), are influential interpretations. Alan Dawley, *Struggles for Justice: Social Responsibility and the Liberal State* (Cambridge, MA: Harvard University Press, 1991), interprets the period from the perspective of economic class and gender. Charles W. Calhoun, *The Gilded Age: Essays on the Origins of Modern America* (Wilmington, DE: Scholarly Resources, 1996), contains fourteen chapters on topics about the late nineteenth century. John Milton Cooper Jr., *Pivotal Decades: The United States, 1900–1920* (New York: W. W. Norton, 1990), offers a readable overview of the early twentieth century. Excellent regional views of changes in the nation are C. Vann Woodward, *Origins of the New South* (Baton Rouge: Louisiana State University Press, 1951) and Rodman Paul, *The Far West and the Great Plains in Transition, 1859–1900* (New York: Harper and Row, 1988).

Economic change in the Gilded Age is surveyed in Fred A. Shannon, *The Farmer's Last Frontier: Agriculture, 1860–1897* (New York: Harper and Row, 1945); Edward C. Kirkland, *Industry Comes of Age: Business, Labor, and Public Policy, 1860–1897* (New York: Holt, Rinehart & Winston, 1961), and Walter Licht, *Industrializing America: The Nineteenth Century* (Baltimore, MD: Johns Hopkins University Press, 1995). An interesting supplement to these studies is Ruth S. Cowan, *A Social History of American Technology* (New York: Oxford University Press, 1997). Glenn Porter, *The Rise of Big Business, 1860–1920* (Arlington Heights, IL: Harlan Davidson, 1992), is a superb introduction to the growth of corporations and changes in the economy. A more comprehensive survey of the subject is Alfred D. Chandler, *The Visible Hand: The Managerial Revolution in American Business* (Cambridge, MA: Harvard University Press,

1977). The processing and distribution of basic commodities in the nation's midsection is the subject of William Cronon, *Nature's Metropolis: Chicago and the Great West* (New York: W. W. Norton, 1991), a book that is well written and informative.

Matthew Josephson, *The Robber Barons: The Great American Capitalists, 1861–1901* (New York: Harcourt, Brace, 1934), is the classic indictment of the great entrepreneurs of the Gilded Age. Ron Chernow takes a more balanced view of these gaints of industry in *Titan: The Life of John D. Rockefeller, Sr.* (New York: Random House, 1998); and *The House of Morgan: An American Banking Dynasty and the Rise of Modern Finance* (New York: Atlantic Monthly Press, 1990). The reader can ride the rails vicariously in Albro Martin, *Railroads Triumphant: The Growth, Rejection, and Rebirth of a Vital American Force* (New York: Oxford University Press, 1992). Melvyn Dubofsky, *Industrialism and the American Worker, 1865–1920* (Wheeling, IL: Harlan Davidson, 1996), is a succinct overview of workers in the period between Reconstruction and World War I. Other illuminating studies of labor include David Montgomery, *The Fall of the House of Labor: The Workplace, the State, and American Labor Activism, 1865–1925* (New York: Cambridge University Press, 1987); Walter Licht, *Working for the Railroad: The Organization of Work in the Nineteenth Century* (Princeton, NJ: Princeton University Press, 1983); and Alexander Keyssar, *Out of Work: The First Century of Unemployment in Massachusetts* (New York: Cambridge University Press, 1986).

Patterns of life in the Gilded Age and Progressive Era are etched in Hal S. Barron, *Mixed Harvest: The Second Great Transformation in the Rural North, 1870–1930* (Chapel Hill: University of North Carolina Press, 1997); John S. Gilkeson, *Middle-Class Providence, 1820–1940* (Princeton, NJ: Princeton University Press, 1986); Glenda Riley, *The Female Frontier* (Lawrence: University Press of Kansas, 1988); Thomas J. Schlereth, *Victorian America: Transformations in Everday Life, 1876–1915* (New York: HarperCollins, 1991); and Jessica H. Foy and Thomas Schlereth, eds., *American Home Life, 1880–1930: A Social History of Spaces and Services* (Knoxville: University of Tennessee Press, 1992). The commercialization of leisure is examined in Steven A. Reiss, *Sport in Industrial America, 1850–1920* (Wheeling, IL: Harlan Davidson, 1995). The development of higher education and the social sciences frames Allan G. Bogue's *Frederick Jackson Turner: Strange Roads Going Down* (Norman: University of Oklahoma Press, 1998), a biography of the famous historian.

The epic saga of the peopling of America is told by Roger Daniels, *Coming to America: A History of Immigration and Ethnicity in American Life* (New York: HarperCollins, 1990). The diversity of immigrant groups and ethnic culture is revealed in John E. Bodnar, *The Transplanted: A History of Immigrants in Urban America* (Bloomington: Indiana University Press, 1985); Timothy J. Meagher, ed., *From Paddy to Studs: Irish American Communities in the Turn of the Century Era, 1880 to 1920* (Westport, CT: Greenwood Press, 1986); and Judith Smith, *Family Connections: A History of Italian and Jewish Lives in Providence, Rhode Island, 1900–1940* (Albany: State University of New York Press, 1985). Biographical studies of two key figures in the African-American community disclose many dimensions of its history. See Louis R. Harlan, *Booker T. Washington*, 2 vols. (New York: Oxford University Press, 1972, 1983); and David L. Lewis, *W.E.B. DuBois—Biography of a Race, 1868–1919* (New York: Henry Holt, 1993). James Borchest, *Alley Life in Washington: Family, Community, Religion & Folklife in the City 1850–1970* (Urbana: University of Illinois Press, 1980), offers a revealing portrait of everyday life among blacks and whites in the nation's capital.

Ellen K. Rothman, *Hands and Hearts: A History of Courtship in America* (New York: Basic Books, 1984), examines how men and women formed family bonds; and Mark C. Carnes, *Meanings for Manhood: Construction of Masculinity in Victorian America* (Chicago: University of Chicago Press, 1990), focuses on gender roles. The adaption of women to changes in American society can be sampled in Susan Porter Benson, *Counter Cultures: Saleswomen, Managers, and Customers in American Department Stores, 1890–1940* (Urbana: University of Illinois Press, 1986); Deborah Fink, *Agrarian Women: Wives and Mothers in Rural Nebraska, 1880–1940* (Chapel Hill: University of North Carolina Press, 1991); and David Kennedy, *Birth Control in America: The Career of Margaret Sanger* (New Haven, CT: Yale University Press, 1970). Two women who led important crusades, one against liquor and the other to protect consumers, are portrayed in Ruth Bordin, *Frances Willard: A Biography* (Chapel Hill: University of North Carolina Press, 1986); and Kathryn Kish Sklar, *Florence Kelley and the Nation's Work: The Rise of Women's Political Culture, 1830–1900* (New Haven, CT: Yale University Press, 1995). Linda Gordon's *Pitied but Not Entitled: Single Mothers and the History of Welfare, 1890–1935* (New York: Free Press, 1994) argues that conflicts along class, partisan, and gender lines marked efforts to aid poverty.

Robert W. Cherny, *American Politics in the Gilded Age, 1868–1900* (Wheeling, IL: Harlan Davidson, 1997), is a solid introduction to politics in the generation after the Civil War. A classic commentary on government in Gilded Age America is James Bryce, *The American Commonwealth*, 2 vols. (New York: Macmillan, 1890); despite its age, the work retains surprising utility. H. Wayne

Morgan, *From Hayes to McKinley: National Party Politics, 1877–1896* (Syracuse, NY: Syracuse University Press, 1969), is a comprehensive account of presidential elections and administrations. The dynamics of popular politics are examined in Richard J. Jensen, *The Winning of the Midwest: Social Political Conflicts, 1888–1896* (Chicago: University of Chicago Press, 1971); Paula Baker, *Moral Frameworks of Public Life: Gender, Politics, and the State in Rural New York, 1870–1930* (New York: Oxford University Press, 1991); J. Morgan Kousser, *The Shaping of Southern Politics: Suffrage Restriction and the Establishment of the One-Party South, 1880–1910* (New Haven, CT: Yale University Press, 1974); Paul Kleppner, *Continuity and Change in Electoral Politics, 1893–1928* (New York: Greenwood Press, 1987); John M. Allswang, *A House for All Peoples: Ethnic Politics in Chicago, 1890–1936* (Lexington: University of Kentucky Press, 1971). The Populist challenge to the major parties is the subject of Robert C. McMath Jr., *American Populism: A Social History, 1877–1898* (New York: Hill and Wang, 1993).

Reform was a dominant theme of politics in the early twentieth century. Changes in public life during the era are skillfully summarized in Arthur S. Link and Richard L. McCormick, *Progressivism* (Arlington Heights, IL: Harlan Davison, 1983). Important interpretations of progressivism include Richard Hofstandter, *The Age of Reform* (New York: Random House, 1955); Gabriel Kolko, *The Triumph of Conservativism* (Glencoe, IL: Free Press, 1963); and Richard L. McCormick, *From Realignment to Reform: Political Change in New York State* (Ithaca, NY: Cornell University Press, 1981).

Morton Keller's volumes constitute a monumental survey of public policy and government during the Gilded Age and Progressive Era: *Affairs of State: Public Life in Late Nineteenth-Century America* (1977), *Regulating a New Economy: Public Policy and Economic Change in America, 1900–1933* (1990), and *Regulating a New Society: Public Policy and Social Change in America, 1900–1933* (1994), all published by Harvard University Press (Cambridge, MA). Ballard C. Campbell, *The Growth of American Government: Governance from the Cleveland Era to the Present* (Bloomington: Indiana University Press, 1995), places the Gilded Age and Progressive Era within broad dimensions of change in the American political tradition. Jon C. Teaford, *The Unheralded Triumph: City Government in America, 1870–1900* (Baltimore, MD: Johns Hopkins University Press, 1984), documents the enormous contributions that urban officials made to life in the late nineteenth century. Conflicts over social policies divided many communities in the decades around 1900, a point made clear in James C. Mohr, *Abortion in America: The Origins and Evolution of National Policy,*

1800–1900 (New York: Oxford University Press, 1978); David J. Pivar, *Purity Crusade: Sexual Morality and Social Control* (Westport, CT: Greenwood Press, 1973); William O'Neill, *Divorce in the Progressive Era* (New Haven, CT: Yale University Press, 1967); Theda Skocpol, *Protecting Soldiers and Mothers: The Political Origins of Social Policy in the United States* (Cambridge, MA: Harvard University Press, 1992).

The presidents have attracted more scholarly attention than any other political subject concerning America, except possibly war. Solid studies of the presidents of the era include Allan Nevins, *Grover Cleveland: A Study in Courage* (New York: Dodd, Mead, 1932); Allan Peskin, *Garfield* (Kent, OH: Kent State University Press, 1978); Lewis Gould, *The Presidency of William McKinley* (Lawrence: University of Kansas Press, 1980), and *The Presidency of Theodore Roosevelt* (Lawrence: University of Kansas Press, 1991); and Alexander S. George and Juliette L. George, *Woodrow Wilson and Colonel House: A Personality Study* (New York: Dover, 1964). Most presidents are the subject of several biographies, some published in several volumes. *The American National Biography*, 24 vols. (New York: Oxford University Press, 1999) cites the most important literature about each president, in addition to including a full sketch. This collection also contains biographical essays and references about notable women and men from all walks of life.

America's venture into world affairs during the Gilded Age and Progressive Era included participation in two wars. The first conflict is discussed in Gerald F. Linderman, *The Mirror of War: American Society and the Spanish-American War* (Ann Arbor: University of Michigan Press, 1974); David F. Trask, *The War with Spain in 1898* (New York: Macmillan, 1981); and Stuart Creighton Miller, *"Benevolent Assimilation": The American Conquest of the Phillippines, 1899–1903* (New Haven, CT: Yale University Press, 1982). The Cuban intervention in 1898 triggered a new level of American activity in the Caribbean and the Pacific, which is the subject of Lester Langley, *The Banana Wars: United States Intervention in the Caribbean, 1898–1934* (Lexington: University Press of Kentucky, 1985); and Richard D. Challener, *Admirals, Generals, and American Foreign Policy, 1898–1914* (Princeton, NJ: Princeton University Press, 1973). Regarding the second military engagement, one may consult Ross Gregory, *The Origins of American Intervention in the First World War* (New York: W. W. Norton, 1971); and Thomas J. Knock, *To End All Wars: Woodrow Wilson and the Creation of the League of Nations* (New York: Oxford University Press, 1992). The home front is the subject of David M. Kennedy, *Over Here: The First World War and American Society* (New York: Oxford University Press, 1980).

Index

ISBN 0-8420-2734-3

9 780842 027342

90000 >